ELEMENTARY CURRICULUM IMPROVEMENT

By

Dr. Marlow Ediger
Professor Emeritus of Education
Truman State University
201 W. 22nd. Box 417
North Newton KS 67117
United States of America

&

Dr. Digumarti Bhaskara Rao
M.Sc., M.A., M.A., M.Ed., Ph.D.
Reader
R.V.R. College of Education
Guntur–522 006
Andhra Pradesh
(India)

DISCOVERY PUBLISHING HOUSE
NEW DELHI-110002

First Published - 2003

Reprinted - 2016

ISBN: 978-81-7141-740-7

Elementary Curriculum Improvement

Published by:

DISCOVERY PUBLISHING HOUSE PVT. LTD.

4383/4B, Ansari Road, Darya Ganj

New Delhi-110 002 (India)

Phone: +91-11-23279245, 43596064-65

Fax: +91-11-23253475

E-mail: discoverypublishinghouse@gmail.com

sales@discoverypublishinggroup.com

web: www.discoverypublishinggroup.com

Printed at:

Infinity Imaging Systems

Delhi

To

a great statesman

Dr. Rayapati Srinivas

M.B., B.S.

President

District Congress Committee, Guntur

Former Chairman

Zilla Parishad, Guntur

Preface

Elementary education is the foundation for any educational programme. In order to lay a good foundation at elementary level, a sound elementary curriculum is required. Hence, the elementary curriculum is on continuous appraisal and modification to meet the needs of the individual as well as the society.

This book on Elementary Curriculum Improvement is meant for helping the curriculum designers and text book writers in developing a progressive elementary curriculum, guiding the pre-service and in-service elementary teachers in becoming efficient teachers, supporting the educational administrators and supervisors in guiding effectively the personnel involved in elementary education. This book will help many a people involved in elementary education.

Prof. Marlow Ediger

Dr. D. Bhaskara Rao

Contents

Aristotle and the Curriculum

Aristotle (384-322 B.C.), an Athenian philosopher, is still much revered today. Mortimer Adler (1902) and the late Robert Maynard Hutchins (1899-1977) are/were Aristotelian in their philosophical beliefs. St. Thomas Aquinas (1225-1274) joined the thinking of Christianity of his day with the thinking of Aristotle, resulting in the official beliefs of the Catholic church today. The thinking of Aristotle then is a living and not a dead system of beliefs. Plato was the teacher of Aristotle. Pertaining to comparison of Plato and Aristotle, Ulich wrote:

> There is first a remarkable difference in their attitudes toward life. When Plato observes, he does so in order to transcend reality toward the sphere of the ideal. Aristotle, on the other hand, prefers to dwell on his observations and their objects. He examines and describes, and if he transcends things, he goes through them, whereas Plato treats them as symbols. Plato represents the more intuitive, mathematical, and dialectical type of philosopher. Aristotle, though he is all that, too, is also the collecting and systematic scientist. Plato's attitude toward the world is such that its surface does not concern him as something ultimate. Consequently, he is not only the enthusiast and the radical reformer, in spite of his emphasis on conservatism, harmony, and balance; he is at the same time the artist, full of humor and irony. Often enough he may have gone with his master Socrates where nobody could see them and there split with laughter over the world's folly—which is not to say that they did not weep over it the next hour.
>
> Aristotle does not indulge in such caprice. He was first Plato's most sagacious disciple; but later his conscience no longer allowed him to follow his master. The Platonic-Romantic type may call Aristotle dry, but at least he tries to be reliable, as far as he is in his power.

A Hierarchy of Living Things

Aristotle believed that all living things (plants and animals) had numerous things in common, such as growth, reproduction, and decay. Living things whether plant or animal have the tendency to grow from infancy to adulthood. Also, each reproduces their own kind. Dogs beget dogs while human beings beget their kind. Living things also die and decay.

Higher than plants, according to Aristotle, was animal life. Animals, as well as human beings, can use their senses. The senses of sight, hearing, touch, taste, and smell may then be utilized in functional situations. Plants do not possess these senses. Animals and persons can also move and use locomotion to benefit and enhance their well being, whereas plants are stationary.

Human beings are higher on the scale of development than animals and thus possess practical and theoretical reason. Practical reason emphasizes the use of the Golden Mean. The Golden Mean stresses the avoidance of extremes, such as eating too little or too much, and being too aggressive or too meek in life.

Atistotle stated that man is a rational being and the highest level of reason is pure contemplation. Pure contemplation would emphasize removing oneself from the real world and into an environment where thought for its own sake would be emphasized. The contemplator would reflect upon ethics and morality in a conducive atmosphere. Naturally, a moderate to high income person would/could have time for contemplation compared to a lower income individual.

Durant wrote:

> As Aristotle walked wandering through his great zoological garden, he became convinced that the infinite variety of life could be arranged in a continuous series in which each link would be almost indistinguishable from the next. In all respects, whether in structure, or mode of life, or reproduction and rearing, or sensation and feeling, there are minute gradations and progressions from the lowest organisms to the highest. At the bottom of the scale we can scarcely divide the living from the 'dead'; "nature makes so gradual a transition from the inanimate to the animate kingdom that the boundary lines which separate them are indistinct and doubtful"; and perhaps a degree of life exists even in the inorganic. Again, many species cannot with certainty be called plants or animals. And as in these lower organisms it is almost impossible at times to assign

them to their proper genus and species, so similar are they; so in every order of life the continuity of gradations and differences is as remarkable as the diversity of functions and forms.

The lowest level of things were the nonliving, according to Aristotle. Soil, rocks, stones, wood, among others, would come lowest in the hierarchy, as compared to living things. The lowest level of that which is living would be plants. Plants can grow, reproduce, and die but they cannot utilize sensation nor move. Higher than plant life are animals. The latter have and can use their senses, as well as move around. However, animals cannot reason. They do not possess abilities to think rationally. Only human beings can emphasize the Golden Mean and contemplate for its own sake.

Causes for Happenings

Aristotle believed that definite causes were in evidence for happenings on earth. Thus, effects had a cause or causes. Cause and effect thinking was then in evidence. Which causes did Aristotle emphasize?

Aristotle believed in a prime mover. The prime mover made and ordered the universe. But, the prime mover that set things into motion was uncaused. An uncaused prime mover was then in evidence. After the universe or world was set into motion, a clocklike precision of the earth of world was in evidence. The prime mover may be considered as God. Although, the prime mover was a separate concept from God, as perceived presently in western society.

Aristotle believed in a material cause. Matter is inherent in a material cause. Items such as rock, metals, word, and stone are represented in material causes.

Next, Aristotle believed in a formal causes. The matter in the material cause is used to make an item which possesses form. Material to formal causes or potentiality to actuality represents change from matter to form. Depending upon what is wanted the material cause (wood) may become a chair, a table, or a toy.

There has to be a force which changes matter or material cause (potentiality) to formal cause (actuality). Supposing a carpenter takes a log from a walnut tree to make a box. The walnut tree is the material cause whereas the box is the formal causes. The process or prodcedure utilized to change from material to formal cause is the efficient cause. The efficient cause moves the matter (wood) to a formal cause (box). A worker is the efficient cause.

Finally, as a fourth cause, Aristotle emphasized a final cause. The final cause is the use that a maker or doer will emphasize in the finished product. The final cause stresses a blueprint that the efficient cause will make out of the formal cause. There is always matter or a material cause which ends in a definite form or formal cause. The efficient cause works to change matter into form. The ultimate use of the end results is the final cause. Aristotle believed in a soul which permeates the human being. Unlike his teacher Plato who emphasized mind-body separation, Aristotle believed the soul to provide form (formal cause) of the human being.

Logic in Aristotlian Thinking

Aristotle emphasized the concept of logic as a means or method in arriving at truth. Inductive thinking was one approach in gaining truth. Being a biologist, Aristotle carefully observed plants and animals to arrive at generalizations. Thus, from specific observations of numerous plants and animals, Aristotle developed conclusions. From the specific to the general, in part he emphasizes the concept of generalizations. The more numerous the observations made pertaining to each classification of knowledge, the more accurate each generalization should be. Aristotle arranged from simpler to more complex forms of life in a hierarchical manner. Thus, from the inanimate to the highest level of development (the reasoning human being) represented the range of development from the simple to the complex. In between these two extremes, plants and animals were arranged in ascending order of complexity.

Aristotle emphasized ten categories pertaining to knowledge to be utilized in logical thinking. These categories are the following:

1. substance, such as boy, girl, cat, and dog;
2. place, such as a region or exact location;
3. quantity, such as the precise length and width of objects;
4. quality, such as the goodness, badness, or neutralness of an object or item;
5. relation, such as greater than, lesser than, or equal to;
6. having, such as items or objects possessed or owned;
7. passion, such as hurt received from a deed or action;
8. action, such as performing or doing;
9. time, such as today, yesterday, or tomorrow;
10. situation.

Aristotlian logic has generally been credited with a deductive procedure. To reason deductively, Aristotle emphasized a major premise, a minor premise, and a conclusion. Numerous history of education textbooks emphasize the following as an example of Aristotle's thinking:

1. All men are mortal (major premise);
2. Socrates is a man (minor premise);
3. Therefore, Socrates is a moral (conclusions).

The major premise represents a broad statement, highly general in nature. Certainly, one cannot disagree with the above listed major premise. It is true, without qualification. Thus, the major premise should not be needed in further sequentially steps in logical thinking. The minor premise—Socrates is a man—can be verified with the utilization of authority-such as textbooks in history, as well as in philosophy. The conclusion is realized as a result of reasoning involving the major and minor premise.

Hutchins, Adler and Aristotle

Robert Maynard Hutchins (1899-1977) and Mortiner Adler (1902-) were/are strong proponents of the thinking of Aristotle. Both emphasized students study the *Great Books of the Western World* which both completed editing in 1952. The thinking of Aristotle is a component part of the *Great Books,* in addition to numerous other great thinkers of the past.

Both Dr. Hutchins and Dr. Adler believed that secondary and under-graduate curricula should emphasize the classics. The classics consist of writings of authors whose thinking is enduring. A recent writer's contributions could not be included due to its recency. The endurance of the thinking of recent writers is not known. It takes time for any writer to reveal that his/her ideas are enduring and not temporary. Plato (427-347 B.C.), Aristotle (384-322 B.C.), St. Augustine (354-430), St. Thomas Aquinas (1229-1274), Frances Bacon (1561-1626), John Locke (1632-1704), Descartes (1596-1650), David Hume (1711-1776), among others, have presented vital ideas and content. These ideas have not been temporary in importance. Rather, the content has remained significant throughout the centuries regardless of geographical areas. Time has not diminished the importance of the thinking of the above-named philosophers. Other thinkers and philosophers had their day in terms of salience; however, their works have been transitory and temporary.

Hutchins and Adler believed strongly in liberal education. Liberal or general education provides those ideas, philosophies, and subject matter necessary for all students to gain and secure a common core of values. The values have not diminished in importance but have remained vital and relevant. With a common core of values, students may communicate and share ideas with each other. An agreement then is in evidence pertaining to set of enduring beliefs. Too frequently, values and beliefs in society have changed much in time and space. Students then cannot grasp upon the changeless. Instead, the changing in terms of goals in life are constantly in evidence.

Both Hutchins and Adler would deemphasize/eliminate vocational training classes from the secondary or high school level of schooling, as well as from the undergraduate level in college and university. Vocations in significance in society change. Jobs and occupations continuously change in their importance. Stability is definitely not in evidence. Thus, vocational training and selection must come after the undergraduate years of schooling. Proper habits must be developed within students prior to the training period for vocational education. Development of worthwhile habits comes from reading and reflecting upon the thinking of great philosophers whose ideas are permanent and stable.

Brubacher wrote:

> Hutchins attacked the naturalism of the progressive-education position. His objection was to the romantic and anti-intellectualistic character of its naturalism rather than to naturalism itself. In its stead he favoured a naturalistic philosophy of education based on natural law. By observing the uniformities of nature, education could be stabilized, he maintained. Uniformity is determined in Aristotelian fashion by distinguishing that which is essential to a thing's constitution from that which is merely an accident of its individuality. While the particular is not to be neglected in education, neither is the universal to lose its position of chief importance. The Aristotelian influence is clear also in Mortimer J. Adler (1902-). Not only did he define education as Aristotle did as the habituation of native capacities in virtue, but his confidence in the unchanging nature of man led him to assert that the aim of education should be the same for all men in all times and in all places.

To further stress the significance of perennialism which advocates enduring ideas in space and time, O'Neal wrote:

> Absolute Truth. For the intellectualist, Truth is not man-made, and it is no private matter. On the contrary, there are certain truths and

values that exist independent of being known. These qualities do not 'exist' (from the Greek exstasis, 'to stand out') so much as they 'subsist', or undergird, all personal experience. They do not 'adhere' to Being so much as they 'inhere' within Being, and constitute the very essence of the world as we know it. These essential qualities of Being (which may be defined in a variety of different ways, ranging from the abstract concept of beauty or the formal principles of mathematics to the basic laws of physics) are 'absolute' in the sense that they have no context, but rather, constitute the very ground of Being.

First Principles. Behind the flux of transitory existence, then, there lies an intransitive (or, at the very least, imperceptibly evolving) core of meaning, an irreducible set of metaphysical first principles, that are not derivative in the sense of growing out of experience but fundamental in the sense that they cause us to experience the world in the way in which we do. Implicit within Being there are certain 'essential' and abstract properties that exist independent of the 'accidental' aspects of life and which constitute the very centre of universal meaning.

There is, then, such a thing as absolute knowledge (Truth), and this knowledge transcends mere personal experience. As philosopher Mortimer Adler notes "...philosophy does not exist unless it is absolute and universal knowledge—absolute in the sense that it is not relative to the contingent circumstances of time and place; universal in the sense that it is concerned with essentials and abstracts from every sort of merely accidental variation".

Criticism of the Thinking of Aristotle

There are numerous criticisms of the thinking of Aristotle, as would be true of any philosopher's beliefs.

Pure contemplation, no doubt, would be for wealthy individuals who have time for leisure. Also, it takes purpose and intelligence to emphasize contemplation or pure thought outside the framework of reality or the real world. Pure contemplation then would not stress the involvement of many, many individuals.

Pure contemplation does not involve action or a doing concept. Contemplating outside the framework of putting thoughts into action makes for passive individuals. John Dewey (1859-1952) believed that thought must not be separated from action. He felt that thoughts involved the gathering of data or information. The data or information must be utilized to solve identified problems. The problems identified are those that are relevant in society. Thus, content must be utilized to solve problems, according to John Dewey.

Aristotle, instead, stressed thinking in its pure form. The contemplation is valuable in and of itself. To John Dewey, thought is important or instrumental in solving real, life-like problems.

Aristotle stressed a hierarchy from the lowest to the highest of the inanimate to the animate. Among human beings, practical reason was lower in the hierarchy than pure contemplation. Aristotle, in his hierarchical beliefs, believed that slaves were born into the institution of slavery. Slaves were larger in size, physically, compared to other human beings. They were stronger generally than other classifications of individuals. John Dewey believed that all individuals should utilize intelligence to solve problems. Solving problems then is not the role of the elite only, but the right of all persons.

Aristotle believed that manual labour degraded the individual. Manual labour also distorted the shape and form of the body. A well educated person does not live by working physically with the hands. Instead, upper class persons use the Golden Mean in everyday life, but above all, the highest good is to have time for thought and contemplation. Upper class persons, too, according to Aristotle, would perform exercises which developed a graceful, fully harmonized body.

John Dewey emphasized physical activities in education and in schooling. Thus, cooking and manual training activities were inherent in ongoing lessons and units. Subject-matter was utilized to solve problems in cooking and manual training activities. Thus, the manual and the academic were not separate but integrated entities. Physical labour was not degraded by Dr. Dewey. Recreation was not for upper class persons alone, but for all as individuals interact with others in society. The inanimate and the animate are not separated from each other in a hierarchical manner. All are needed to identify and solve problems in society. Thought by all is needed as data to remedy problematic situations.

Aristotle emphasized that "man is a political animal". Human beings need to be educated for citizenship and as members of the state. The individual becomes fulfilled only, as members of a nation. Individualism is not emphasized as a goal by Aristotle. Rather, the state and citizenship goals become paramount.

John Dewey emphasized concepts pertaining to the individual interacting with others in society. In society, problems need to be identified and solved. The identified problem(s) may pertain to improving laws, rules, and regulations in society. Certainly, pupils in a classroom should have a voice and be involved in decision-making pertaining to standards of conduct in the classroom and in school.

Implications for the School Curriculum

With the philosophy of Aristotle, which implications might be relevant in the school curriculum?

1. students should become proficient in classifying information. Out of the mass amount of subject-matter studied in any lesson or unit, students, need to be able to organise its content. Classifying skills are vital to develop within students to achieve order and organisation of subject-matter.
2. citizenship education needs to be stressed in the classroom. Definite objectives, learning activities, appraisal procedures need to be emphasized in developing quality citizens.
3. learners need opportunities to learn utilizing both inductive and deductive procedures. With inductions, students are guided to develop generalizations from specifics. The teacher needs to be a good asker of relevant questions to guide students to achieve inductively. Students also need to develop feelings of curiosity and inquisitiveness in order to stimulate the raising of questions and attain vital generalizations.

   In deductive methods, the teacher supplies viable generalizations to students who in return utilize that which has been presented by the instructor.
4. the cultivation of the intellect is a very relevant goal. High levels of thinking need to be emphasized in students attaining intellectual goals. An academic, not an actively centred curriculum, would tend to emphasize the development of the intellect within the framework of a subject centred curriculum.

REFERENCES

Brubacher, John S. *A History of the Problems of Education*. Second Ed. New York: McGraw-Hill Book Company, 1966.

Durant, Will. *The Story of Philosophy*. New York: Pocket Books, 1958.

O'Neal, William F. *Educational Ideologies*. Santa Monica, California: Goodyear Publishing Company, 1981, p. 157.

Ulich, Robert. *History of Education Thought*. New York: American Book Company, 1950.

2

Immanuel Kant and Education

Immanuel Kant (1724-1804) emphasized idealism as a philosophy of education. Kant believed that categories in the mind made for cause and effect thinking. In his *Critique of Pure Reason*, Kant stressed that in the natural environment, happenings have causes. Supernaturalism definitely does not prevail as numerous religious thinkers of his day as well as presently may emphasize. Rather, in the natural world, there are causes for each affect of happening. If rain falls, causes are in evidence for this phenomenon. Or, when snowstorms transpire, scientists can provide reasons for this occurrence. The mind has or contains categories which perceive cause and effect. Although Kant did not write specifically for educators, there are tremendous implications in his philosophy for the school and class setting. Certainly, in teaching science, Kant would have stressed students thinking in terms of causes for happenings in the scientific arena.

Kant and Moral Education

Immanuel Kant in his *Critique of Practical Reason* wrote about moral developing of students. In the morality arena, cause and effect thinking is not to be stressed. Rather, each person has an 'ought' or 'oughts' that need emphasizing. Whether it makes for happiness or not, a person ought to behave in a certain way. What provides the guidance needed to behave in a designated way? Kant states that a person should act and react which must become universal. The categorical imperative, emphasized by Kant, stressed the utilization of the Golden Rule. Thus, any human being should perform deeds and acts to others which he/she would desire in return. In other words, only do to others what you would want them to do to you.

To emphasize the Categorical Imperative further, Kant believed that persons should be treated as ends and not means to an end. A means to an end would emphasize using others as stepping stones for one's own personal gratification. Rather, human beings, according to Kant, should become ends. Emphasizing the Golden Rule in everyday living stresses treating each person as an end.

Moral education then should receive primary emphasis in the curriculum. Kant's guidelines in stressing morality include the following:

1. morality should stress universals in space and time. Moral guidelines are not specific but flexible such as the Golden Rule. Flexibility in implementing the Golden Rule makes moral generalizations applicable to any place or region on the face of the earth, as well as applicable in any period of time. The time of application could be in the past, present, or future;
2. mortality in its manifestations may not bring happiness necessarily to the personal self. It could be painful to apply the Golden Rule. Certainly, just acts and deeds may not always bring contentment to the doer;
3. it is a duty to treat others as ends and not as means to an end. Duty is different from desire or wish;
4. each person has the freedom to choose. Hopefully, ethical rather than unethical values will be chosen. Each person then possesses free will;
5. individuals are entirely responsible for their choices whether they be moral or immoral;
6. human beings are born as being good individuals. However, wrong decisions can be made pertaining to the unethical and the immoral;
7. students must be taught to be thinking, reasoning individuals. The goal in education is to develop the moral being.
8. self-discipline is necessary to curb the undesirable choices and decisions in life;

9. human nature is improved through education and schooling;
10. cultivation of the mind or intellect is a major goal of education. The intellect must develop into a being who is able to think critically, as well as analyze information;
11. individuals need to emphasize the concept of wisdom when developing the rational powers;
12. predictions in science do not interfere in the decision-making arena. Cause and effect then is not involved in reasoning and in thinking;
13. Kant's *Critique of Practical Reason* states that the individual makes choices and decisions in the ethical domain. In his *Critique of Pure Reason*, Kant emphasizes that nature stresses causes and effects.

Scruton wrote:

Two questions now arise. In what does the objectivity of the categorical imperative consist? And how is it defended? The objectivity of the categorical imperative consists in three separate properties. First, it makes no reference to individual desires or needs, indeed to nothing except the concept of rationality as such. Hence, it makes no distinctions among rational agents, but applies, if at all, universally, to all who are subject to the dictates of reason.

(It therefore governs reasoning about ends and not about means.) Secondly, the rational agent is constrained by reason to accept the categorical imperative: this imperative is as much a fundamental law of practical reason as the law of non-contradiction is a law of thought. Not to accept it is not to reason practically. Like the law of non-contradiction, therefore, it cannot be rationally rejected. Thirdly, to accept such a principle is to acquire a motive to act—it is to be persuaded to obedience. Since the imperative makes no reference to any desire, but only to the faculty of reasoning as such, it follows that, if all those three claims can be upheld, practical reason alone can provide a motive for action. Hence the ground of Hume's scepticism—which is that reason is inert, and that all practical reasoning is merely subservient to desire—is cut away. Moreover, the moral law becomes not just universal, but necessary, for there is no way of thinking practically that will not involve its overt or covert affirmation. The categorical imperative has 'objective necessity', and achieves this by abstracting from all needs and desires, all 'empirical determinations'. It represents the agent as bound by his rational nature alone.

Kant and Experience in the Real World

Immanuel Kant was an idealist. He believed strongly in the use of reason. The Categorical Imperative can only be realized through reason. Reason is an end and not a means to an end in the Categorical Imperative. Thus, one can reason morality and standards that are therein.

Kant believed that knowledge begins in experience. Securing content from experiences, Kant labeled as a posteriori. Contact and interaction with the actual, real world provides experiences for persons. Individuals learn from these situations. A posteriori as a term emphasizes empiricism or the empirical world. Opposite of a posteriori is a priori. A priori stresses that which is true but not experienced.

Kant wrote:

> There can be no doubt that all our knowledge begins with experience. For how should our faculty of knowledge be awakened into action did not objects affecting our senses partly of themselves produce representations, partly arouse the activity of our understanding to compare these representations, and, by combining or separating them, work up the raw material of the sensible impressions into that knowledge of objects which is entitled experience? In the order of time, therefore, we have no knowledge antecedent to experience, and with experience all our knowledge begins.
>
> But through all our knowledge begins with experience, it does not follow that it all arises out of experience. For it may well be that even our empirical knowledge is made up of what we receive through impressions and of what our own faculty of knowledge (sensible impressions serving merely as the occasion) supplies from itself. If our faculty of knowledge makes any such addition, it may be that we are not in a position to distinguish it from the raw material, until with long practice of attention we have become skilled in separating it.
>
> This, then, is a question which at least calls for closer examination, and does not allow of any off-handed answer—whether there is any knowledge that is thus independent of experience and even of all impressions of the senses. Such knowledge is entitled a priori, and distinguished from the empirical, which has its sources a posteriori, that is, in experience.
>
> The expression 'a priori' does not, however, indicate with sufficient precision the full meaning of our question. For it has been customary to say, even of much knowledge that is derived from empirical

sources, that we have it or are capable of having it a priori, meaning thereby that we do not derive it immediately from experience, but from a universal rule—a rule which is itself, however, borrowed by us from experience. Thus we would say of a man who undermined the foundations of his house, that he might have known a priori that it would fall, that is, that he need not have waited for the experience of its actual falling. But still he could not know this completely a priori. For he had first to learn through experience that bodies are heavy, and therefore fall when their supports are withdrawn.

In what follows, therefore, we shall understand by a priori knowledge, not knowledge independent of this or that experience, but knowledge absolutely independent of all experience. Opposed to it is empirical knowledge, which is knowledge possible only a posteriori, that is, through experience. A priori modes of knowledge are entitled pure when there is no admixture of anything empirical. Thus, for instance, the proposition, 'every alteration has its cause', while an a priori proposition, is not a pure proposition, because alteration is a concept which can be derived only from experience.

Kant, A Priori, and A Posteriori

Kant believed that all knowledge comes from the use of the senses initially. A posteriori knowledge emphasizes that which comes from experiences in the real world. Selected leading philosophers, past and present, have believed that what is knowable comes from experiences only. John Dewey (1859-1952) believed that experience is all that can be known. These experiences occur in the here and the now. One experiences as the individual interacts with society in its diverse realities.

Immanuel Kant believed that a posteriori knowledge (experience) is not adequate. There also is knowledge that is independent of the world of experiences and that is a priori. A priori knowledge is true and correct independent of any observer. Thus, Kant believed that a posteriori knowledge (experience) is important, but it does not go far enough. A posteriori can provide human beings only with what exists or what is and not what should be. The experiences of human beings can be described in terms of what is or what exists presently. It cannot tell us what should be or what ought to be.

In the Categorical imperative, Kant emphasized a priori knowledge. The Imperative is an ought, regardless of a person's wishes, wants, and hope. The Categorical Imperative is universal and endures in space and time. A priori are necessary truths and are analytic not synthetic truths. Analytic truths are inherent in definitions, such as a definition for Imperative. Since a priori means prior to experience, it applies to propositions, judgements, concepts, ideas, or notions. No instances of experience apply to a priori truths. A proposition can be known after vital inherent concepts are acquired. A priori statements cannot be both true and false. Rather, they are absolutely a priori. Thus, a triangle has three sides only, and not other numerical values.

A posteriori truths come from experiences. The senses are utilized to secure information. In the here and the now, individuals interact with the social and natural environment. Content is secured through these interactions. The result is a posteriori.

Kant was a strong idealist in philosophical thought. Even though he believed that knowledge came through the use of the senses, rationalism or ideals were central to Kant's thinking. Thus, moral standards can be developed through reason and not through empiricism. The latter stresses what is whereas the former emphasizes what should be. Idealists tend to believe that the senses do not provide adequate, accurate information. Truth then can be secured outside the framework of experience(s) . These are priori truths. A priori are necessary truths. The utilization of the senses is not necessary in the a priori realm. The world of experience, however, may be utilized to substantiate the a priori. Idealists tend to emphasize universal truths that hold true in all places and in all times. The Categorical Imperative of Kant stressed universality in terms of moral criteria.

Analytic truths are a priori. They are true outside the realm of experience. The predicate is contained in the subject. In the sentence—All teachers of students are human beings—the words "are human beings" does not add any new meanings to the subject 'teachers'. Thus, the predicate is contained in the subject.

A posteriori truths are synthetic and accrue through experience. Synthetic truths are empirically based. In the statement—Half of the teachers are men and the other half and the other half are women—is based on observation or the world of experience. The predicate is definitely not contained in the subject.

Transcending Experience

Kant believed that the mind rises above or transcends the world of experience. The mind operates in terms of categories, such as time, space, and thought categories. What is experienced through the senses is developed into perceptions. Perceptions developed depend upon the purposes of the involved person. The mind then selects what is to be learned. What is learned is classified; thought is involved. Content acquired is classified in terms of time and space. The concepts of time and space are a priori. They are independent of any person's experiences. Thus, the categories of time and space are necessary, absolute, and true. Pure reason is a priori since it is independent of personal experiences of human beings.

John Locke (1632-1704) believed that all knowledge comes from experience in the real world. The environment then imprints itself upon the mind of the learner. The mind being like a blank sheet at birth is the Tabula Rasa theory. With sensations from the environment, reflection is then possible, according to Locke. With sensation or the utilization of the five senses, content is imprinted upon the mind of the student. Reflecting upon the impressions upon the mind, the individual may then think, classify, doubt, believe, value, and will. Immanuel Kant, however, emphasized that both a priori (prior to experience) and a posteriori (pertaining to experience) knowledge was in evidence for individuals. The categories of the mind emphasize thought, space, and time. The mind then transcends experiences in the here and the now.

Kant believed that only phenomena could be known. The nomena could not be known. However, Immanuel Kant speculated about and on the nomena. In his Transcendental Dialectic, Kant developed the following thesis and antithesis:

1. God exists versus God does not exist;
2. there is a beginning versus there is no beginning in terms of the development of the universe;
3. the universe is finite versus being infinite in its dimensions in space.

Immanuel Kant further posited in the Transcendental Deductive Theory that there is a God, even, though empirical evidence is lacking. Also, Kant posited the existence of a Soul for human beings. Along with the Soul, Kant also stressed immortality for people. Good persons then in the here and the now should be rewarded in the hereafter. The Transscendental Deductive theory then posits (empiricism lacking) that a good person on the planet Earth will be rewarded in the hereafter. God, the Soul, and immortality are there so that the reward is possible.

In Conclusion

The philosophy of Immanuel Kant has numerous implications for the curriculum. Students must be guided to become moral human beings. A thinking, reasoning person is necessary in order to become moral.

Castell and Borchert wrote:

> All imperatives command either hypothetically or categorically. The former represent the practical necessity of a possible action as means to something else that is willed or might be willed. The latter would be that which represented an action as obligatory of itself without reference to some other end.
>
> If an action is good only as a means to something else, then the imperative which commands it is hypothetical only; but if it is conceived to be good in itself, that is, without reference to any further end, the imperative which commands it is categorical.
>
> The hypothetical imperative only says that the action is good for some purpose, actual or possible. The categorical imperative declares an action to be binding in itself, without reference to any purpose or end beyond itself.

REFERENCES

Castell, Alburey and Borchert, Donald M. *An Introduction to Modern Philosophy*. New York: The Macmillan Company, 1976.

Kant, Immanuel. *Critique of Pure Reason*. London: The Macmillan Company, 1956.

Scruton, Roger. *From Descartes to Wittgenstein*. London: Routledge and Kegan Paul, 1981.

3

Johann Pestalozzi and the Curriculum

Johann Pestalozzi (1746-1827) was a Swiss educator who had his numerous successes and failures in teaching students. Pestalozzi's methods were well ahead of his day. He placed much emphasis upon the concrete in teaching-learning situations; whereas other educators basically emphasized the abstract phase of instruction with its rote learning and memorization emphasis. Robert Ulich wrote:

> With this truth in mind, Pestalozzi now attacks the "artificial methods of schooling" of his time, which prefers "words to things" and forges "ahead of the free, slow, and patient course of Nature," and gives man a superficial polish which gratifies the superficial standards of modern civilization but conceals the lack of natural power within a person. From such unsound education results "the wretched and exhausting pursuit of the mere shadow of truth".
>
> Only men educated in the "road of Nature" can understand and estimate one another, because they will develop a pure sense of simplicity and uprightness. They will also know that man can use his strength and knowledge best only in clearly defined situations. In this context Pestalozzi emphasizes the necessity of vocational and class education. This may sound surprising to those who know Pestalozzi as the prophet of equality in education; yet the two aspects are, at least from Pestalozzi's point of view, not contradictory. For his concept of equality means not uniformity but the full acknowledgment of nature as it develops diversely in different men and relates them thus to different strata and vocations of life.

> Everybody has to follow the "road of Nature," but it is not the same road for everybody. The less gifted have to go through other experiences and choose other tasks than do those endowed with unusual talent. If a school tried to treat the two in one and the same way, it would kill the talent in the talented, and the possibility of proper and practical adjustment for the average, and neither of them would be happy. So differentiation is inevitable, and it contributes to the richness of human life. But above all variety starts the unity of humanity, and those who put the differences above the unity reverse the order of nature. Therefore the same Pestalozzi who is for a differentiated society and education can also say:
>
> Whoever departs from this natural order and lays artificial emphasis on class and vocational education or training for rule or for service, leads man aside from the enjoyment of the most natural blessings to a sea of hidden dangers.
>
> A society with a differentiated training of youth, which does not at the same time acknowledge the democratic right of all to develop and serve mankind according to their particular abilities, is a "class society" in the negative and dangerous sense of the term. It can only end in catastrophe, as did the absolutist and patriarchical society of the eighteenth century, whose downfall Pestalozzi clearly anticipated.

Methods of Instruction

Johann Pestalozzi believed very strongly in utilizing concrete materials (real objects) in teaching students. In his day, teachers started with abstractions and symbolic learning activities for students. Rather than starting with the abstract which lead to rote learning, Pestalozzi advocated having students experience the real and the concrete. Or, saying the same or similar idea, Pestalozzi recommended learners start with the simple and move to the complex in ongoing activities.

How long the concrete stage of learning relate to each curriculum area? In the area of science, students would study and learn from diverse sedimentary, metamorphic, and igneous rock. Or, if students were studying insects, real insects would be studied. Thus, students might learn about the head, thorax, and abdomen of selected insects. Later in sequence, learners would read and write on topics pertaining to what was studied in the concrete.

In the mathematics curriculum, students using concrete materials, would count, add, subtract, multiply, and divide utilizing real objects. Ultimately, students would learn the abstract and the symbolic after the concrete phase of learning had been experienced.

In a lesson involving discussions, Pestalozzi believed that related objects should be discussed. Object lessons were important for students in order that the concrete to the abstract concept was emphasized in ongoing lessons. Pupils then would attach meaning to what was being learned rather than sheer memorization of subject-matter being emphasized.

Atkinson and Maleska wrote:

> Pestalozzi insisted that the natural instincts of a child should provide the motives for learning. He considered cooperation and sympathy, rather than compulsion or physical punishment, the proper means by which to achieve discipline. Influenced by Rousseau, he believed that free expression would allow the natural powers of the child to develop. Since it is nature that gives the drive to life, he maintained, the teacher's responsibility is to adapt instruction to each individual according to his particular changing, unfolding nature as required at the various stages of his development. Pestalozzi looked upon the child as a unity made of moral, physical, and intellectual powers—all of which could be developed harmoniously through education.
>
> Sense perceptions, thought Pestalozzi, are vitally important in the development of a child's mind. Among the younger pupils especially this would call for reliance upon observations of actual things and natural objects rather than upon books and reading. To help a child develop his sense of touch, sight, and sound, Pestalozzi designed an entire series of object lessons as instructional aids for mastering the fundamentals of language, number, and form. He advocated proceeding from the concrete to the abstract and from the particular to the general, using everyday objects like animals, plants, and tools.
>
> All this greatly impressed visiting educators at a time when children were studying Latin with very little understanding of its meaning. Furthermore, Pestalozzi had developed his methods in such fine detail that it became evident a definite system of training would be necessary to permit teachers to study the child more closely if they were to guide his personal development and to adjust instruction to his particular requirements and interests.

When studying geography, students would see actual geographical phenomena such as plains, plateaus, rivers, and lakes. From these concrete learning situations, students would be aided by the teacher to develop clay models of what had been observed. Later on, students read about geographical concepts acquired during the excursion as well as when the related models were mode.

Pestalozzi believed the following criteria to be significant in teaching:

1. Reality rather than abstractions should be in evidence in the school curriculum in initial student learning.
2. The semi-concrete (models and illustrations) should follow realistic concrete experiences.
3. Students should master each step of learning prior to progressing to the next ordered activity or experience.
4. Physical punishment of pupils, in general, should be eliminated. Discipline based on love should be experienced by all students.
5. The use of the senses in learning is vital. These senses include the traditional utilization of touch, smell, taste, hearing, and sight. Developing the senses in learning should receive paramount emphasis.

Pestalozzi would definitely oppose:

1. rote learning of content without students understanding what has been learned;
2. drill and practice without developing pupil interest in ongoing activities and experiences;
3. survey approaches in teaching-learning situations without students attaining content in depth;
4. physical punishment of students without emphasizing students enjoying ongoing activities and experiences;
5. forced discipline upon pupils without developing spontaneous quality behaviour within students.

Eby Wrote:

Several Principles of special application to mental development were recognized. The first of these is that one must proceed from the known to the unknown. When once stated, this idea appears so self-evident that it seems incredible that anyone should ever have pursued the opposite course. And yet, absurd as it certainly was, much of the instruction of children before this time attempted, as someone has remarked, "to teach the unknown by means of the incomprehensible." A most flagrant example of this was the practice of teaching children to recite Latin or the catechism before giving them the meaning of the words. Against all such instruction Pestalozzi vehemently protested.

Another principle which Pestalozzi recognized is that instruction must proceed from the concrete to the abstract, or from the particular to the general. This principle formed the central theme of all his

> ideas on intellectual culture. The practice of teaching words before the child has a direct experience of the things they designate, he looked upon as a terrible mistake—a mistake which was to blame for most of the evils of the time. Clearly, however, as he recognized this principle, he did not show how the process should be carried to its completion. His absorption in the art of sense impression kept him from explaining how the mind develops the power of abstract thinking.
>
> ...In the attempt to follow out these principles in actual instruction, Pestalozzi encountered a subtle difficulty which never ceased to baffle his thought. The lack of psychological knowledge, together with his inability to express his ideas clearly, greatly misled him. He never perceived the distinction between the logical and psychological knowledge, together with his inability to express his ideas clearly, greatly misled him. He never perceived the distinction between the logical and the psychological order of subject matter. It was largely this failure to discriminate between these two methods of approach which made him constantly declare that "the art of instruction" depends "on the existence of physico-mechanical laws." It was this confusion, which made him say that he would "mechanize instruction." His methods never got away from this grievous error. It is recognized today that instruction may adopt and follow out one of two divergent lines of procedure. These have been called the psychological and the logical order of subject-matter.

Pestalozzi was a strong believer in vocational education. Vocations in his day tended to emphasize the concrete in its actual life's situations. Thus, gardening, cabinet making, growing crops, raising livestock, laying bricks, among others, were stressed. In Pestalozzian schools, initially, students helped with the farm work and other manual activities. Thus, pupils in the world of work and on excursions learned from the concrete. Concrete, semi-concrete, and abstract learnings were emphasized in diverse academic areas, such as in arithmetic, science, geography, reading, as well as in the different areas comprising the language arts.

To further stress the concrete, vocations were brought into the activities and experiences of students. Thus, the manual training movement was emphasized not only by Pestalozzi but also by other educators, such as Emmanuel Fellenberg (1771-1844). Manual training schools were popular in Fellenberg's day but they tapered off in significance as the decades went by. One reason for their decline was the incorporation of machines thus lessening the utilization of physical training to do manual labour types of work.

Pestalozzi was extremely optimistic in terms of what schooling could do for any single individual. In fact, Pestalozzi taught orphans in his first school. These were indeed unfortunate persons. Their lot had been poverty and ignorance. Pestalozi believed that through education the orphans could become productive, self-supporting persons in society. Situations and remedies were more complex than Pestalozzi originally believed them to be. However, he had unwavering faith in what schools and education can do for a student. Pessimissim was definitely not a part of his philosophy of education.

In Closing

Pestalozzi's major goal in education was to develop the well-rounded personality. Thus, the intellectual powers of the student were significant to develop. Intellectual goals were predominate in mathematics, science, geography, as well as reading and the language arts. However, other objectives were also important such as social development of learners. Harsh discipline methods were not emphasized. In fact, discipline was based upon loving the child and emphasizing self-discipline. Students would find learning activities so interesting that spontaneous obedience was stressed.

Goals emphasizing physical endeavours also became paramount. To manipulate items and objects in the concrete and to take excursions with teacher guidance stressed the importance of the physical being.

Pestalozzi's goals in education could be contrasted with those of Johann Friedrich Herbert (1776-1841) and Friedrick Wilhelm Froebel (1782-1852). Herbert believed the major objective in education to be the development of the moral person. A study of history and literature emphasizing the noble lives of persons might then assist students to become moral beings. Froebel advocated the development of the creative person. To develop the creative person, Froebel developed unique materials, such as gifts and occupations whereby students would manipulate the inherent materials.

Pestalozzi became a very famous educator. Leading statesmen and educational personnel came to visit his schools. His ideas in education, in general, remain with us today.

Brubacher wrote:

> Ever since the social culture had been reduced to written symbols and education had taken the social short-cut of vicarious learning

through the written or printed word rather than through direct experience, one of the most persistent aberrations of education had been that the oncoming generation had often memorized the literary form of their social culture without always comprehending its actual meaning. Of this difficulty reformers of nearly every century had been aware. Yet, though many had urged that comprehension and memorization go hand in hand, little or nothing had been done to mark out the steps in facilitating understanding. Few teachers realized, as Pestalozzi so clearly did, that "When a third person, to whom the matte is clear, puts words into my mouth with which he makes it clear to people in his own condition, it is not on that account clear to me, but it is and will remain his clear thing, not mine, inasmuch as the words of another cannot be for me what they are to him—the exact expression of his own idea, which is to him perfectly clear."

The only way to correct this misunderstanding between teacher and pupil, according to Pestalozzi, was for the teacher to commence with sense impressions of the object of the lesson. Only after time for these impressions to take effect had elapsed should the teacher proceed to the naming of the object. Once named, the object could be studied as to its form; that is, its various qualities could be discussed and compared. Finally, with the abstraction of its essential as against its accidental qualities, the object was ready for definition. This, in brief, is what Pestalozzi so frequently refers to as the essence of his method, teaching everything through number, form, and language. In this way language and observation or experience are always so closely linked that education should henceforth be well on its way to eliminating forevermore rote memory without comprehension.

REFERENCES

Atkinson, Carroll and Maleska, Eugene T. *The Story of Education*. New York: Chilton Book Division, 1962.

Brubacher, John S. *A History of the Problems of Education*. New York: McGraw-Hill, Inc. 1966.

Eby, Frederick. *The Development of Modern Education*. New York: Prentice-Hall, Inc., 1952.

Ulich, Robert. *History of Educational Thought*. New York: American Book Company, 1950.

The Student and the Psychology of Learning

The teacher of elementary school children needs to be well versed in principles of learning which educators recommend should be used in teaching pupils. When following these criteria or guidelines, pupils can be assisted in achieving to their optimum. Too often, teachers have violated important principles of learning when teaching pupils thus underachievement has become a part of learners. A good environment for learning is provided when the teacher follows acceptable guidelines in teaching pupils.

Purpose in Learning

The teacher needs to develop or maintain purpose for learning within pupils. Pupils may learn very little from ongoing learning activities if they 'see' little or no purpose in what is being learned. Learners must sense a reason for learning selected facts, concepts, and generalizations. Too frequently, the classroom teacher has merely assigned a certain number of pages for pupils to read from a textbook with no readiness activities involving purpose for reading. The teacher, perhaps, merely stated the following: "Read pages 110 to 113 for tomorrow and answer questions five, six, and seven at the end of the chapter." It is no wonder that many learners fail to sense purpose for reading.

If pupils are to read content from a basal reader, for example, the teacher can guide pupils in a discussion pertaining to the related pictures in the textbooks. Pictures from the teacher's file could also be utilized. As these pictures are being discussed, the teacher could print the related new words on the chalkboard that pupils will be encountering in their reading. These words should be printed in neat manuscript style and their meaning discussed. Pupils can then obtain a mental image of these words from the chalkboard and utilize these learnings in recognizing new words which they will meet in print. They should also be able to recall the meanings of the new words when reading so that meaningful learning may take place. As the pictures and related new words are being discussed, pupils should ask questions and identify problem areas. Pupils can then read to find information to answer these questions or problem areas. Thus, a purpose is involved in reading and that is to get needed information which the learner desires. Students learn more if they sense that a purpose is involved in learning that if no reasons exist for participating in a given learning activity.

Interest in Learning

It is important for teachers to select learning activities which capture the interests of pupils. Pupils should learn more if they are interested in a given learning activity as compared to having a lack of interest. Too often teachers have not considered the interests of pupils when selecting appropriate learning activities. Thus, learners do not achieve to their optimum. The teacher can construct an interest inventory whereby pupils can respond in checking what is of interest to them. For example, on this interest inventory, all pupils could check their hobby or hobbies from those listed by the teacher. Space should be left for writing in their hobby or hobbies if they are not listed. Hobbies which pupils have can become a definite part of ongoing learning activities in a given unit. For example, stamps from a collection, pertaining to a unit of study of Great Britain, can become a part of the learning activities on that country. Or, a rock collection could become a definite part of a science unit pertaining to the changing surface of the earth. On the interest inventory, some pupils may indicate positive attitudes toward listening to music of other lands. Certainly these musical recordings can be brought into selected social studies units when they relate to the nations or areas of the world being studied. Teachers need to study various interest inventories and develop an instrument which would give data on ways of capturing the interests of pupils.

Pupils, generally, will show little interest in a given learning activity which is excessively complex. For example, pupils who read well below grade level will not be interested in reading content from books which are written for the grade level they are presently in. The words, terms, and ideas being presented from these textbooks will not be on the understanding level of pupils. Thus, interest in learning will lag. Nor will talented and gifted learners generally be interested in content which is written well below their present achievement level in reading. These learners will generally be bored and feel a lack of challenge in learning activities which have excessively low standards.

Some learning activities have a tendency to capture pupil interest more as compared to other kinds of activities. Well selected films, filmstrips, pictures, slides, excursions, and records can generate much pupil interest if properly introduced. Pupils from different achievement levels in a group can generally benefit from these learning activities. They can interpret and gain content on different achievement levels.

Learning activities involving discussions can make for a lack of interest on the part of learners if the ideas being discussed contain excessively difficult vocabulary terms which learners do not understand or if the discussion activity is carried on for too long a period of time.

Meaning Attached to Learning

To benefit adequately from ongoing learning activities, pupils need to understand that which is being learned. Too frequently, pupils have memorized facts, statements, and conclusions without really understanding or attaching meaning to what has been learned. Or, pupils have memorized content for a test resulting in a rapid rate of forgetting. If pupils attach meaning to what has been learned, an improved retention rate should thus result. All teachers should be highly interested in having pupils retain as much as possible of what has been learned.

For learning to be meaningful for pupils, the teacher must assess the learner in terms of his present achievement level. Thus, in initiating or introducing a unit, the teacher should develop some kind of pretest which will assist in determining present achievement levels of pupils. This could involve the use of a variety of evaluation techniques. Paper-pencil tests could be used as well as discussions. Not all evaluation, of course, should be done through the use of paper-pencil tests. Tests such as these will not adequately measure how well pupils can utilize a microscope in science or how well pupils can construct and make models related to ongoing social studies units.

Once pupils have been pretested, the teacher needs to adjust objectives in a unit of study. The objectives should then be attainable for pupils. Careful selection of learning activities or determining an appropriate instructional sequence for learners is then important. If the objectives are too difficult for pupils to realize, meaningful learnings will then not occur. Learning activities which are too difficult for pupils make for a lack of meaningful learnings on the part of children. The teacher needs to pay careful attention to proper sequence when pupils are pursuing ongoing learning activities. The other extreme in sequence could pertain to the teacher duplicating what learners already have mastered or learned in previous units of study. Thus, it is important that the teacher think in terms of good sequence when providing learning activities for pupils.

The teacher can be misled in providing for meaningful learning activities for pupils if the type of pretest utilized is not in harmony with the learner's present achievement level. For example, a first grade pupil will not reveal what he knows in a given unit of study if he is asked to respond in writing to essay items in a pretest situation. Nor would he reveal present achievement levels, generally, if he were asked to read and respond to complex true-false, multiple-choice, completion, or matching items. Each child must be pretest using an appropriate evaluation technique which is in harmony with child growth and development characteristics.

Motivating the Learner

Pupils who lack motivation will not have the necessary energy level to become actively involved and benefit fully from ongoing learning activities. The teacher must think of strategies which assist learners to achieve to their optimum due to appropriate motivation. Forcing learners to memorize a given set of facts, generally, would make for situations where learners lack motivation. In some situations, teachers want to depend upon scolding or embarrassing learners in order to 'encourage' learning. Sooner or later, teachers discover that under such circumstances pupils learn to dislike learning, teachers, as well as the school as an institution. Pupils may come to the conclusions that school is an unhappy place and learning is something to be shunned. A few teachers still feel that pupils learn only when they are forced to and that learning occurs only in situations involving drudgery. These teachers may think and feel that learning cannot be enjoyable for children and in their deeds emphasizes that 'learning' can come about largely when experiences for children are made unpleasant through regurgitation of facts, rote learning, and drill.

The teacher rather needs to think of stimulating pupils so that an inward desire to learn will result. A good bulletin board developed at different intervals when units are taught can do much to assist pupils in asking questions whereby a desire exists to get data in answer to these questions. In developing these bulletin board displays, the teacher needs to think of possible questions pupils may raise pertaining to the pictures contained thereon. Can the bulletin board display help develop an inward desire to learn on the part of pupils? This question needs to be answered in the affirmative by classroom teachers. The teacher can also develop interesting learning centres pertaining to different units of study. This should assist learners in identifying important problem areas thus motivating pupils in developing an inward desire to learn. The teacher can also utilize films and filmstrips in teaching. These aids to learning must be on the understanding level of pupils and have content which would stimulate pupil curiosity. Learning activities need to be selected carefully by teachers so that pupil motivation for learning will be at its optimum.

Providing for Individual Differences

Too frequently, all pupils in a classroom are on the same page at the same time when a given textbook is utilized in the classroom. Situations such as these do not provide for individual differences within a classroom. For some time, educators have recognized that pupils differ from each other in capacity, achievement, interests, energy level, and home background, among other factors. Common sense would say that not all learners then can be at the same place at the same time when utilizing textbooks for a given lesson or lessons.

Some pupils learn more from a particular learning activity as compared to others. For example, a third grade pupil with below average achievement may not benefit as much as possible from a third grade textbook since it is generally written for average achievers. However, this same pupil may learn much from studying and discussing content from audio-visual aids which pertain to ongoing units of study. Pupils have different learning styles. It behooves the classroom teacher to select learning activities which provide for different learning styles within a classroom.

In addition to different learning styles, pupils achieve at various rates of speed. There are many different approaches and methods available to the teacher to use in order that individual differences within a classroom can be provided for. For example, in the individualized reading programme, each pupil would select his own library book to read. A pupil may be in the fifth grade, but he is reading on the third grade level. Thus, a library book is selected by this child which is on his reading level. He also selects a book which contains content which is interesting and meaningful. Another student who is in the fifth grade may be a talented and gifted learner. This student may select and read library books which are on the seventh and eighth grade levels. He should select library books which are interesting and challenging. Having completed reading a library book, the pupil reveals how well he has comprehended the contents of that book. Once learners have selected a library book, they read at their own unique rate of speed. Child A should not compare himself with Child B in terms of difficulty of the library book being read or in terms of rate of speed in reading. Each child is unique with his own interests, capacity, and achievement. Following the completion of reading a library book, the child may have a conference with his teacher. The teacher must eventually get to know the contents of various library books well. He will need to assess the child's comprehensions in gaining ideas from reading. Questions asked by the teacher should not destroy interest in reading; rather, the learner should be stimulated in wanting to engage in reading more complex library books with continued improvement in the area of comprehension. In the conference, the teacher can also evaluate the breadth of content pupils are reading when selecting various library books for the individualized reading programme.

In discussing individualized reading, the one of the writers has attempted to describe how pupils can select library books which vary in complexity as far as reading levels are concerned. Each pupil, then, ideally selects a library book which is on his reading level. The classroom setting needs to have an ample number of library books dealing with various reading achievement levels. Each learner also will differ from others in the rate he is reading content. Each child in a class needs to be successful in achievement so that optimal growth can take place.

Balance Among Objectives

It is important for the teacher to think in terms of some kind of balance among objectives. If a teacher only emphasizes cognitive domain objectives which deal with the use of the intellect, pupils will not develop as well as possible in other facets of development. Cognitive objectives, of course, are of utmost importance for pupils to achieve; however, psychomotor and affective domain objectives should also be stressed. Psychomotor domain objectives deal primarily with the use of the muscles such as in making and constructing objects and models, repairing objects and items, dramatizing situations, performing folk dances, and playing games. Affective domain objectives pertain to attitudinal development of pupils. All pupils need to have positive attitudes toward learning. Positive attitudes will assist learners to achieve at their optimal rate in cognitive and psychomotor domain objectives. Each pupil should develop positive attitudes toward himself as an individual so that an adequate self concept may result. Certainly, learners need to have wholesome attitudes toward others so that good human relations can then be in evidence. A lack of respect toward classmates generally results in behavioural problems. Feelings of respect toward others are the heart of democratic living. Pupils should develop wholesome attitudes toward others. All individuals desire to be respected.

Cognitive domain objectives are important for learners to achieve. An ample number of understandings need to be developed and understood so that critical and creative thinking can be emphasized in problem solving activities. Life in society demands that individuals become highly proficient in problem solving. All human beings face problems in life which require the best solutions possible. There is no better place to emphasize problem solving than in the elementary school years. The environment in school can be structured for pupils so that problem solving activities can be stressed. The teacher needs to structure an interesting learning environment in the classroom which will guide learners to identify important problems. In introducing a unit, an attractive bulletin board display can capture pupil curiosity whereby questions are asked to begin learning activities which involve the problem solving approach. These questions need to be adequately delimited so that related data or information can be gathered. Further stages of problem solving can then be stressed such as developing and testing hypotheses, and revising the original hypotheses, if necessary. The teacher heeds to think of numerous learning activities that stimulate pupil curiosity which is basic to identifying problems or questions when using the problem solving approach. Thus, it is important for the teacher to stress cognitive, as well as psychomotor and affective domain objectives. One domain of objectives such as the affective or attitudinal dimension may hinder or help achievement in the other domains—the cognitive and psychomotor.

A different classification scheme which may be utilized in an attempt to provide for balance among objectives is understandings, skills, and attitudes. When studying a unit on Great Britain, for example, learners need to develop important understanding pertaining to agriculture, manufacturing, urban living, family living, transportation, and communication. Pupils, of course, would not understand the people of Great Britain unless generalizations are developed pertaining to the above-named areas.

Pupils also need to develop an adequate number of skills such as reading, writing, speaking, listening, using the card catalog, using reference materials, making and constructing objects and models, and working effectively in groups.

Attitudinal objectives would deal with the same category as affective domain objectives. Again, it is of utmost importance for pupils to develop wholesome attitudes toward themselves and others so that an adequate self concept exists and good human relations are in evidence.

Success of Learning

The teachers must select objectives, learning activities, and evaluations, techniques which assist learners in developing feelings of success. Nothing is gained by having pupils develop feelings of failure. Much money is wasted each year in 'teaching' pupils when they experience failure and frustration. The teacher's task is to teach pupils rather than failing or flunking individuals in the elementary school. Too often, teachers have felt that their role is to pass or fail pupils rather than guide them to achieve to their optimum. A teacher may think and feel that he has high standards for pupils when rigid standards are utilized to determine grades that pupils should receive. All teachers should realize that tests can be written which are excessively difficult and all learners in a class could receive failing marks or grades. Tests can be written which are excessively easy and most learners could get very high or excellent marks or grades. What is important is that pupils realize objectives through carefully selected learning activities. The objectives may need to be properly adjusted after a pretest has been administered in beginning a new unit of study.

Pupils who experience excessive failure generally develop an inadequate self concept. They feel they can't achieve well because of experiencing much failure; thus, a lack of successful accomplishment results.

Learning activities need to be adjusted to the present achievement level of each child. Careful attention needs to be paid to sequence so that pupils may experience success in ongoing learning activities. Teachers need to reward pupils with praise if each pupil is doing better than formerly. All pupils then can receive praise regardless of capacity or present achievement levels. Praise for improved performance generally spurs pupils on to greater efforts.

Respect for Pupils

It is of utmost importance for teachers to respect all pupils under his or her influence. As was mentioned previously, pupils differ from each other in capacity and achievement. Thus the teacher needs to respect pupils regardless of capacity and achievement levels. The slow learner, as well as average and talented achievers, need to be assisted in realizing their optimum achievement. Provisions need to be made in the classroom which will provide for each individual pupil.

Pupils come to school from different socio-economic levels. Some of these pupils wear more expensive clothing than others. Some are neat and tidy. Others wear old clothing which may not be as clean as the teacher would desire it to be. However, the teacher must realize that pupils can come from unfortunate home situations. An inadequate income may be the lot of some parents. Misfortune such as illness, death, unemployment, and dissension may afflict a considerable number of homes in a given community. Thus, the child in such an environment cannot achieve to his optimum. He may worry so much over the home environment that little time is left for thought, study, and learning. By having much knowledge about each individual pupil, the teacher can use this information to do a better job of teaching. Certainly, the information, used properly by the teacher, should assist in providing for individual differences. Teachers become much more tolerant and understanding of learners if they understand each child's home background and experience.

A child in the elementary school may speak nonstandard English due to models presented in the home environment. Too frequently, teachers have felt that nonstandard English should be criticized so that pupils will want to speak standard English. Teachers may have corrected pupil's spoken language until there is little desire left to speak, especially in the teacher's presence. Pupils will gradually learn standard English when listening to the teacher who presents an example or model to follow. Learners may also get examples pertaining to the speaking of standard English when listening to recordings, tapes, films, and the voices of others who speak English which is generally acceptable to middle class Americans. Pupils should not be forced to change from nonstandard to standard English. Generally, forced changes placed on learners make for negative attitudes toward the teacher and school.

The teacher should respect pupils who come from minority groups such as those who speak a foreign language in the home or those who come from homes whose religious preferences are different from those of others in the class setting. Pupils of different races need to be accepted as individuals who deserve the best in education and other opportunities regardless of creed or religion. Learners should be assisted in developing an adequate self-concept so that optimal contributions can come from all in a democratic society.

In Summary

There are important criteria that should be followed by teachers when providing learning activities for pupils. Pupils should sense a purpose or purposes for learning. Thus, learners would feel that a reason or reasons exist for participating in specific learning activities. Teachers need to select those learning activities which would capture pupil interest. It is of utmost importance that learners understand what is being taught so that meaningful learning occurs.

If pupils lack motivation, a lower energy level will be available for ongoing learning activities. Teachers should work in the direction of stimulating pupils so that an inward desire to learn will result. Pupils achieve at different rates of speed and at different achievement levels thus making it necessary to provide adequately for each child in the classroom. Intellectual development on the part of learners is important but is not the only category of objectives that should be emphasized when teaching pupils. There needs to be some kind of balance based on rational thought among the following categories of objectives—understandings, skills, and attitudes. Attitudes affect the degree to which a pupil will develop to his optimum in understanding and skills objectives. Attitudes are changed in some cases by obtaining more information. Developing appropriate attitudes can help in realizing understandings and skills. Each category of objectives affects other categories such as positive attitudes toward learning affect achievement in objectives which pertain to understandings. Learners need to be successful in learning and be respected by others.

REFERENCES

Ediger, Marlow and Digumarti Bhaskara Rao, *Psychology and Curriculum*. New Delhi, India: Discovery Publishing House, 2004.

Ediger, Marlow and Digumarti Bhasakra Rao. *Philosophy and Curriculum*. New Delhi: Discovery Publishing House, 2003.

5

Grouping Pupils in the Elementary School

Numerous approaches have been recommended by educators in grouping pupils for instruction. Certainty does not exist as to which plan of grouping is best. Each recommended approach of grouping pupils seemingly contains strengths as well as weaknesses. Teachers, principals, supervisors, and parents must consider and assess each of these approaches in grouping pupils for instruction. The psychology of learning is important as well as child growth and development characteristics when making a final decision-making pertaining to grouping pupils for instruction.

Faculty members of an elementary school need to become thoroughly knowledgeable as to the various possibilities that exist in grouping pupils for instruction. Each plan should be evaluated in terms of acceptable criteria or standards. No thinking person would advocate new approaches to grouping without being fully knowledgeable about their strengths and weaknesses. It is important that there be widespread acceptance of a new plan for grouping before it is implemented. Teachers, principals, supervisors, and parents should be in much agreement about a new plan for grouping before it is implemented. Each elementary school should also study thoroughly the present plan being used for grouping pupils for instruction. Thus, a gap may be noticed between where the school is presently in the area of grouping pupils for instruction as compared to where it should be.

One of the most important tasks involved in implementing a new plan for grouping pupils may well be to get parental acceptance. Parents can be satisfied with the most traditional plan of grouping available. The lay public then must reach a stage of disequilibrium whereby they no longer are satisfied with the status quo. The following approaches may be utilized to develop this state of disequilibrium within the lay public:

1. Talks given at Parent-Teacher Association meetings pertaining to new plans of grouping pupils for instruction.
2. Ideas about new plans for grouping being injected when parent-teacher conferences are held.
3. Newspaper articles bringing in items pertaining to new approaches in grouping pupils for instructional purposes.
4. The possibilities of presenting concepts and generalization pertaining to grouping pupils on a local television or radio station should be explored.
5. Talking informally to parents at open house and on other occasions about grouping pupils for instruction.
6. Faculty members of an elementary school should discuss creative approaches in informing the lay public relating to proposed innovations in the schools.

Any plan for grouping pupils is not a panacea. It is a means to an end but not an end in and of itself. The new plan of grouping pupils for instruction should aid in improving the curriculum. It should guide in improving teaching-learning situations in the elementary school. Too frequently faculty members have felt that a new plan for grouping pupils should solve all ills in an elementary school. A newly implemented plan for grouping pupils could present many new problems to the involved school. If a team of teachers cannot work together cooperatively, the innovation may cause more grief than improvement over previous plans of grouping. As another example, in a departmentalized plan for grouping pupils, learners may not develop well emotionally and socially if the teacher goes overboard for teaching subject-matter only. Intellectual development of pupils to be sure is important; however equally important is physical, social and emotional development.

Plans for grouping pupils have been misunderstood by teachers, principals, and supervisors. For example, there are elementary schools which are called 'nongraded schools' by name only. Teachers by example in their teaching may be emphasizing the use of fifth grade materials, for example, in teaching all fifth graders regardless of capacity and achievement levels. The nongraded philosophy is definitely not being implemented in cases such as these. "Turn teaching" has been confused with team teaching. In turn teaching, each teacher does his or her own preparing for teaching with no cooperative endeavours involved in planning together with other team members in terms of objectives, learning activities, and evaluation techniques. Each teacher then takes his turn in teaching in large group sessions as well as working with smaller groups, and individual pupils. As will be discussed later, team teaching emphasizes that members of a team plan together teaching strategies for a given set of learners. It is important that teachers, principals, and supervisors understand the basic underlying principles that each plan emphasized in grouping pupils for instruction.

There will, no doubt, be different interpretations for the philosophy or rationale behind each plan for placing pupils into groups; however, there will be considerable agreement also in interpretation of the underlying principles pertaining to each plan of grouping. For example, the nongraded elementary school states the importance of pupils experiencing continuous progress. Hardly could pupils experience continuous progress if all pupils in a class are on the same page at the same time when utilizing the basal reader, for example, as a learning activity. The only exception to this case could pertain to a class of pupils which are highly homogeneous in terms of reading achievement. This would indeed be rare, however, when thirty pupils, for example, would make up the total number in a class setting. Even then there would be individual differences that need to be provided for.

The Nongraded School

The nongraded elementary school has much to offer in terms of helping learners to be successful. As was stated previously, a basic principle underlying this approach to grouping is that pupils should experience continuous progress. Teachers can be "overly ambitious" in wanting learners to achieve thus causing pupils to lose out in the ongoing activities. It is no wonder then that pupils experience failure and eventually develop or maintain feelings of inadequacy. Pupils should feel that they are achieving to their optimum thus feelings of success become a part of the child.

In the nongraded elementary school, it is important that teachers attempt to determine reading levels of pupils as early as possible. Pupils are generally grouped homogeneously based on reading achievement. It is good if an elementary school has at least three roomfuls of pupils of a given chronological age. If there were only two roomfuls of eight-year-olds, for example, it would be difficult to group them homogeneously. The range of achievement in reading in each room would be great indeed. With three roomfuls of pupils of a given chronological age, the chances are fairly good of achieving some degree of homogeneity in grouping pupils for instruction within each classroom. More homogeneity would be possible in grouping if there were more than three roomfuls of pupils on a given age level. Within each classroom pupils could be further grouped into three different achievements levels in reading. Pupils should be placed in the reading group which is in harmony with their level of achievement. Flexible grouping is important. It is important to put pupils in another group if they demonstrate that the original group they were placed in was not in harmony with their present achievement level. Teachers must evaluate pupil achievement continuously to determine the group that each child would benefit most from. At the end of a specific school year, the teachers should record where learners left off in terms of materials used and skills mastered. This would be important so that pupils do not repeat unnecessarily previous materials read and skills mastered. With the beginning of a new school year, the teacher would need to do some reviewing of what learners had learned previously since some forgetting, of course, will have occurred of previously developed learnings. The teacher would also need to engage in reteaching that which necessitates doing this.

The sky is the limit in pupil achievement in the nongraded school as long as there is continuous progress for learners and success in evidence. Thus, for example, pupils who would be in the sixth year beyond kindergarten of the nongraded schools could be reading from and using seventh and eighth grade materials provided this harmonizes with their capabilities presently in reading. A slower group of pupils in the same age group may be reading from and using fourth grade reading materials since this harmonizes with their present achievement level. The teacher would accept pupils where they are presently in reading achievement and help them to progress continuously.

Ideally, there should be no failures in the nongraded school. No one, of course, basically likes to be a failure or have feelings of failure. In the graded school concept, some pupils have repeated a grade since they did not achieve up to grade level in reading achievement or did not realize standards set by the teacher. Some cannot achieve up to grade level standards since they lack the necessary capacity, interest, motivation, or home background. For others, it is not challenging enough to realize fifth grade standards, in reading, for example, if they are in the fifth grade. Their capacities, interests, and motivation would demand realizing a higher level of achievement than the grade level they are in presently. The nongraded school emphasizes the importance of providing for individual differences. If pupils fail in the graded school, they may use the same materials over again for the next school year. Certainly, this does not help learners to achieve continuous progress. He may even have the same teacher again which constantly can remind him of failure! These examples do not exemplify basic underlying principles of the nongraded school.

There are, of course, some weaknesses of the nongraded school. If pupils would be grouped homogeneously continuously, there would be no opportunities within the school setting for pupils to interact with other children of different capacity and achievement levels. Certainly life in society does not operate that way. Individuals interact with others of different capacities, interests, achievement levels, and background knowledge.

There are teachers who may not wish to teach the slowest group of pupils. They may not have the knowledge, patience, interest, and poise to work with the slowest group of achievers. The attitudes and feelings of the teachers, no doubt, will be reflected within learners. To make matters worse, parents may not have the necessary positive attitudes to accept the fact that their child is in the slowest group. Certainly parental attitudes will also be reflected within their children. Parents in the home reveal their feelings toward school to their children.

Sometimes, parents speak openly about their feelings toward school in front of their children. And even if words are not used in communicating feelings and attitudes, the child in the home or school generally is able to understand nonverbal communication.

It should also be pointed out that pupils grouped among the top achievers could develop negative attitudes toward those who achieve less well and have less capacity. In the class setting, teachers need to guide pupils in accepting and respecting others. Respect for others is the heart of democratic thinking.

The Self-Contained Class

Too often, educators have been prone to criticize heavily the more traditional approaches to grouping pupils for instruction, such as the self-contained classroom. Tradition does not in and of itself make a concept or idea bad. There are many traditions in life, which, no doubt, will remain with us forever. However, many customs, beliefs, values, and ideals change due to living in a changing society. Respecting others in the home, school, and community will always be an important ideal to strive toward. Critical thinking, creative thinking, and problem solving, no doubt, also will always remain important skills for individuals to develop.

The self-contained classroom concept is based on the idea that a teacher can get to know pupils well by teaching them for the major part of the school day. Music, art, and physical education could be taught by special teachers. By knowing children well, the teacher should be able to do a good job of providing for individual differences. The teacher can get to know well the child's interests, needs, and abilities in a self-contained class. Teachers have numerous opportunities to become thoroughly familiar with the home background of each child in a self-contained classroom.

A further advantage of the self-contained class is that teachers can help pupils sense the relationship of knowledge. The teacher, for example, can guide learners to sense that social studies and science are related. In units on air, land, noise, and water pollution, the teacher can guide learners in understanding basic scientific principles and generalizations pertaining to this problem in society. Children could also study the effect that pollution has on man. Thus science and social studies would be emphasized as being related. When a committee of pupils reports findings to the class pertaining to research conducted on pollution, the language arts area of speaking is involved. Thus, a teacher in a self-contained class has many opportunities to guide learners in relating knowledge so that it is not conceived to be in isolation. Too frequently, pupils have felt and thought that knowledge is compartmentalized and cannot be related. In problem solving, knowledge which is related will be used in arriving at solutions. In daily living, it is important to be able to solve problems. Solutions to these problems generally require content which is related. Too often, individuals who compartmentalize knowledge have a difficult time in using what has been learned in the process of problem solving.

Disadvantages of the self-contained classroom can also be listed. A teacher may find it difficult to teach the different curriculum areas well be in a self-contained classroom. Can a teacher do justice in teaching reading and the language arts, social studies, science, mathematics, and perhaps, art and physical education? It certainly does require keeping up with the many separate areas that make up the elementary school curriculum. Sometimes a teacher will say that he does not like to teach science or he does not feel competent in teaching science. That curriculum area then may be slighted and minimized by the teacher. There has been a trend in some elementary schools to departmentalize selected curriculum areas on the intermediate grade level. A teacher who has a strong background of course work in science and elementary education could then teach science to several classrooms of pupils. Other teachers could then select curriculum areas to teach in which they have a strong background of course work on the college and / or university level. Teachers should teach the curriculum area or areas in which they have the strongest background knowledge in content as well as in methodology. Elementary school pupils in many cases are aware of strengths and weaknesses that teachers have. It takes good teachers to help pupils achieve to their optimum. Subject-matter knowledge of teachers, of course, is not the only important consideration or important factor in teaching. The teacher must like children and have an inward desire in wanting them to achieve to their optimum. The good teacher is respectful of children and shows the necessary patience in working with all learners so they can feel successful in learning.

The self-contained classroom then has its strengths and weaknesses as do all plans in grouping pupils for instruction. Since the self-contained room is a traditional plan for grouping, it has come under considerable criticism. However, one must realize that this plan emphasizes that the teacher should know pupils well by being with a given class for a major part of a school day. Pupils in this plan for grouping can be assisted in relating knowledge. The time allotted to each curriculum area in the self-contained room can be flexible. If the teacher needs more time for teaching mathematics in a given school day, perhaps it is feasible to shorten the time devoted to teaching social studies. On a different day, needed additional time can be given for the teaching of elementary school social studies. In other words in the self-contained classroom, flexibility in scheduling different curriculum areas of the elementary school is possible.

Departmentalization

Departmentalization emphasizes the importance of teachers being well prepared to teach in their area or areas of speciality. Thus, an elementary school teacher, for example, may teach only mathematics or only reading. The teacher in a departmentalized elementary school generally has a strong background of course work in the area he is teaching. For example, a social studies teacher will have much course work in the social sciences together with ample course work in elementary education. The student may have a double major in the two areas previously mentioned, or have a major in elementary education with a minor or an area of concentration in the social sciences. Thus, the teacher should be well prepared in terms of credit hours in a given academic area on the college and/or university level to teach in a departmentalized school. This teacher would generally have fewer daily preparations to make in a departmentalized plan as compared to the self-contained classroom. The teacher in a departmentalized school may teach social studies, for example, to five fifth or sixth grade classes.

Not many elementary schools emphasize departmentalization on the primary grade levels. The subject-matter knowledge needed on these grade levels is generally not a major problem; however, it is very important for these teachers to be warm, friendly, understanding, and help each child realize his optimum potential.

It becomes difficult to correlate or integrate different curriculum areas in the elementary school when departmentalization is emphasized strongly. Each curriculum area may become an isolated domain unto itself. Various curriculum areas can be correlated or integrated in a departmentalized plan of grouping if teachers teaching the separate academic areas plan together. They could plan together how science and social studies may be correlated so that pupils sense degrees of relationship between these two curriculum areas. For example, when fifth grade pupils would be studying a unit on the "Age of Discovery" in social studies, they could also be developing science principles and generalizations pertaining to magnetism in a unit on "Magnetism and Electricity." With the use of steel needles and a magnet, pupils could develop resultant magnets by stroking the needles in one direction on the magnet. The magnetized needle could then be placed on a cork which is floating in a pan of water. Pupils could observe the poles of the magnetized needle. Understandings could be developed by learners pertaining to like poles of magnets repel whereas unlike poles attract. The magnetized needle would behave in a similar way in relationship to the north and south magnetic field on the surface of the earth. Compasses became important for sailors during the "Age of Discovery" when new lands and water routes were being explored and discovered.

As a further example, reading and social studies could be correlated in a departmentalized plan of grouping pupils if teachers from these two curriculum areas would plan together. If pupils are studying a unit on "Colonization in the New World" in social studies, the basal reader may have selected stories that relate to that period of time. Thus pupils would have additional opportunities to learn more about the dolonists in Colonial America in the curriculum area of reading and this could be correlated with the related ongoing social studies unit. Ample time would need to be given by teachers for planning from the different curriculum areas being taught in a departmentalized plan of grouping so that subject-matter areas or different academic disciplines may become related in the thinking of pupils. Correlation for the sake of correlating is to be frowned upon. Correlating and integrating of content are important when it helps pupils to develop interest, purpose, and motivation for learning. Also, pupils should not think in terms of isolated, fragmented knowledge to the point of memorizing unimportant facts for test purposes or under threat from teachers and parents. An excessive number of isolated facts which are learned by pupils make retention of learning a major problem. Generally, pupils will retain learnings longer if knowledge is perceived as being related rather than as isolated, unrelated bits of information.

Homogeneous versus Heterogeneous Grouping

Educators have long debated and discussed the pros and cons of homogeneous versus heterogeneous grouping of pupils. Some have stated that homogeneous grouping is not as democratic as it could be since pupils of a similar level of achievement would be placed in a specific group. For example, the top achievers in mathematics in the sixth grade would be in one room in an elementary school followed by the second best achievers being in a different room. Other levels of mathematics achievement would be in separate rooms with the slowest learners in this curriculum area being grouped in a room by themselves. It has been felt by some educators that pupils need to interact with others regardless of achievement levels. Principals, supervisors, and teachers could provide situations whereby learners work and play together with others regardless of capacity and achievement levels even though homogeneous grouping is emphasized for several curriculum areas. For example, pupils could be grouped heterogeneously in physical education, music, and art. This type of plan for grouping pupils emphasizes heterogeneity in several curriculum areas of the elementary school. For other curriculum areas, homogeneous grouping could be emphasized such as in mathematics, the language arts, social studies, and science.

Teachers may find it easier to teach a given group of learners if homogeneous grouping is in evidence as compared to heterogeneous grouping since the range of achievement will not be as great within a class. However, teachers may not like to teach a class of slow learners as well as those who achieve at a faster rate of speed. The attitude of the teacher, of course, may be reflected within learners. Since the range of achievement in a class may be very great in heterogeneous grouping, it may pose a problem for some teachers in providing for individual differences. In certain methods of teaching it may not matter much if heterogeneous or homogeneous grouping is utilized. For example, in individualized reading, each pupil basically selects his own library book to read. He generally selects a book which is on his reading level. His own reading of the library book will involve a pace which should be in harmony with being able to comprehend the contents adequately. Each pupil in a class will read at a different rate of speed. Also each learner will select a library book which differs in complexity from other library books selected for reading by other children in the classroom. Thus, individual differences can be provided for regardless of capacity and achievement levels of pupils in a class or group. Following the reading of a library book, the teacher may have a conference with the pupil. The teacher can then get data on the learner having comprehended the contents of the library book as well as evaluating pupil interest, enthusiasm, and purpose for reading the book. The teacher can also evaluate the quality of oral reading of the child when the latter reads a section of the library book orally. The teacher can record the results of the conference for future reference. Comparisons can be made of conferences held with each pupil from one time to the next to notice changes in behaviour.

In using individualized reading in the classroom, it is obvious that heterogeneous or homogeneous grouping would not be a major problem. It becomes more of a problem when utilizing basal readers if the teacher feels that all learners in a class or in a group should be at the same place at the same time in using a specific series of these readers. It is only common knowledge that learners in a class differ in capacity, achievement, interest, and motivation. Thus, learners in a class cannot be held to the same achievement without detrimental results. For some pupils the expected uniform standards of achievement of traditional teachers will be too difficult where frustration and failure may be the end result. For other learners these standards may be excessively low resulting in boredom and a lack of enthusiasm. The teacher must provide for individual differences regardless of the plan of grouping.

Team Teaching in the Elementary School

A rather recent innovation in grouping pupils for instruction is team teaching. The term 'team' implies that teachers work together cooperatively in determining objectives, learning activities, and evaluation techniques when teaching a specific set of learners. Team teaching needs to be differentiated from 'turn teaching'. In turn teaching, each teacher does his own planning for teaching and then takes his turn teaching pupils either in a large group or small group sessions. Other teachers also take their turn teaching these learners. However, there is little or no interaction among teachers when planning the objectives, learning activities, and evaluation techniques.

Democratic planning is very important when team members work together. Team teaching emphasizes that members learn from each other in planning sessions. Thus, inservice education is an inherent part of team teaching as a plan in grouping pupils for instruction. If a leader or member of teaching team would be very domineering or autocratic, the chances are that individuals, of course, would not learn from each other. There needs to be mutual respect of personalities and ideas presented when team members select the best objectives, the best learning activities, and the best evaluation techniques to be utilized in teaching a given set of learners.

The talents of each teacher should be utilized when providing learning activities for pupils. For example, when large group instruction is utilized in teaching ninety pupils, each team member's strengths should be analyzed to determine who should do the teaching in the large group session. If pupils are studying a unit on "New England—Past and Present," a team member may have travelled extensively in this area as well as studied its past history thoroughly. This team member may have excellent slides, pictures, filmstrips, and booklets pertaining to the New England area. Thus, large group instruction, no doubt, would heavily involve using the talents of this member of the team. At other times, different members of the team will be utilizing their talents involving large group instruction in team teaching.

After the large group session has been completed, all teachers on the team should guide learners in small group sessions. Here, learners can ask questions pertaining to the content of learning activities presented in large group instruction. Additional learning activities, carefully selected, can be provided in small group sessions. The teacher needs to select activities which are meaningful, interesting and purposeful to learners. Pupils need to be actively involved in ongoing learning activities. A variety of learning activities should be provided for learners in small group sessions. It should be pointed out that in large group instruction, the teaching team must consider and select those learning activities which capture pupil curiosity and are relevant for learners. If activities are not selected carefully, it will be difficult to hold the attention of pupils and valuable time in learning will be lost.

Ample opportunity also needs to be given to pupils to work on individual projects and activities. With the guidance of the teaching team, pupils should work on purposeful projects and activities on an individual basis which relate to the large and small group sessions.

Team teaching has long emphasized the importance of teachers using their time wisely in what they were trained and educated to do. Thus, teachers should teach and plan for teaching rather than performing routine tasks such as collecting lunch and milk money, putting overshoes on pupils, and keeping attendance records. During the school day, there should be time available for planning. Planning should not be done before the school day begins and after it ends only. In team approach, some planning can, of course, be done, during the school day. For example, a team which teaches only social studies in a school year should have a free period each school day when planning can be done.

There are numerous plans available which emphasize basic principles related to team teaching. In the master teacher plan, a teacher would be designated as the leader of the team with status difference. This individual may also receive more salary than other team members due to having additional responsibilities. The master teacher should have demonstrated teaching proficiency in the curriculum area or areas his team is responsible for. His background of course work on the college and/or university level should be strong relating again to the curriculum area or areas his team assumes responsibility for. The master teacher would then be the leader of the team when planning sessions are conducted. He should be able to work together well with others, particularly team members. The team approach in planning sessions involves 'give' and 'take' as far as verbal interaction is concerned. The group rather than the individual determines objectives, learning activities, and evaluation techniques.

Another plan for implementing ideas pertaining to team teaching would involve a team of teachers with no one individual being designated as the leader. Teacher A, for example, would present an idea. This idea could be modified by other team members. Teacher B then could modify, substantiate, or bring in new ideas in the planning session. Each teacher as he or she participates becomes the leader at the time ideas are being presented. In planning sessions, the best of thinking must be emphasized. Each idea must be assessed in terms of its worth and value rather than on who presented the idea or ideas. Selected teachers may feel uncomfortable when their ideas are being evaluated by other teachers in a planning session. A teacher may also feel uncomfortable when teaching in front of other teachers in large group sessions. In other words, team teaching may not be the best approach to use in grouping pupils for instruction as far as all elementary school teachers are concerned. Some teachers, of course, will do a better job of teaching in a self-contained classroom where there is little interaction with other teachers in the school pertaining to actual teaching-learning situations. Team teaching, however, can be very beneficial to many classroom teachers. Team members can learn much from each other in planning sessions if a democratic atmosphere exists. Some teachers are motivated to do a better job of teaching if other teachers are observing them in large group or small group sessions as well as when helping pupils in individual projects. Teachers on teams need to be flexible in their thinking so that ideas can be modified and the best of thinking is then in evidence pertaining to teaching-learning situations. When ideas are constructively criticized in planning sessions, teachers should not be offended at these suggestions. Rather, teachers should perceive this situation as occasions to improve the quality of teaching. Inservice education then becomes a part of the planning sessions.

Grouping within a Class

To provide for individual differences, pupils should have ample opportunities to work in groups. There should be ample times when pupils may select the group they wish to work in. For example, pupils in a class are studying a unit pertaining to Australia. A committee of pupils could be making a relief map of that country. A second committee may be developing a model sheep and cattle station, while a third committee is gathering information from several sources for a report on manufacturing in Australia. Perhaps, a fourth committee would be involved in dramatizing situations relating to wheat farming in Australia. In teacher-pupil planning sessions, cooperative decisions can be made pertaining to the goals each committee is to realize. Ultimately, each pupil can select the committee he would want to participate in.

There will be times when the teacher may appoint individual pupils to work on different committees. If the example given previously pertaining to committee work in a unit on Australia, the teacher could select pupils to work on each of the committees. For example, pupils who do well in reading content may be placed on the committee doing research on manufacturing in Australia. Other pupils having good eye-hand coordination may be appointed to serve on the committee making the relief map on Australia. In other words, the teacher in placing pupil in committees based on learner capacity, achievement, and interest. All pupils should achieve relevant understanding, skills, and attitudes.

The teacher could use the sociometric device to determine committee members. In using this device to evaluate social and personal growth, the teacher could ask questions of pupils pertaining to the following two areas:

1. If you were doing research on Australia, who would be your first, second, and third choice in selecting committee members to work with you?
2. If you were making a relief map or dramatizing a scene relating to Australia, who would be your first choice, second choice, and third choice, in terms of committee members?

The questions need to be worded on the understanding level of pupils. Pupils must feel confident that the teacher will keep the information obtained strictly confidential. The teacher can use the data to determine committee members. Certainly, pupils will do better work in committees if they can get along well with each other as compared to having a lack of harmony. To be sure, a few learners may feel that being on a committee with friends provides situations where "goofing-off" or "having a picnic" is in order. The teacher needs to develop standards or criteria with pupils when emphasizing committee work so that optimum achievement for all will be in evidence.

It can be excellent if interage grouping is emphasized in the elementary school. In society people of different ages interact with others regardless of age levels. Thus, pupils in an elementary school should have ample opportunities to play and work together regardless of age levels.

Having completed the relief map, the research, the model sheep and cattle station, and having practiced dramatizations pertaining to Australia, pupils from other classes of different age levels can be invited to the classroom to observe the ending or culminating of the social studies unit "Living in Australia." In situations such as these, pupils who are visiting the class which is ending a unit on Australia can learn much content as well as methodology in teaching. Perhaps, the visitors may wish to have similar learning activities in their own classroom. When teachers have ample opportunities to view the teaching procedures used by other professionals, the quality of teaching in many cases should improve.

Criteria for Grouping Pupils

Each elementary school should critically evaluate and develop criteria pertaining to grouping pupils for instruction. Criteria that are developed should harmonize with research findings on child growth and development characteristics. The type or plan of grouping that is implemented in the elementary school should help pupils to achieve to their optimum in intellectual, physical, social and emotional development. The following questions should be considered when evaluating different plans in grouping pupils for instruction:

1. Does the plan of grouping pupils aid in providing for individual differences within a specific class?
2. Does the plan provide ample opportunities for pupils to engage in committee work?
3. Would pupils achieve agreed upon objectives most effectively when this plan of grouping is used?
4. Do teachers think and feel that the plan for grouping being considered would assist them in doing the best job of teaching?
5. Does the plan for grouping pupils for instruction harmonize with the architecture of the school?
6. Does the elementary school have ample audio-visual aids and other materials for teaching which would harmonize with the plan being considered in grouping pupils for instruction?
7. Do parents and the lay public adequately understand and accept the new plan for grouping before it is implemented?
8. Would the plan harmonize with revised, up-to-date educational objectives of the local elementary school?
9. Would the plan in grouping pupils for instruction harmonize with what is known about child growth and development characteristics?
10. Would the plan harmonize with the concepts and generalizations of a democracy?
11. Could a teacher learn from other professionals in the elementary school when a specific plan of grouping pupils for instruction is utilized?
12. Do pupils have ample opportunities to interact with learners of different capacity and achievement levels as well as with those of similar capacity and achievement?

13. Would pupils have occasions to work with learners of a younger age level as well as with older children?
14. Would the plan of grouping pupils for instruction provide the child with needed security and status?

Numerous plans exist in grouping pupils for instruction. Each plan has its strengths and weaknesses. Thus, careful evaluation of each plan is important before it is implemented. The nongraded elementary school places primary emphasis upon continuous progress of learners. The self-contained classroom stresses the importance of teachers getting to know pupils well so that this information can be used to do a better job of teaching. Relating of different curriculum areas is also emphasized as being important in the self-contained classroom. The departmentalized elementary school emphasizes the importance of having pupils in a class who are as alike as possible in capacity and achievement. Heterogeneous grouping emphasizes the importance of learners having a variety of capacity and achievement levels within a specific class. In team teaching, teacher strengths must be utilized in teaching a specific curriculum area, such as social studies, science, mathematics, or reading. This would be true of large group and small group sessions as well as in aiding learners in individual study. In a team approach, members have ample opportunities to learn from each other when planning sessions are in operation to determine objectives, learning activities, and evaluation techniques for a given set of learners. Teachers in a team approach have occasions to observe each other in teaching-learning situations. Within a class-setting, the teacher must use a variety of acceptable criteria in grouping pupils for instruction in order to provide for individual differences.

REFERENCES

Ediger, Marlow and Digumarti Bhaskara Rao, *Elementary Curriculum*. New Delhi, India: Discovery Publishing House, 2003.

Ediger, Marlow and Digumarti Bhaskara Rao. *Relevancy in Elementary Curriculum*. New Delhi: Discovery Publishing House, 2004.

6

Providing For Individual Differences

Teachers, principals, and supervisors need to become thoroughly familiar with individual differences among pupils and how to guide each learner to achieve optimal development. Thus, it is important to be highly knowledgeable about traits pertaining to slow learners, average achievers, as well as talented and gifted pupils.

The Slow Learner

Which traits and characteristics do slow learners possesses? Generally, it can be said that slow learners may be described in the following ways:

1. They may come in the category of having IQ's or Intelligence Quotients ranging from 75-90.
2. Their achievement is lower than that of average achievers and will register lower than their present grade level average expectancy.
3. The attention span of slow learners is shorter than that of higher achievers.
4. It takes more time for the slow learners to understand a new process in mathematics as well as to master addition, subtraction, multiplication, and division facts.
5. These learners need more of concrete and semi-concrete learning activities than do faster learners.
6. Slow learners need learning activities which provide proper sequence.

7. More supervision and direction may need to be given to slow learners compared to pupils who achieve at a higher level.
8. A lack of opportunities to learn in the home setting may be the lot of many slow learners.
9. It is necessary for teachers to be patient and understanding in teaching pupils achieving at a slower rate of speed as compared to faster achievers.
10. Slow learners generally ask fewer questions and may reveal less curiosity in the school and class environment as compared to peers of similar age levels.

Talented Pupils

Teachers, principals, and supervisors need to identify and provide adequately for talented learners in the class setting. Talented pupils may reveal characteristics such as the following:

1. having a rather lengthy attention span;
2. possessing the ability to gain understandings and skills quickly;
3. being able to retain learnings well;
4. completing tasks more rapidly than peers in the class setting;
5. showing much curiosity in learning;
6. revealing tendencies of being creative individuals;
7. becoming more independent in learning;
8. having a desire to complete additional work in the school and class setting;
9. possessing knowledge and skills helpful in the areas of problem solving;
10. being able to engage in constructive learning activities when spare time is available in the school and class setting.

Comparing Talented Pupils and Slow Learners

There are always exceptions to statements made about human beings. However, in general the following comparisons may be made between talented pupils and slow learners:

1. Talented pupils retain learnings longer than do slow learners.
2. Talented learners possess more initiative and become more independent in learning as compared to peers in the school and class setting.

3. Pupils with much ability acquire learnings sooner as compared to learners with less capacity.

Learning Activities and Individual Differences

The teacher must select interesting, meaningful, and purposeful learning experiences to provide for individual differences in ongoing units of study in mathematics. Slow learners will need the following kinds of experiences:

1. Concrete phases of instruction need to be emphasized adequately whereby pupils use bean and corn seeds, checkers, crayons, beads, sticks, and other objects to clarify learnings in counting, addition, subtraction, multiplication, and division.
2. The teacher must explain new processes in mathematics thoroughly and patiently to slow learners. Adequate opportunities, of course, must also be given to aid these pupils in learning inductively.
3. Adequate emphasis must be given to help slow learners develop sequential learnings. Too frequently, the teacher wants to 'jump' too far ahead of these pupils in teaching-learning situations. Thus, selected slow learners have been taught addition involving regrouping and renaming (e.g., 48 + 17 = ——; 39 + 18 = ——) whereas these learners need more practice and guidance in simple addition (e.g., 32 + 13 = ——); 43 + 13 = ——).
4. The teacher needs to observe the attention span of slow learners in each learning activity. Thus, slow learners need to experience a new learning activity in mathematics before the preceding experiences become dull and boring.
5. Adequate supervision and guidance must be given to slow learners to aid them in achieving optimal development in mathematics. Thus, the teacher needs to evaluate if these pupils have achieved a desired objective before the next sequential objective is stressed in a new lesson or unit of study. Kindergarten and first grade pupils, for example, should be able to count to ten in a rote manner before counting the number of members in a set of ten.
6. There are many abstract symbols which may be emphasized in teaching-learning situations in ongoing units of study in mathematics. These abstract symbols

include + (plus), × (times), ÷ (divided by), = (equals), and others. Pupils should be guided to attach meaning to these symbols in functional situations. Abstract symbols in mathematics should not be emphasized in ongoing units of study to the point where slow learners feel frustrated and lack feelings of success in the mathematics curriculum.

7. Slow learners may be less creative in finding diverse solutions to a problem as compared to faster learners in the class setting. Thus, for example, a slow learner may be able to find one solution to a problem such as

$$\begin{array}{r} 42 \\ \times 6 \\ \hline 12 \\ 240 \\ \hline 252 \end{array}$$

Other algorisms could include the following:

(a)
$$\begin{array}{r} 42 \\ \times 6 \\ \hline 240 \\ 12 \\ \hline 252 \end{array}$$

(b)
$$\begin{array}{r} 42 \\ \times 6 \\ \hline 252 \end{array}$$

8. Slow learners need ample opportunities to engage in practice and drill activities involving previous learnings obtained from relevant units of study. Thus, slow learners need to experience new learning activities directly related to content mastered previously. If a pupil, for example, has learned in a meaningful, interesting, and purposeful way that 8 + 4 = 12 and 4 + 8 = 12, he/she may practice related learnings in which these addition facts are contained in relevant word problems. Drill as a method of teaching could involve the use of flash cards, games, and the overhead projector to fix specific learnings in the minds of pupils. Thus a pupil may need drill with the use of flash cards pertaining to the following:

$$\begin{array}{r} 8 \\ +5 \\ \hline 13 \end{array} \quad \begin{array}{r} 5 \\ +8 \\ \hline 13 \end{array} \quad \begin{array}{r} 13 \\ -8 \\ \hline 5 \end{array} \quad \begin{array}{r} 13 \\ -5 \\ \hline 8 \end{array}$$

9. Slow learners need to experience objectives in mathematics which are attainable. Presenting of slow learners before a new unit in mathematics is implemented aids in adjusting the new unit to the present achievement levels of these

learners. Objectives for slow learners to attain should not be too difficult nor should they pertain to what these learners have already acquired. Thus, new learnings may be gained by slow learners when achieving desired objectives in mathematics and at the same time success can be inherent in these experiences.

10. Slow learners should be guided to develop feelings of an adequate self-concept. These learners too frequently have experienced failure in mathematics, as well as other curriculum areas. Other pupils in the school and class setting may have minimized the worth and achievement of the slow learner. All pupils in the school and class setting need to be respected for their intrinsic worth regardless of ability, socio-economic level, or creed.

Adequate provision needs to be made for the fast learner in the mathematics curriculum. These pupils need to experience the following:

1. There needs to be less emphasis upon the concrete stage of learning and more emphasis upon abstract learnings. The teacher, however, must observe if these fast students are ready for relevant abstract learnings and guide each pupil to acquire optimal development.
2. The teacher generally needs to give less of explanations to these learners in terms of understanding new concepts and processes in the mathematics curriculum. Talented learners can become quite self-directed and independent in their work.
3. Fast learners can gain mathematical concepts and generalizations readily. These learners with teacher guidance may become relatively independent in sequencing their own learnings.
4. The talented pupil has a longer attention span as compared to the slow learner. Thus, time devoted to the teaching of mathematics should harmonize with the attention span of these learners and result in a balanced programme of learning for pupils in the elementary school.
5. Less direct supervision in mathematics of talented and gifted pupils needs to be in evidence by the classroom teacher. These learners in the class setting can be

independent and responsible in ongoing units of study in mathematics.

6. Talented and gifted pupils may be highly fascinated and challenged when encountering abstract symbols and concepts in the mathematics curriculum. A stimulating environment with interesting, meaningful, and purposeful learning experiences will aid pupils in wanting to acquire relevant abstract content. Thus, for example, talented first grade pupils may attach meaning to abstract concepts, such as lines, line segments, points, and rays. With appropriate sequence in learning talented sixth graders, as a further example, can attach meaning to abstract concepts such as square root, complex numbers, irrational real numbers, and tolerance.
7. Talented and gifted pupils in the mathematics curriculum should be guided to become increasingly independent in their work. Thus, these learners should have ample opportunities to select what to learn, as well as methods of learning. With teacher guidance, these pupils should be guided in evaluating their own achievement in ongoing units of study as well as with a specific problem or area of difficulty being experienced. Talented and gifted pupils with teacher leadership should assess their own progress in units of study dealing with the following:
   (a) sets and mathematical sentences;
   (b) structural ideas or properties in mathematics;
   (c) basic addition, subtraction, multiplication, and division facts;
   (d) algorisms for addition, subtraction, multiplication, and division using whole numbers;
   (e) prime numbers, composite numbers, and integers;
   (f) addition, subtraction, multiplication, and division for fractional numbers;
   (g) addition, subtraction, multiplication, and division using decimals and per cents;
   (h) metric and nonmetric geometry;
   (i) other systems of numeration;
   (j) uses for probability and statistics;

(k) functions in the mathematics curriculum.

8. Talented and gifted pupils should be guided to achieve to their optimum in individual endeavours as well as in committee work in the class setting. The teacher must guide these learners to experience continuous progress in ongoing units of study in mathematics as well as to work together harmoniously with others. Too frequently, the mathematics teacher may emphasize individual efforts on the part of the pupil largely. Thus, committee work on the part of pupils is greatly deemphasized. Certainly, there needs to be rational balance between pupils working on an individual basis as well as within a committee setting. Gifted and talented pupils may work together within a committee to understand a new process, check computations, and/or solve a problem in an ongoing unit of study in mathematics. Talented and gifted pupils could also assist slower achievers in the mathematics curriculum. There are several values inherent in a learning activity of this kind involving fast learners helping slow learners in mathematics units of study:

   (a) Talented and gifted pupils may develop feelings of an adequate self by helping others who need assistance.

   (b) Fast learners may understand previously developed learnings more fully by explaining related content to pupils who learn at a slower rate.

   (c) Talented and gifted pupils may develop wholesome attitudes toward those who experience difficulty in learning.

Talented and gifted pupils as well as those learners who achieve at a slower rate need to develop feelings of being accepted by others, belonging to a group, having security and status in the school and class setting, and being able to participate freely in ongoing learning experiences.

Specific Ways of Providing for Individual Differences

There are numerous ways available to provide for individual differences in the mathematics curriculum. The following approaches, among others, can be utilized to provide for slow learners, average achievers, as well as talented and gifted pupils:

1. using behaviourally stated objectives. Learners of different achievement levels would achieve the same measurable objectives. However, slow learners attain each objective in sequence at a slower rate as compared to average achievers and fast learners;
2. pretesting pupils to ascertain their own individual achievement levels at the beginning of a new school year when using a series of reputable mathematics textbooks. Each pupil depending on his/her present achievement level would be participating in learning activities directly related to pretest results based on content from a series of mathematics textbook. Thus, for example, a fourth grade pupil may be participating in learning experiences involving the use of a third grade mathematics textbook, while a talented and gifted peer may be involved in learning experiences using content from a fifth or sixth grade mathematics textbook;
3. providing learning centres to enrich experiences for talented and gifted pupils who have completed assigned work in ongoing units of study in mathematics;
4. grouping pupils within the class setting to provide for individual differences. Thus, slow learners, average achievers, and fast learners could be taught in separate groups in an atmosphere of respect. The mathematics curriculum would be adjusted to the present achievement level of each of these groups of learners;
5. grouping pupils homogeneously for mathematics instruction on the intermediate grade levels. Thus, if feasible, fast learners could be taught in one class setting, average achievers in a different class setting, with slow learners comprising a third group;
6. using a variety of materials and methods in the mathematics curriculum. Thus, the mathematics curriculum is adjusted to diverse learning styles exhibited by learners. Also, there are more complex learnings in mathematics available for fast learners as compared to other levels of achievement. With the use of concrete materials (real objects or replicas), differences between and among pupils in mathematics achievement may be

more adequately provided for as compared to the use of abstract learnings. Thus, in using a meter stick (a concrete object) in a unit on "Measurement and the Metric System," slow learners may measure the height of selected objects such as a door, window, and desk. Talented learners may use a meter stick to find the area of the classroom or the volume of selected containers;

When abstract learnings are to be acquired in mathematics, it is much more difficult to provide for individual differences. For example, if pupils are to learn to divide the following as a new experience for all learners in a heterogeneously grouped classroom; 8478 ÷ 36, talented pupils will generally develop new understandings much more rapidly as compared to peers of similar chronological age. Thus, if talented pupils are ready for developing learnings pertaining to the previously named division problem slow learners and average achievers may then not possess needed background learnings;

7. accelerating achievement of talented and gifted pupils in the mathematics curriculum. In a nongraded programme of mathematics instruction, fast learners can be guided to experience continuous progress within the framework of a challenging and meaningful curriculum. Thus, for example, in a fourth grade class, selected talented learners may be acquiring relevant experiences based on criteria related to fifth, sixth, or seventh grade level of attainment;
8. organising a mathematics club to provide for individual differences. Selected pupils with teacher guidance may wish to organise a mathematics club as a means of enriching the curriculum as well as providing for individual differences. Thus, at selected regularly scheduled intervals, meetings may be held involving members in the mathematics club. The members may:
   (a) view and discuss content from filmstrips relating to stimulating topics in mathematics;
   (b) identify topics, units and specific problems in mathematics for discussion and evaluation;
   (c) interect with a resource person (high school or university mathematics instructor) involving a challenging area of interest in mathematics.

(d) make models pertaining to learning gained from ongoing units of study in geometry.

In Summary

Teachers, principals, and supervisors need to study, appraise, and implement research findings, pertaining to helping slow, average, and fast achievers realize optimal development in the school and class setting. Thus, educators in the schools need to ask questions and attempt to arrive at solutions pertaining to the following problem areas:

1. How do slow learners differ from average achievers in intellectual, emotional, social, and physical development? How are slow learners different from fast learners in these same four facets of development?
2. How can educational objectives be selected which are attainable for slow, average, and fast achievers?
3. What criteria should be utilized to select learning activities for all pupils in the school and class setting so that each may experience continuous progress in the mathematics curriculum?
4. How can each child's progress in different curriculum areas be evaluated appropriately and thus help to insure the best quality learning experiences possible for each individual learner?

REFERENCES

Copeland, Richard W. *Mathematics and the Elementary Teacher*. Fourth Edition. New York: The Macmillan Company, 1982.

Joyce, Bruce R., and Berj Harootunian. *The Structure of Teaching*. Chicago: Science Research Associate, Inc., 1967.

Kidd, K., *et al*. *The Laboratory Approach to Mathematics*. Chicago: Science Research Associates, Inc., 1970.

National Council of Teachers of Mathematics. *The Learning of Mathematics*, Its Theory and Practice. Washington D.C.: Twenty-First Yearbook, 1953.

National Society for the Study of Education. *Mathematics Education*. Chicago: NSSE, Sixty-Ninth Year Book, 1970.

Turnbull, A.P. and J.B. Schulz. *Mainstreaming Handicapped Students: A Guide for the Classroom Teacher*. Boston: Allyn and Bacon, Inc., 1979.

7

Reading and the Language Arts

Each pupil should develop optimum proficiency in reading. Reading can be a very enjoyable leisure activity. Individuals enrich themselves by engaging in reading activities. In society, it is important for individuals to do much reading and thus remain informed about problems and issues on the local, state, national, and international levels. Each person may then have additional alternatives from which decisions can be made. A broad base of background knowledge may assist learners to increase their proficiency to make decisions.

Each pupil differs from other children in the class setting in achievement, capacity, interests, and motivation for reading. Thus, the teacher must make provision for individual differences among learners in the reading curriculum.

Experience Charts and Reading

In a reading readiness programme for early primary grade children, experience charts may be developed cooperatively by pupils with teacher guidance. The experience chart approach is sound since it is based upon personal experiences of involved pupils. Thus, pupils experience ideas from excursions, filmstrips, films, pictures, slides, or discussions. Following the experience, pupils present content for an experience chart. The teacher in this situation prints the content using neat manuscript letters. Most pupils generally have not developed a writing vocabulary to do the actual writing. After the content has been written in large, highly legible manuscript letters, pupils read what has been written with teacher guidance. The teacher points to words and phrases as they are being read by pupils. Learners then are reading what they have experienced.

The following assumptions support utilizing experience charts:

1. Pupils are actively involved in experiences which provide content for an experience chart.
2. Learners present ideas for the experience chart.
3. Pupils with teacher help read content pertaining to their very own experiences.
4. Learners may notice how ideas are written down utilizing abstract letters in words.
5. The content in the experience chart is familiar to learners since it relates to their own personal lives.
6. The experience chart method may assist pupils to develop interest in reading.
7. Individualization is inherent in using experience charts since each child has unique experience. Each child may then present content for a group or individual experience chart.

Learning Centres and Reading

A different approach to individualize instruction in reading pertains to the use of learning centres. One of these centres might well be a reading centre. Library books should be on diverse reading levels and on various stimulating topics. Ideally each pupil selects an interesting library book to read on the appropriate reading level. Following the reading of a library book, pupil achievement may be evaluated in several ways.

1. Task cards at the learning centre could be written with open-ended questions for pupils to respond to.
2. The teacher and pupil might discuss contents of a library book which the latter has completed reading.
3. The child may choose his/her own approach in revealing comprehension pertaining to content in a library book such as in completing a diorama, a dramatization, a frieze, or a picture.
4. The pupil might share ideas gained from reading a library book within a small group or committee.

Any approach that is used to assess pupil achievement should stimulate learners to do additional reading.

Reading Readiness and Individualized Instruction

There are numerous learning activities which assist pupils in learning to read through a quality reading readiness programme. Providing for individual differences is an important concept for teachers to follow when selecting learning activities in a reading readiness programme.

Background information must be developed within pupils in a quality reading readiness programme. Later, pupils will read much content where familiarity with ideas is important. To aid in developing background information, the following learning activities, among others, may be utilized:

1. Discuss pictures with pupils pertaining to ongoing units of study.
2. Show and discuss films, filmstrips, and slides.
3. Have pupils take an excursion and discuss observations made.
4. View and have follow-up activities pertaining to a telecast on educational television.
5. Develop learning centres with appropriate activities to help pupils achieve relevant background information.

For each of the above learning activities, purpose must be developed within pupils prior to participation. The learning activities can provide for individual differences even though learners at selected intervals may be taught in large group instruction. Pupils may then interpret content from audio-visual materials on their own individual present achievement levels. It is best if most of these activities can be used in small group or committee work. Pupils may then have increased opportunities to interact with other learners in discussing acquired facts, concepts, and generalizations. The frequency of interaction in a discussion per pupil in small group work is greater than would be true of larger groups or the class as a whole.

In a quality reading readiness programme, it is important for learners to experience hearing likenesses and differences in sounds. Thus, for example, a teacher may ask pupils to present words which have the same beginning sound as does the word 'bat.' Pupils may also be asked to give words which rhyme with 'bat.' These activities should aid learners to become increasingly proficient in phonetic analysis. Later, in more formalized programmes of reading instruction, the use of phonetic analysis will aid in unlocking new words.

In a reading readiness programme pupils begin to make associations between symbol and sound. When pupils are reading from an experience chart with teacher guidance, they may well notice specific letters in words and make the proper associations with sounds.

When selected objects are labelled in a class, pupils ultimately will also make associations between symbols and sounds. If they cannot identify the abstract word, the real object will tell its meaning, such as the labelled abstract word 'chair' on a real chair. Pupils learn to identify individual words at different rates of speed. Provision may then be made for individual differences.

Pupils should have ample opportunities to browse through interesting and appealing library books containing quality pictures. Illustrated books have a tendency to provide for individual differences when chosen by pupils. Learners may then interpret illustrations on their own individual achievement level. The teacher also needs to read library books to pupils in a reading readiness programme. Thus, pupils may become motivated in wanting to learn to read.

Further learning activities in a reading readiness programme might consist of pupils advancing at individual levels of achievement in noticing configuration clues. Experiences in noticing configuration clues must be provided in proper sequence for each learner. Among others, these learning activities may include the following:

1. Pupils make a cross on which word looks different from two other words (man lonely man).
2. Learners place an 'X' on which letter appears different from two other letters (h h a).

Gross discriminations need to be made by pupils followed in sequence by those involving finer discriminations. Fine discriminations are involved in which a word or letter looks different in appearance from the remaining words/letters in each of the following sets:

1. house hen house;
2. b b 1;
3. horse hill hill;
4. a a b.

Basal Readers and the Pupil

Basal readers are used quite frequently in elementary school classrooms. Teachers need to utilize the manual directly related to the basal reader in a creative manner. Too frequently, the manual is utilized rigidly. Suggestions pertaining to objectives, learning activities, and assessment procedures found in manuals of basal readers should be adapted to individual differences in the class setting. The manual can give teachers many excellent suggestions to use in teaching-learning situations. The following criteria are recommended in helping pupils achieve to their optimum when basal readers are utilized:

1. Basal readers should be on the present achievement level of pupils when learning activities are provided.
2. Prior to reading a given selection, pupils should have adequate readiness activities such as:
   (a) gaining adequate background information;
   (b) seeing new words in manuscript print and attaching meaning to these words;
   (c) establishing purposes for reading. The purposes may pertain to questions which require answers from reading a given selection.
3. Following the reading activity, pupils should have appropriate follow-up activities, such as:
   (a) discussing purposes or answers to questions after reading a given selection;
   (b) writing a summary of main ideas read;
   (c) developing an illustration, frieze, mural, or diorama;
   (d) reading additional literature related to the content read;
   (e) selecting stories and books written by the same author;
   (f) reading selected portions orally;

(g) writing diverse forms of poetry;
(h) dramatizing selected sections of the content;
(i) developing a related bulletin board display.

Basal readers have been misused by classroom teachers. Certainly, teachers must apply relevant principles of learning in teaching-learning situations involving the use of basal readers. These principles would include:

(a) providing for individual differences;
(b) attaching meaning to what has been learned;
(c) stimulating learners in desiring to learn;
(d) praising pupils for improved performance regardless of past achievement;
(e) diagnosing pupil difficulties and working toward remediation;
(f) having learners achieve at their own optimum unique rates of achievement;
(g) selecting interesting learning activities;
(h) having pupils sense reasons for participating in ongoing learning activities;
(i) providing sequential learning for learners;
(j) having pupils voice their concerns and interests in selecting reading materials;
(k) maintaining balance among objectives pertaining to learning word recognition techniques, reading for a variety of purposes, and reading for enjoyment.

There are selected procedures which have been used in situations involving the use of basal readers which definitely cannot be recommended. Among others, these include the following:

1. All pupils in a class being on the same page at the same time in a basal reader.
2. Every learning activity in the manual being utilized in teaching-learning situations for all pupils in the class setting.
3. Pupils rigidly developing learnings pertaining to phonetic analysis and other word recognition techniques when they already are reading proficiently.

4. Teachers emphasizing recall of information largely, when purposes for reading are being pursued on the part of pupils. Higher levels of thinking also need adequate emphasis, e.g. critical thinking, creative thinking, and problem solving.
5. Little emphasis being placed on pupils reading for enjoyment.
6. The same or similar methodology being used rather continuously in teaching reading.
7. Content in basal readers not being correlated or integrated with other curriculum areas in the elementary school.
8. Teachers not diagnosing pupil difficulties in reading adequately and not working toward remediation of problems.
9. Pupils not being taught in terms of using child growth and development characteristics.
10. Recommended principles of learning not being utilized in teaching-learning situations.
11. A lack of teacher knowledge or enthusiasm in teaching reading.

The teacher of reading needs to engage in self-evaluation to determine which trends in a modern reading curriculum should be emphasized in teaching-learning situations in the class setting.

Linguistics and Reading

Selected specialists have emphasized the importance of linguistic approaches in guiding learners to achieve in reading. According to the one linguistic school of thought in beginning reading instruction, pupils should learn to read words which have rather through consistency between symbol and sound. Pupils may then learn to read sentences in which words follow a specific pattern in pronunciation and spelling. Thus, the teacher might guide pupils in learning to read sentences containing the following words:

man fan Dan pan tan

ban can Nan ran van

Or, pupils in beginning reading could learn to read words such as the following in sentences:

bet net pet vet

met let set wet

It is difficult, of course, to write sentences with involved words following a pattern such as in the above named 'man' family or 'bet' family of words. This approach in the teaching of reading has been acceptable by some teachers. However, in the curriculum area of spelling, pupils in many units of study, learn to spell words where patterns are important. Thus, pupils are learning the structure of words such as in the following set where the initial consonant can be changed and a new word results: pat, rat, fat, cat, bat, hat Nat, and sat.

There are advantages that linguistic approaches in the teaching of reading emphasize. These implications may also hold true for spelling. Among others, the advantages include the following:

1. Pupils can be aided in reading instruction by noticing how selected words pattern rather consistently between symbol and sound.
2. Learners develop understandings pertaining to structure of related words following a general or specific pattern.
3. Pupils may learn to identify new words when thinking of related patterns.
4. Learners develop a positive approach in identifying new words when viewing structure or pattern of words.

Disadvantages in using linguistic approaches in the teaching of reading might be the following:

1. Monotonous reading activities may be experienced by pupils, especially in beginning teaching-learning situations.
2. There might be a lack of relationship in terms of how pupils speak using functional sentences as compared to reading content in beginning reading using selected linguistic approaches.
3. Many words are spelled in an irregular manner in the English language and do not pattern well, such as 'my', 'sigh', 'I', and 'lye'. These words contain the long 'i' sound.

In using linguistic approaches in the teaching of reading, pupils encounter more of irregularly spelled words as they progress through the elementary school years. There also are irregularly spelled words which follow a pattern, such as 'blight, 'flight', 'might', 'plight', 'sight', and 'night'.

Specific Objectives and Reading

Selected teachers, supervisors, and administrators advocate the use of specific objectives in the teaching of reading. These objectives are written in a precise manner. It is possible to measure if pupils have achieved specific objectives after instruction. Through observation, as one method of appraisal, the teacher can evaluate if pupils have or have not achieved the desired ends. Specific objectives must be selected carefully, prior to instruction, by those involved in teaching pupils. Thus, relevancy is an important concept to emphasize in selecting specific objectives for pupils to achieve.

The following are examples of specific objectives which pupils may achieve on their own unique achievement level:

1. The pupil will voluntarily read a library book and be able to answer three out of four questions correctly in evaluating comprehension.
2. The learner will pronounce correctly 95 per cent of words encountered in reading a selection from the basal reader.
3. Reading a story of his/her own choosing, the pupil will state the main idea in the selection.
4. Having identified a problem in any curriculum area, the pupil will select five reference sources to gain a relevant solution.
5. The pupil will present at least three generalizations related to content read from a self-selected library book.
6. The learner will analyze a selection in reading by identifying three opinions given by the writer.
7. After completing the reading assignment, pupils will assess content in terms of presenting two accurate statements and two inaccurate statements.
8. The learner will tell a story pertaining to content read using appropriate sequence of sentences.
9. Following the reading of content in social studies, the pupil will give five facts contained in the selection.
10. Having read content pertaining to five story problems in mathematics, the pupil will tell in his/her own words information needed to provide viable solutions.

It is important for teachers to write significant objectives when specificity is important. Too frequently, specific objectives are written which can be stated quickly and may then represent irrelevant learnings. Each objectives in reading must be evaluated thoroughly in terms of acceptable standards.

Determining Reading Levels

One of the most important problems facing teachers of reading is to determine reading levels of individual pupils. Once this has been accomplished, the teacher has a further responsibility in finding materials which are beneficial to each individual. How can the teacher determine present reading levels of each pupil in the class setting?

1. The school may use standardized achievement tests to determine reading levels of pupils. These tests need to be assessed in terms of being valid and reliable. Grade equivalent test results from standardized tests may provide guidance to teachers in determining reading levels of learners on an individual basis.
2. The teacher may mark off approximately 100 running words in a basal textbook. The content has not been read previously by the pupil. The learner orally reads the selection to the teacher. Generally, pupils should pronounce 95 to 98 per cent of the words correctly, if the involved book has content on the instructional level of the learner. The teacher also must select, with great care, four questions covering the selection to be read by pupils. Each pupil basically should be able to answer correctly three out of the four questions to assess comprehension in reading.

The figure given pertaining to correct word pronunciation as well as reading comprehension are approximate. If pupils, for example, pronounce 75 per cent of the words correctly in a selection, comprehension will suffer. Thus, this book being considered is not on the instructional level of individual pupils. Or, if a pupil continually pronounces all words correctly without previous practice and can continually respond correctly to all relevant questions asked to assess comprehension, the book being considered will generally be too easy for the learner. The textbook might then be considered to be on the recreational level of reading. There is no room for growth in recognising new words in reading on the part of individual pupils if, without previous practice, the child can pronounce 100 per cent of the words correctly. Thus, in a quality reading programme, there is room in each lesson for pupils to learn to identify a few new words as well as be challenged in the area of comprehension.

The teacher then has an important responsibility in determining reading levels of individual pupils. Appropriate materials must be obtained to assist each pupil in achieving optimally in reading.

Evaluating Reading Achievement

In assessing pupil achievement in reading, teachers need to ask themselves, among others, the following questions:

1. Did I guide each child in learning to read to his or her highest potentials?
2. Were reading materials provided for each child's own unique level of achievement?
3. Did pupils engage in more independent reading than formerly?
4. Were pupils guided in developing proficiency in word attack skills so that comprehension of content was at an optimal level?
5. Did it appear that pupils enjoyed learning activities involving reading?
6. Were pupils developing optimal skills in reading for a variety of purposes?
7. Did learners have ample opportunities to assess their own achievement in reading?
8. Were pupils permitted to make an adequate number of choices in terms of selections to be read?
9. Did each child achieve stated objectives in reading instruction?
10. Were attitudinal objectives emphasized adequately as well as skills and understanding objectives in teaching-learning situations?
11. Did pupils develop appropriate appreciations toward quality literature in the reading curriculum?
12. Were pupil difficulties in reading diagnosed adequately?

13. Was remedial reading instruction emphasized adequately for needy learners.
14. Did I attempt to determine reading levels of each pupil?
15. Were appropriate learning activities selected to provide for individual differences?
16. Did I use valid evaluation techniques in assessing learner achievement?
17. If pupils did not achieve desired objectives, did I attempt to determine causes for this happening to remedy identified deficiencies?

In Summary

There are many innovations in the teaching of reading. Teachers, principals, and supervisors must become thoroughly familiar with new methods of teaching. New approaches in teaching reading should be evaluated thoroughly before being introduced in an elementary school. Objectives in reading must be carefully selected for pupils to achieve. Learning activities to achieve desired ends, as well as appraisal procedures to evaluate achievement, need to provide for individual differences among learners.

REFERENCES

Ediger, Marlow and Digumarti Bhaskara Rao. *Teaching Reading Successfully*. New Delhi, India: Discovery Publishing House, 2000.

Ediger, Marlow and Digumarti Bhaskara Rao. *Language Arts Curriculum*. New Delhi: Discovery Publishing House, 2003.

Ediger, Marlow and Digumarti Bhaskara Rao. *Teaching Language Arts Successfully*. New Delhi: Discovery Publishing House, 2004.

Microcomputers in the Reading Curriculum

The microcomputer era is increasingly becoming important in the school and class setting. Prior to the utilization of microcomputers, the following methods of reading instruction, among others, have been utilized:

1. basal readers with its accompanying manuals. The manuals provide objectives, teaching suggestions, and evaluation procedures to notice student achievement. Basal readers are published by commercial companies and represent a rather popular method in the teaching of reading. Contents in these readers provide common learnings for a given set of students in a classroom;
2. individualized reading with its emphasis upon using trade or library books, not basal readers. Each student selects his/her own library book to read sequentially. Methods of appraising comprehension and achievement from reading a library book involves the utilization of a conference with pupil and teacher participation;
3. language experience approaches involve personal as well as group activities which provide background information. The experiences of learners from excursions and/or audio-visual information provide students with content for the experience chart. The teacher, generally in manuscript letters, records ideas presented by pupils from the excursions or audio-visual presentation. Pupils with teacher guide read the recorded ideas;

4. the Initial Teaching Alphabet (ITA) which has selected new or modified symbols to record words in a rather consistent sound (phoneme) and symbol (grapheme) relationship. Thus, the letters 'oo' in moon are printed 'ω' to represent consistency between phoneme and grapheme. Or, the 'ow' sound in how are written 'ou' to emphasize consistent sound symbol relationships. The long i sound (as in my, high, dye, I, pie, and light) is always printed i.e. The following symbols, as examples, are printed the same in ITA as compared to traditional spelling—b, d, f, h, k, l, m, n, p, r, s, t, v, w, y, and z;
5. linguistic procedures with its emphasis upon patterns. The patterns might involve words, such as ban, can, fan, man, pan, ran, and tan to be utilized within sentences. Young children in the early primary years may learn that an initial consonant is changed in the above named list and a new word results, *e.g.* changing the letter 'b' to the letter 'c' changes the word 'ban' to 'can.' In sequence, as learners progress through the grades, they experience patterns where less consistency between grapheme and phoneme is in evidence.

Linguists also emphasize students understanding sentence patterns, such as:

1. subject-predicate;
2. subject-predicate-direct object;
3. subject-linking verb-predicate adjective;
4. subject-linking verb-predicate nominative;
5. subject-predicate-indirect object-direct objects.

Microcomputer usage can incorporate philosophies in the teaching of reading from:

1. basal readers;
2. individualized reading;
3. language experience approaches;
4. the Initial Teaching Alphabet;
5. linguistic methods.

Psychology of Microcomputer Instruction

Software utilized in microcomputer teaching situations must follow definite criteria. Certainly, the programme utilized must fit in to a specific lesson being taught. Thus, if reading for facts is being emphasized, the software being used should directly relate to having students read to acquire salient facts.

Within the framework of microcomputer experiences, learners need to achieve sequence or appropriate order. Steps too difficult to achieve or learnings that lack challenge need to be avoided. New learnings then need to be attained by pupils and yet the content acquired is feasible or possible in its acquisition.

Content presented in software must be meaningful for involved learners. Understanding what is being learned from microcomputer use is very important. Sometimes, pupils experience tasks which lack meaning. Role learning and memorization of subject-matter for a test might then be an end result. It behooves the teacher to choose software which provides students with meaningful subject-matter.

Students need to experience success in ninety per cent of their response, approximately, to receive adequate reinforcement. If pupils feel successful, an increasingly adequate self concept should be in evidence. Feelings of failure tend to decrease the value of the personal self. Lower self esteem increases the likelihood for more failure on the part of student learning.

Individual differences among learners need adequate provision. In selected programmes, pupils may give the correct commands by typing the letter f (fast), a (average), or s (slow) in terms of the rate or speed of the software and microcomputer presentation. If the pupil cannot predetermine the f, a, or s in frame presentation on the monitor, a learner can respond more quickly than others pertaining to a multiple choice item. Students individually need to achieve optimally.

Quality attitudes need to be developed within students. A variety of activities based on present achievement levels should aid in developing effective attitudes within pupils. Microcomputer instruction is one means of providing for individual differences. Use of textbooks, workbooks, worksheets, films, filmstrips, slides, video tapes, pictures, transparencies, and study prints provide additional experiences for pupils. With diverse learning styles, each pupil needs to experience those activities which assist on an individual basis to achieve as much as possible.

In looking at educational psychology, learners need to experience those activities which are sequential, meaningful, interesting, understandable, purposeful, reinforcing, and attainable.

Purposes of Microcomputer Instruction

There are numerous means of utilizing personal computers in teaching students in the area of reading. Tutorial programmes provide pupils with new learnings. Thus a programme might emphasize each of the following uses in terms of developing word attack skills:

1. phonics in assisting learners to associate sounds with symbols;
2. syllabication in guiding pupils to divide words into syllables and thus unlock unknown words;
3. structural analysis in which students learn to divide words into prefixes, suffixes, and root words;
4. configuration clues whereby learners perceive shape or form of specific words for identification purposes;
5. picture clues whereby a picture provides the identification of unknown words;
6. context clues in helping students to identify a word within the cónfines of a sentence. The unknown word must make sense with other words contained in that sentence.

Students also need to become proficient in diverse comprehension procedures. Thus, students need to develop skill in reading to:

1. follow directions in a meaningful manner;
2. acquire factural content;
3. determine sequential ideas;
4. separate facts from opinions, fantasy from reality, and accurate from inaccurate statements in reading critically;
5. achieve novel, unique ideas as is true in creative reading;
6. develop main ideas or generalizations;
7. solve problems;
8. achieve satisfaction in recreational reading;
9. skim or scan specifics, such as names, dates, and places.

Certainly, reading for diverse purpose or kinds of comprehension is significant. Each of the above named types of comprehending needs to be emphasized in a quality reading curriculum. Individual purposes require a different kind of comprehension. Not all types of comprehension in reading is done at the same rate of speed. Thus, skimming or scanning for a specific item of information is achieved more rapidly as compared to reading to understand directions. In skimming or scanning, a specific name, date, or place is being located on a page of content and not all words, by any means, need to be read on a printed page or pages. However, in gleaning directions, each word needs to be read carefully so that the end product when following the directions will turn out satisfactorily. If a learner does not understand directions being read, a wrong outcome will, no doubt, follow in whatever is being made.

Dennis and Kansky wrote:

> One view of education pictures the student on one end of log and the teacher on the other. Teaching takes place as dialogue between teacher and student in which the questions and statements of each are a response to the questions and statements of the other. When not used to the exclusion of other instructional schemas, this is a powerful instructional technique. We call it *tutoring*.
>
> Computers have been shown to be an effective and economical resource for tutoring. The quality of the tutoring, of course, is a function of the computer programmes available. The problem for the designer of such programmes is to make the computer behave as if it were a very knowledgeable and creative teacher who is engaged in a dialogue with a single student for the purpose of helping that student to develop important new thoughts. The designer must make the dialogue rich enough to account for variations in student achievement, interest, and learning style. In view of the complex nature of such programmes, it should come as no surprise that the supply of them is meager.

In addition to tutorial programmes, diagnostic and remediation is significant. Specific errors need to be pinpointed in diagnosing pupil difficulties in reading. After diagnosis has been emphasized, then remediation needs to take place. Remediation emphasizes taking care of difficulties emphasized in the concept of diagnosis. Areas of diagnosis may emphasize ties emphasized in the concept of diagnosis. Areas of diagnosis may emphasize:

1. substituting one or more words in place of those contained in context in reading;
2. omitting a word or words being read;

3. mispronouncing words;
4. repeating words identified correctly;
5. inability to recognize a word;
6. hesitation but identifying the word correctly;
7. inserting one or more words;
8. making reversals.

Additional uses for microcomputers include drill and practice, as well as simulations and games. Wright and Forcier listed the following criteria for software selection for drill and practice, as well as simulations and games:

Criteria for Drill and Practice Programmes	*Criteria for Simulations and Games*
1. Format is interactive	1. Clear directions
2. User can establish the pace	2. Simple keyboard/paddle use
3. Provision made for a progression in levels of difficulty	3. Varying levels of difficulty
4. Items at same level of difficulty can be selected at random	4. Realistic situation for role-playing
5. Employs motivational techniques	5. High level of interest maintained throughout
6. Rewards presented for correct responses	6. Results predicated on user input
7. Incorrect responses handled appropriately	
8. Teacher can modify content	

In Summary

There are numerous methods available in reading instruction. These include use of basal readers, individualized reading, language experience approaches, Initial Teaching Alphabet, and linguistic procedures.

The psychology of microcomputer instruction stresses:

1. sequence in learning;
2. meaningful content;

3. interest in subject-matter;
4. readiness to learn;
5. purpose for learning;
6. reinforcement to motivate students;
7. providing for individual differences;
8. positive attitude development.

Purposes in microcomputer instruction include:

1. tutorial;
2. diagnostic and remediation;
3. drill and practice;
4. simulations and games.

Microcomputer instruction should assist pupils individually to attain optimally. Thus, courseware chosen for students must follow appropriate criteria. Flake, *et al*. provide, among others, the following criteria in choosing courseware:

1. *Educational content and value*: Is the content accurate? Clearly presented? Appropriate for the intended audience? Free of stereotypes? Important? Does the programme seem to achieve its objectives? Is it easily integrated with classwork?
2. *Mode of instruction*: Is the programme intended to teach concepts principles, skills, visualization, and/or problem solving? Is the appropriate form of instruction being used; that is, is it an appropriate form of instructional materials, such as simulation, tutorial, drill and practice, visualization materials, problem-solving materials?
3. *Technical features*: Did you have any technical problems with the programme? Is the layout visually attractive? Are graphics, colour, and sound used effectively to enhance instruction? Could you modify the programme?
4. *Ease of use*: Are the instructions clear? Can students operate the programme easily? Control the pace? Review the instructions? End the programme? How is inappropriate input handled?
5. *Motivation*: Does the programme hold students' interest? Do students want to use it again? Does the programme vary when repeated?

6. *Feedback*: Is the feedback positive and constructive? Appropriate for the grade level? Immediate? Varied? Does it provide help or an explanation?
7. *Record keeping*: Are student records stored on disk for later retrieval? What information is stored? For how many students? Is the recordkeeping system easy to use? Is it reasonably secure?
8. *Documentation*: Are the written instructions clear? Well organised? Comprehensive? Are the objectives, prerequisites, and intended audience specified?
9. *Summary and recommendations*: What are the programme's strengths? What are its weaknesses? Does it take advantage of the computer's capabilities? Does it involve the learner in the learning process? How does it compare to others with similar objectives? Would you buy and use it?

REFERENCES

Dennis, Richard J., and Robert J. Kansky. *Instructional Computing*. Glenview, Illinois: Scott, Foresman and Company, 1984, page 14.

Wright, Edward B., and Richard C. Forcier. *The Computer: A Tool for the Teacher*. Belmont, California: Wadsworth Publishing Company, 1985, page 158.

Flake, Janice L., *et al.*, *Fundamentals of Computer Education*. Belmont, California. Wadsworth Publishing Company, 1985, pages 326 and 327.

9

Which Words Should Pupils Learn to Spell?

One issue, among others, in the spelling curriculum pertains to who should determine which spelling words pupils are to master.

Learners need to become proficient spellers in order to communicate ideas effectively in writing. Pupils should not learn to spell a specific set of words merely for the sake of doing so. Rather, selected spelling words need mastering because of their use in diverse purposeful writing experiences. Learning to spell words correctly has transfer values. Hopefully, pupils individually will then perceive purpose in learning to spell a reasonable number of words within the framework of flexible time limits.

Which methods might be utilized to determine relevant words for learners to master in the spelling curriculum?

Utilizing Recommended Commercially Prepared Textbooks

There are teachers, principals, and supervisors who advocate pupil's mastering sequential weekly lists of words from reputable spelling textbooks. These educators may believe that relevant spelling words for pupil mastery can be determined rather accurately by writers of spelling textbooks. Preparation time is saved by teachers when using the learning activities in the adopted spelling textbook. Otherwise, the teacher needs to choose spelling words for pupils to master, as well as learning activities to guide pupils in learning to spell each word correctly.

In utilizing the contents of a reputable spelling textbook, an underlying assumption might be that each week's list of spelling words, as well as the related learning activities, are sequentially arranged for learners. The teacher, however, must also adapt the use of the spelling textbooks to the present achievement levels of pupils.

Advantages given in using reputable spelling textbooks in teaching pupils may include the following:

1. Time is saved in preparing for teaching in that objectives, experiences, and evaluation procedures are already preplanned for teacher consideration and usage.
2. Generally, a considerable amount of time and money has gone into the development of appealing, reputable spelling textbooks. Teachers and pupils can benefit from efforts put forth by companies and their writers in developing quality basal textbooks in spelling.
3. Content in spelling textbooks does provide for individual differences among selected pupils. There are learning activities for slow learners, average achievers, and talented pupils. The teacher may add additional learning activities in spelling to provide for diverse levels of achievement in the class setting.
4. Spelling words in recognized textbooks, in many cases, are based on research results to determine which words pupils in society use most frequently in writing.

Disadvantages involving the use of basal textbooks in teaching spelling might include the following:

1. The majority of pupils in the school/class setting need to experience a variety of activities in learning to spell. The use of textbooks is one method of teaching spelling.
2. Pupils need to transfer learnings obtained from one situation to another. Spelling textbooks and their use may not give pupils needed assistance to apply previously developed learnings to new writing situations.
3. Boredom and a lack of interest in learning may accrue if the majority of learnings for pupils in spelling come from the sequential use of a textbook.
4. The words pupils are required to learn to spell may not meet the personal needs of a learner in functional writing situations.

Units of Study and the Spelling Curriculum

There are selected educators who recommend that lists of words in spelling come largely from ongoing units of study in social studies, science, mathematics, and reading. Pupils may then experience the correlated curriculum, e.g. correlate (relate) social studies and spelling. The number of words each pupil is to learn to spell depends upon present individual achievement levels. Teacher-pupil planning may be utilized to determine the number of spelling words the latter is to master in a given period of time. Thus, for example, in a unit on "Visiting the Farm," pupil A may master the following spelling words in a one week cycle: grain, wheat, corn, soybeans, tractor, combine, plow, disk, automation, inventions, sheep, hogs, and cattle. Words should be chosen based on their functional use in diverse writing situations.

Disadvantages given for obtaining spelling words for mastery from ongoing units of study may include the following:

1. It might be difficult to choose useful spelling words from selected ongoing units of study.
2. It could be rather limiting in scope to assist pupils to learn to spell only those words which come from present units being studied.
3. It might be difficult for the teacher to assist pupils to perceive purpose in learning to spell words from certain units of study.

There are advantages in assisting pupils to master the spelling of words from units of study in diverse curriculum areas.

1. Students can perceive that learnings are related and not isolated in the school curriculum. Lists of spelling words may then come from different academic areas in the school curriculum.
2. Pupils may practice the correct spelling of words in diverse learning activities, such as in writing poems, plays, stories, announcements, outlines, as well as in notetaking.

Research Studies and the Spelling Curriculum

There are educators who recommend pupils learn to spell words which specific research studies have indicated to be relevant. Rinsland in 1945 identified 100 words most frequently used by pupils in spelling. By mastering the spelling of essential words, pupils might then be able to cut down considerably on the number of words misspelled in diverse writing situations.

Fitzgerald in 1951 identified 350 most useful spelling words for learners to master in the elementary school. These words are identified by grade levels—second grade, third grade, fourth grade, fifth grade, and sixth grade. If pupils master the correct spelling of words from the Fitzgerald study, fewer spelling errors might then be in evidence in written products.

Objective methods in research can be utilized to identify spelling words for mastery learning by pupils. Attempts have been made in research studies to weed out irrelevant words contained in spelling lists. If pupils practice the correct spelling of words having low utility values, fewer misspelled words may then not be an end result in written work.

Not all problems in the spelling curriculum, of course, are solved when utilizing research results. For selected pupils, other spelling words may be more functional to master than those identified in research studies. It is indeed difficult to provide for individual differences. The curriculum area of spelling is no exception!

These questions need careful consideration in any plan of spelling instruction:

1. Which criteria may be utilized to determine how many spelling words each pupil should master in a given period of time?
2. Which learning activities should the teacher provide in order that pupils may retain correct spelling of relevant words?
3. How should pupil achievement in spelling be evaluated?

Word Lists Versus Functional Writing Situations

There are numerous language arts specialists who emphasize the use of lists of words for pupils to master in spelling. Pretesting based on words in a list is then recommended so that the pupil does not study the spelling of a word already mastered. According to selected research studies, word lists and the use of pretests assist pupils to learn the correct spelling of words more readily and with better transfer results compared to other methods and approaches.

Lists of spelling words might come from the following sources:

1. basal weekly lists from reputable spelling textbooks;

2. lists of words selected from ongoing units of study;
3. word lists as identified by research studies;
4. words chosen for a specific writing activity, e.g. needed words to write a business or friendly letter.

Major concerns in having pupils master the spelling of words from specific lists, largely or solely, might well include the following:

1. It tends to isolate the spelling of words from functional writing situations, e.g. writing announcements, summaries, and outlines.
2. Rote learning may be emphasized compared to utilitarian goals in the curriculum.
3. Lists of words to master in spelling may not meet the personal writing needs of a pupil.
4. If a common learnings list of spelling words is provided for all to master, who is in a position to ascertain which these words should be?

Instrumentalism and the Spelling Curriculum

Instrumentalism as a philosophy of education advocates what is being learned is useful in achieving other goals. Words in spelling are not mastered for their own sake, but rather they possess utilitarian values. Learning to spell words then is useful. Why? To communicate ideas in real life situations. If, for example, pupils are studying a unit on the Middle East, selected pictures, brochures, pamphlets, and books need ordering. The materials are needed to solve problems that pupils identified pertaining to the Middle East. Thus, letters will need to be written by learners individually or in committees to order these free or inexpensive materials. As the writing activity commences, specific words are identified in spelling which need mastering. Pupils may then perceive purpose in learning to spell words since each word is functional or instrumental to the objective-writing a business letter to get needed materials pertaining to the Middle East area of the world.

In Summary

There are numerous approaches to guide teachers in selecting vital spelling words for pupils to master. The teacher may utilize reputable spelling textbooks, units of study in diverse curriculum areas, research study results, word lists, and instrumentalism as a philosophy of education, to determine needed spelling words for pupil mastery. There are other methods which may be utilized. These include:

1. using contracts which specifically indicate the number of words an individual pupil is to learn to spell. Pupil-teacher planning generally is involved in determining these words. Both sign the contract and indicate the due date for mastery learning. The number of words for any particular child to master in spelling must be reasonable;
2. having each pupil learn to spell those words misspelled in daily functional writing situations. Whichever words are incorrectly spelled by a child are placed on a list for mastery learning.

The language arts teacher needs to study diverse methods/ approaches of teaching spelling. Providing for individual differences and assisting each pupil to achieve optimally represents recommended criteria in the teaching of spelling.

Norton wrote:

> Considerable research in spelling diagnosis, instructional programmes, and teaching techniques provide clear guidelines for spelling instruction. Following a review of research that spans more than fifty years, Hillerich (1982) identifies the following effective procedures and instructional approaches:
>
> 1. Determine the appropriate instructional spelling level for each student.
> 2. Teach the list of high-frequency words using a research-based approach.
> 3. Teach generalizations about apostrophies and word endings.
> 4. Provide experiences with homophones.
> 5. Teach dictionary skills along with ways of spelling various sounds.
> 6. Develop a desire to spell correctly when the writing is designed for an audience other than an informal group.
> 7. Encourage considerable writing to help children develop an understanding that writing is the only reason for learning to spell.
> 8. Provide children with many meaningful writing experiences that reinforce the automatic spelling of their security lists.

REFERENCES

Fitzgerald, J.A. *A Basic Life Spelling Vocabulary*. Bruce Publishing Co., 1951.

Horn, Ernest. *Teaching Spelling: What Research Says to the Teacher*. AERA of the National Education Association, 1962.

Norton, Donna E. *The Effective Teaching of Language Arts*, Second ed. Columbus, Ohio: Charles E. Merrill Publishing Co., 1985, pages 187-188.

Rinsland, H.D. *A Basic Writing Vocabulary of Elementary School Children*. New York: The Macmillan Company, 1945.

10

Spelling in the Curriculum

Correct spelling of words needs adequate emphasis in teaching-learning situations. Why? Proficient communication is aided when written or typed content contains words which are correctly spelled. A quality language arts curriculum then must place thorough emphasis in aiding students to spell words correctly.

Criteria for a Quality Spelling Programme

Whatever decisions are made in life, standards or criteria are utilized. In teaching and learning situations, the teacher needs to:

1. select worthwhile goals for students to attain. Trivia must be omitted in the curriculum. In spelling, the words students are to master need to be significant presently, as well as in the future. There is much for each to learn. It behooves the instructor to choose carefully those words for learners to spell correctly which are salient and relevant;

2. emphasize the concept of balance in the curriculum. Thus, in spelling pupils need to develop vital understanding, as well as skills and attitudes. All three kinds of objectives need to be stressed. Understanding goals are not adequate in and of themselves, such as learners acquiring facts, concepts, and generalizations related directly to definitions or meanings of spelling words. Rather, skills (utilizing the newly mastered spelling words in functional writing) and attitudes (positive feelings in wanting to learn to spell words correctly) are equally significant goals.

Skills then pertain to the use of what has been achieved within the framework of understanding goals. Attitudes reveal a desire to increase the levels of understanding and skills;

3. guide pupils to perceive purpose or reasons for mastering a given set of spelling words. When inductive methods are utilized, the teacher guides students in discovering reasons for learning to spell selected words accurately. With a deductive method, the language arts instructor explains reasons as to why students need to learn to spell words correctly within a spelling unit. In using extrinsic rewards to aid students to perceive purpose in spelling, awards and announced ahead of time as to the number of words a learner needs to spell correctly in order to receive a prize, a badge, or certificate for achievement. Exhortation may also be used by the teacher to promote perceived purpose. Thus, the teacher stresses the importance of learning to spell words correctly. However, reasons are not given. With exhortation the teacher could say, "It's very important for you to learn to spell these words correctly in unit one in our spelling textbook."

The teacher needs to utilize the four above-named means of guiding students to perceive purpose early in a spelling unit as well as frequently.

Norton wrote:

> Many current articles deal with the writing crisis in American schools. Poor spelling is often cited as a major problem with children's writing. The school programme must help students learn to spell the words they need to know; provide instruction in reliable spelling generalizations; develop an understanding of word meanings and vocabulary; equip the speller with more than one strategy for spelling-word attack; incorporate spelling into all areas of the curriculum; proceed from sound diagnostic evaluation; and provide for the development of motivation, positive student attitudes and sound habits for studying spelling and proofreading.
>
> Diagnostic approaches to spelling instruction stress the placement of students on appropriate spelling instructional levels. In addition to instructional placement, the diagnostic teacher also analyzes the types of errors a child makes in writing. This information is used to individualize the spelling programme for each child. Informal tests for spelling placement, spelling generalizations, and error analysis can be developed by the classroom teacher.

Spelling words are selected according to several different criteria. The frequency-of use approach stresses that spelling instruction should be based on the words that are the most frequently used. Consequently, it is believed that words most frequently used in writing should be taught first, words commonly used by children in a specific grade should be taught in that grade, and words needed in other content areas should be taught in the appropriate grade. Another quite different selection criterion emphasizes the phonic regularity of words. The words selected for this approach would follow a consistent spelling pattern. Some linguists and psycholinguists also stress the consistency of spelling patterns in words of similar meanings. Thus, spelling instruction should allow students to compare, contrast, and categorize words according to root words, word origins, and similarities, in structural patterns.

Several techniques have proven valuable in a developmental approach to spelling instruction. The corrected-test method allows immediate feedback, and liberates students from the systematic study of words already mastered. The self-study method allows students to master their own individualized spelling words. An inductive approach to teaching spelling generalizations allows students to discover and use the reliable spelling generalizations.

Remedial spelling approaches have been developed for the more disabled speller. The Fernald approach has been useful with learning disabled children. In this multisensory method, the child looks at the word, traces the word, then writes the word without looking at it. Spelling games are useful for reinforcing and motivating the remedial spelling student. Spelling should not, however, be taught as an isolated subject. Students, whether remedial, regular developmental, or gifted, require many opportunities to use spelling in meaningful situations.

4. choose a variety of interesting learning activities for students. To achieve interest within learners, diverse activities need to be in the offing. The experiences may include:
   (a) activities contained in spelling textbooks, workbooks, and worksheets;
   (b) commercial and teacher developed games;
   (c) crosswood puzzles in which the list being studied in spelling provides answers for the vertical and horizontal lines;
   (d) computerized drill, practice, and games
   (e) spelling bees where competition is wholesome and educational;

(f) purposeful, practical experiences including writing friendly and business letters, announcements, plays, poems, stories, and skits;

(g) pantomimes, creative dramatics, and formal dramatizations.

5. evaluate student achievement comprehensively. Diverse procedures need to be utilized to appraise learner progress. The evaluation procedures may include:

(a) teacher developed tests;

(b) standardized tests;

(c) learner abilities to spell words correctly within the framework of functional writing situations;

(d) weekly results from students being tested on lists of words contained in spelling textbooks being utilized in the classroom.

6. assist students to utilize correct spelling of words. Students who utilize what has been learned are less likely to forget subject-matter acquired. The teacher needs to provide situations in which pupils may use that which has been learned.

Retention in learning is a perennial problem. Human beings feel and believe that an inadequate amount of content has been retained. Retaining the correct spelling of words is no exception. Teachers need to think of means and methods of helping students remember understandings and skills achieved.

Utilitarian theorists believe that useful spelling words need to be mastered by students. If students learn to spell words correctly which have been identified as being functional, errors in spelling would decline greatly. With utilitarian words mastered by students in spelling, learners might then study what is useful. What is useful will be utilized frequently. That which is used tends not to be forgotten.

Burns and Broman wrote:

> Some spelling programmes are based on the theory of social utility; that is, words are selected on the basis of their importance in the different spelling activities of life. There are a number of investigations about spelling vocabulary, but perhaps the most important one is by Ernest Horn. He studied letters of bankers, excuses written to teachers by parents, minutes of organisations and committee reports,

letters of application and recommendation, the works of well-known authors, letters written in magazines and newspapers, personal letters, business letters—a total of 5 million words and 36,000 different words. From this, the most important 10,000 words were selected as basic words, according to these criteria:

1. The total frequency with which the word was used in writing.
2. The commonness with which the word was used by everyone, regardless of sex, vocation, geographical location, educational level, or economic status.
3. The spread of the word's use in different kinds of writing.
4. The cruciality of the word as evidenced by the severity of the penalty attached to its misspelling.
5. The probable permanency of the word's use.
6. The desirability of the word as determined by the quality of the writing in which it was used.

Horn suggested three criteria for introducing these basic words in the spelling programme:

The most important words should be introduced in the beginning grades and those of lesser importance in the later grades.

The simplest words should be introduced in the beginning grades and the more difficult words in the later grades. Those words that are used often or needed in the curriculum activities of children should be introduced when appropriate.

7. guide students to perceive patterns in the correct spelling of words. There are numerous sets or word families which follow a pattern. For example, first grade pupils need to learn to spell correctly the following: ban, can, fan, man, pan, van, tan, and ran. With a change in the initial consonant of each of the above named words, a new word emerges. Another pattern of words for young learners to master in spelling include bat, cat, hat, mat, pat, rat and sat. Inductively (by discovery) and deductively (through meaningful explanations) pupils need to observe that selected English words form a pattern in spelling. Even the following irregularly spelled words—rough, cough, through, and thought follow a pattern emphasized in the 'ough' letters. Linguists are strong advocates of students noticing pattern which assists in spelling words correctly. Young peoples should study words which pattern in phoneme (sound)—grapheme (symbol) relationships contained in a family such as bet, met, set, let, yet, and get.

In sequence, as learners progress through the diverse grade levels, words containing less of consistency between phonemes and graphemes can be emphasized such as bake, cake, fake, make, rake, and sake. Each of these words contains a silent 'e' ending and might well be appropriate, as an example, for second graders. On the third grade, students might learn to spell words which gradually contain less relationship between phonemes and graphemes. These include my, pie, sigh, island, aisle, rye, and ride. Each of the above-named words contains a long 'i' sound as a linguistic element. As a final example, sixth grades might well learn to spell words which pattern with the vowel sound as in the word blue. The letters 'ue' in sound pattern with to, too, two, rheumetism, flu, new, and soon.

Petty, *et. al.* wrote:

The basic goal in spelling instruction is to teach children to spell the words they use in their writing. This means the writing they do in school and the writing they will do after their school years. Of course it is impossible to determine all of the words any person may need to spell in a lifetime, but everyone should learn to spell the words that are most frequently written. It is also important to encourage children's increasing awareness of the structure of their language and how aspects of this structure relate to spelling specific words. Finally, a positive attitude toward spelling correctly and habits which support this attitude need to be developed.

Since spelling requires putting into written form words that are familiar from speaking, reading, and listening, two important abilities are needed. One of these is the ability to recall how words look—the words that the child has studied and those that have frequently appeared in his or her reading. The other basic ability is that of associating letters and patterns of letters with specific sounds. These two abilities become closely allied in the spelling efforts of most children, and both are influenced by the children's understanding of syntactic and morphemic aspects of the language.

A good speller naturally must know the letters of the alphabet and how to write them in both lowercase and uppercase forms. He or she should know how to alphabetize words and how to use this knowledge to find the spellings of words in dictionaries and glossaries. He or she should be able to pronounce words clearly and accurately and to use a dictionary, including its diacritical makings and key words, as well as phonetic and structural aids to help with pronunciations.

Good spellers, no doubt, have developed quality methods in learning to spell words accurately. Those students doing poorly in spelling may need to develop methodologies which work in spelling words correctly. Which methodology might the teacher assist students in acquiring?

(a) each student needs to look at a word carefully prior to studying its spelling. The sense of sight must be emphasized so that configuration clues might be utilized by the learner. A student cannot master a set of words in spelling unless he/she attends carefully to each new word. Some words are longer than others. Selected words are taller or shorter as far as individual letters within a word are concerned. Thus, distinguishing features must be observed prior to learning to spell that word;

(b) students individually need to be able to pronounce each word correctly. Incorrect pronunciation of words can well make for spelling errors. Also students need to listen to the sounds within a word to associate sounds with symbols. Irregularities in spelling need to be noticed by the student. A learner can over-generalize on the use of phonics. Phonetic analysis may also not be utilized adequately by the student in learning accurate word spelling;

(c) the involved student may now close his/her eyes and attempt to see the new word being studied. The mental image is then checked against the correct spelling of the word in print;

(d) students individually may now write the new spelling word from memory. The written word needs to be checked against the accurately printed word being studied;

(e) the student should now write the new word in isolation as well as within sentences to show mastery.

9. provide a quality learning environment to develop positive attitudes within students. Quality feelings toward any curriculum area, including spelling, assists learners to achieve more optimally. Pupils need to feel that spelling words correctly is important in communicating ideas in writing. Appropriate courtesy and manners are also expressed when words are accurately spelled. The receiver

of written content develops certain impressions of a writer if words are spelled correctly or incorrectly. When letters of application for a position or job application forms are completed by an applicant, certainly, words that are misspelled will influence an employer.

How can a teacher then assist students to feel that spelling words correctly in writing is important?

(a) Pupils need to look at written products in which words are spelled incorrectly. Here nonexamples are used in teaching-learning situations. Students might then notice how effective communication is hindered through incorrect spelling of words.

(b) Learners need to receive responses to business and friendly letters written. Reasons exist for writing business or friendly letters. These reasons might include to order free or inexpensive materials for an ongoing unit being studied in the classroom A business letter then needs to be written. Correct spelling of words in the letter assists in communicating ideas. To correspond with friends, relatives, and acquaintances, friendly letters need composing by students. Politeness in writing and effective communication demands that words be accurately spelled.

Microcomputer Use in the Spelling Curriculum

With an increased number of microcomputers and software available in spelling, students might experience a relatively new kind of experience. There are selected philosophies that may be emphasized in microcomputer instruction.

Tutorial programmes provide opportunities fo: pupils to experience new learnings in spelling. With proper debugging of the software, students may experience sequential learnings in spelling. Adequate opportunities in the programme should be given to pupils to interact or respond to questions or multiple choice items contained in a programme. A reward system must be in evidence which reinforces correct answers given by learners.

Kemp and Dayton wrote:

Tutorials attempt to emulate a human tutor. Instruction is provided via text or graphics on the screen. At appropriate points a question or problem is posed. If the student's response is correct, the computer moves on to the next block of instruction. If the response is incorrect the computer may recycle to the previous instruction or more to one of several sets of remedial instruction, depending upon the nature of the error.

Diagnostic and remediation programmes are significant for selected pupils. The concept of diagnosis emphasizes the need to determine specifically which problems pupils experience in spelling. The following may cause difficulties for students in learning to spell words accurately:

1. words that do not follow a grapheme-phoneme relationship, e.g. one, two, rough, and high;
2. words that represent spelling demons, e.g. always (allways), occur (ocur), running (runing), and rabbit (rabit). Words in parenthesis stress incorrect spellings;
3. words that are easily mispronounced;
4. words that are homonyms, e.g. hear-here; their, there, they're; bear, bare; and wait, weight;
5. words that are heteronyms, e.g. subject (My favourite *subject* is geometry) and Don't *subject* the child to hard work);

Quality software needs to pinpoint specific errors in spelling of a student. Remediation efforts must then follow.

Di Stefano, Dole, and Marzano wrote:

Hagerty (1981) found that the majority of words third graders and fifth graders misspelled in writing were high frequency words that had little phoneme-grapheme representation, like 'sed' for 'said' and 'becuz' for 'because'. Using the words that students misspell in writing, you can have students develop a student dictionary based on each individual's misspelled words.

Drill and practice are vital in spelling. Otherwise pupils may not retain the correct spelling of words. Forgetting can be quite rapid for many students. It behooves the teacher to assist pupils to remember that which has been learned by students. Transfer of learning is also important. If students, for example, have mastered the spelling of a list of words, they must reveal increasingly that the new words can be spelled correctly in functional, utilitarian writing situations.

Software emphasizing drill and practice must:

1. relate to those words students need more help in to retain/remember their correct spelling;
2. emphasize relevance or usefulness in everyday writing situations;
3. provide for success in achievement;
4. indicate a need for reviewing the correct spelling of selected words;
5. reflect student interests and purposes.

Too frequently, drill and practice activities are boring to learners. A lack of challenge is involved in the routine and mundane. A sheer lack of interest may then follow. A meaningless curriculum is an end result. Students fail to achieve vital goals, as a consequence. Certainly learning activities involving drill and practice should be stimulating to students so that sequential learning can follow.

Dennis and Kansky wrote:

> Associative learning, as required for success in a spelling competition, calls for the services of some kindly soul who will sit for hours pronouncing words and checking your spelling against that of the ruling lexicographer. You can claim success (learning) when spaced presentations of the pronunciation of sarcophagus (the stimulus) are met by your unerring verbal dissection s-a-r-c-o-p-h-a-h-u-s (the response). The procedure is known as drill. It's not a very exciting activity for your partner, so you might want to try shouting in order to ensure his or her consciousness.
>
> Textbooks and teachers are not the most effective resources for drills. Textbooks cannot respond with the flexibility needed to shape the student's learning. Teachers cannot give each individual student the time needed to fix all of the associations that are part of education. Using a teacher to carry out such a tedious, unrewarding task is as unforgivable as using a Ming vase as a paperweight.
>
> The computer has been shown to be an effective drillmaster in promoting associative learning. Students achieve mastery of such associations quickly and show high levels of retention. And for reasons that are anyone's guess, students appear to be highly motivated to engage in drill activity with a computer.

Games can be an enjoyable method of learning for students. One of the writers observed a teacher made game utilized in the classroom to challenge students to learn to spell words. A pupil would spin a spinner with the numerals one to five spaced congruently for the spinner to point to. For example, flipping the spinner with the finger, a student spins a value of three. Five piles of congruent cards are placed face down. Pile one has the easiest words while stack five has the most difficult words to spell. Piles one, two, and three are more complex than stack one and less complex than pile five, in a hierarchical manner. With the spinner pointed to number three, an opponent picks up a card from pile three turning it face up. The opponent pronounces the word to the involved student who must correctly spell orally or in writing the spelling word pronounced by the opponent in order to move three spaces forward on the game board. Each player takes his/her turn to cross the finish line.

There are selected excellent programmes for microcomputer utilization emphasizing the gaming approach. CompuCat Spell is a game for pupils to play in the area of spelling. The following are inherent in the game:

1. rules are presented for two players to play at a time;
2. there are three different games in the above-named software;
3. the involved students can select slow, average, or fast for the speed of the software presentation;
4. ten, twenty, thirty, or forty points can be earned for each question answered correctly;
5. the student must respond to a question on the screen before a 'cat' jumps from block one to block ten. If the learner does not respond within this allotted time, he/she loses ten points;
6. extra bonus points can be earned in the game. This is indicated when a 'cat' moves across the top of the screen. One extra bonus point frame has the following item:

   A pup is a:

   1. dug
   2. dig
   3. dog
   4. dag

The learner needs to type the correct numeral on the terminal to receive an extra point.

7. each student can receive a printout of results of the game played. The printout, among other items, contains the number of questions answered correctly, questions missed, and total questions answered. The printout also contains the correct answers to items missed by the involved student;
8. sound is available for reinforcement of correct responses given by students;
9. the manual contains a scope and sequence chart of content contained in the software, such as game one containing short and long vowel monosyllables; short and long vowels; synonyms, antonyms, and word meanings; as well as students choosing correct spelling of sound-spelled words.

Computer managed instruction (CMI) can save much time in developing the spelling curriculum. One means in utilizing CMI is to permit the microcomputer to check the results of student achievement in spelling in:

(a) pretests to ascertain where a student is presently in achievement;

(b) criterion checks to determine how well students are achieving goals as a unit progresses;

(c) post tests in measuring gains at the completion of a unit.

Tests results of students may be stored and retrieved, as needed, in computer managed instruction. A printout of measurable objectives in spelling together with the related learning activities to achieve each goal may be sent home to parents. The printout would show which objectives a student has achieved and which goals need achieving. Parents' support may then be enlisted, as homework for the involved pupil, to assist their offspring in sequential goal attainment. The classroom teacher, the parents, and the pupil might then know which specific objectives in spelling the latter individually has attained and which are left to achieve.

Pertaining to storage and retrieval of information, Grossnickle, *et al*. wrote:

> The power of a computer depends largely on two factors:
>
> 1. Its ability to store and retrieve large amounts of information quickly.
> 2. Its ability to make decisions.

A high level of technical programming skill is required to take full advantage of the decision-making power of the computer. However, using relatively inexpensive software and with the basic technical knowledge, it is possible for a beginner to store and retrieve information.

Information fed into a computer is usually lost when the computer is turned off, but with proper peripheral equipment, information can be stored on cassette or disk. Although a disk drive costs almost half as much as a computer, it is almost essential for efficient school use. Storage and retrieval are nearly instantaneous with a disk drive, and are far more time-consuming with cassette.

In Conclusion

There are selected criteria which teachers need to utilize in selecting objectives and learning activities in spelling. These include:

1. significant objectives need to be selected for pupils to achieve;
2. understandings, skills, and attitudinal goals need to be stressed in goal attainment for learners. Emphasizing only one of the above categories in teaching deemphasizes the concept of balance in the curriculum;
3. perceived purpose needs to be developed for learning;
4. a variety of activities and experiences must be in the offing in the spelling curriculum;
5. diverse procedures need to be utilized to assess learner progress;
6. students need to use the correct spelling of new words in functional writing situations;
7. patterns and irregularities need to be observed by students in spelling;
8. appropriate methodologies should be used by pupils in learning to spell words accurately;
9. positive attitudes toward spelling, as a curriculum area, need to be developed and maintained.

Microcomputer utilization has numerous objectives for pupils to attain. Thus, microcomputers may be used for:

1. tutorial instruction;
2. diagnosis and remediation;

3. drill and practice;
4. the playing of games;
5. computer managed instruction purposes.

The spelling curriculum must reflect the interests, needs, and purposes of students. Each learner needs guidance to attain optimally in spelling.

REFERENCES

Burns, Paul C. and Broman, Betty L. *The Language Arts in Childhood Education*. Fifth ed. Boston: Houghton Mifflin Co., 1983.

CompuCat Spell. New York: McGraw Hill Book Company, 1985.

Dennis, J. Richard and Kansky, Robert J. *Instructional Computing*. Glenview, Illinois: Scott, Foresman and Company, 1984.

Grossnickle, Foster E. *et. al. Discovering Meanings in Elementary School Mathematics*, Seventh ed. New York: Holt, Rinehart and Winston, 1983.

Kemp, Jerrold E. Dayton, Deane K. *Planning and Producing Instructional Media*. New York: Harper and Row, Publishers, 1985.

Norton, Donna E. *The Effective Teaching of Language Arts*. Second ed. Columbus, Ohio: Charles E. Merrill Publishing Co., 1985.

Petty Walter T. *et. al. Experiences in Language*. Fourth ed. Newton, Massachusetts: Allyn and Bacon, Inc. 1985.

Stephano, Philip Di, Dole, Janice, Marzano, Robert, *Elementary Language Arts*. New York: John Wiley and Sons, 1984.

Stewig, John Warren, *Exploring Language Arts in the Elementary Classroom*. New York: Holt, Rinehart and Winston, 1983.

Handwriting: Issues and Problems

Students need to exhibit legible handwriting. Why? Effective written communication must contain legibility in order to convey content from the sender to the receiver. Ideas in writing are difficult to comprehend when the inherent subject-matter contains illegible penmanship.

There are diverse schools of thought emphasizing methods of teaching handwriting. Pros and cons are then in evidence pertaining to objectives, learning activities, and evaluation procedures. Which issues and problems are relevant to consider in the handwriting curriculum?

Separate Subjects Versus Correlation

There are selected specialists in the teaching of handwriting who advocate a separate subjects curriculum. Thus, a separate period of time each day would be set aside for handwriting instruction. Definite sequential objectives are established in implementing each daily lesson plan. Learning activities for pupils to achieve the desired ends are in evidence. Ultimately, learners are appraised to ascertain if objectives have been attained.

Advocates of the separate subjects curriculum believe that learnings from daily lessons in handwriting will transfer to writing experience for students in all curriculum areas. What has been achieved in penmanship is transferable to writing experiences in science, social studies, mathematics, physical education, and the fine arts.

Somewhat toward the other end of the spectrum are educators believing that handwriting needs to be taught as correlated with each academic area whenever writing experiences are being implemented. In the writing of outlines, reports, classroom notes, plays, stories, and summaries, students need to exhibit legible handwriting. Thus, in developing an outline of subject-matter containing main divisions, subdivisions, and details, students should reveal the concept of legibility in handwriting. Specific errors made in handwriting need diagnosis and remediation. Handwriting then is taught as needed and not in emphasizing separate class time for penmanship instruction. Within the confines of students developing outlines, quality handwriting is stressed in proofreading the final written product.

An issue is then in evidence involving teaching handwriting as a separate subject as contrasted with legibility in final written products being emphasized in each curriculum area.

Behaviourism versus Humanism

Behaviourists recommend utilizing precise, measurable objectives in teaching. After handwriting instruction, it can be measured if a student has not achieved the stated objective(s). The objectives are stated prior to teaching and learning. These ends may be developed a year ahead of the time of the implementation in the classroom. The teacher or a committee of teachers may do the writing of these predetermined objectives.

The behaviourally stated objectives need to be arranged in ascending order of difficulty. Each student on an individual basis achieves ordered goals. No student need wait for other learners to catch up with the former. Nor should slower achievers be on a uniform level of attainment with those who achieve at a more rapid rate.

Reinforcement theory is significant in behaviourism as a psychology of learning. The teacher needs to guide students to relate the stumulus (S) with the response (R). The S may be the specific learning activity for the student to participate in. The R is indicated by students revealing what has been learned from the (S) stimulus. To connect the S with the R, success in learning needs to be in evidence. This strengthens the S and the R in S—R theory of learning.

With reinforcement theory, diverse rewards need to be utilized. These include verbal praise, inexpensive prizes, badges, and certificates for outstanding achievement. Learning activities need to be sequential in order that each student experiences continuous progress and success.

S—R theory of learning emphasizes a technology of learning. The objectives need to be highly precise. Why? Opportunities to learn with learning activities must match in a precise manner with the stated objectives. Evaluation of pupil progress is only in terms of the measurably stated objective(s). A definite method of teaching is then in evidence. A technology of instruction is an end result.

Pertaining to technologies of instruction, McNeil wrote:

> Individually prescribed instruction (IPI) and mastery learning are other examples of curriculum produced by technologists. Instructional objectives, arranged in an assumed hierarchy of tasks, are the keystone of the system, and lesson materials are built around that arrangement. The objectives are the intended outcomes of instruction. Each pupil must master them before going on to the next step in the learning hierarchy. Mastery is indicated by successful responses to criterion-referenced tests matched to the content and behaviour specified in the objective. Objectives in the teaching of mathematics, for example, or grouped by topics such as numeration, place value, and subtraction.

Lesson materials are matched with the objectives and allow the pupil to proceed independently with a minimum of teacher direction. The pattern for involving the pupil with the system has three parts:

1. Finding out what the pupil already knows about the subject. Usually a general placement test is administered to reveal the pupil's general level of achievement. The pupil is also given a pretest to reveal specific deficiencies.
2. Giving the pupil self-instructional materials or other carefully designed learning activities. Such activities focus on one of the specific deficiencies previously identified.
3. Giving the pupil evaluative measures to determine his or her progress. Such measures help the teacher decide whether to move the pupil ahead to a new task or to provide additional materials or tutoring.

Advocates of the S—R theory of learning stress the following advantages in utilizing their approach in teaching:

1. The teacher can measure if a student has/has not been successful in learning. Behaviourally stated ends are specific and not general. The latter kinds of objectives leave much leeway in interpreting if a student is or is not achieving. The teacher needs to be certain that pupils are learning by measuring accomplishment against the stated behavioural objectives.
2. Learning experiences may be selected which have purpose and the inherent purposes are to guide learners in goal attainment. The activities are not in evidence for the sake of having something for pupils to do. Rather, students are to achieve predetermined objectives. Each objectives must be worthwhile, relevant, and significant. Thus, quality learning opportunities assist students to attain definite objectives.
3. Evaluation techniques are definite and pinpoint if a learner has or has not measured up to having attained the behaviourally stated objectives. Thus, the technique(s) of appraisal are valid. Evaluation is emphasized in terms of a student having achieved objectives. The learning activities selected also pinpointed the precise ends. Therefore, validity is inherent in evaluation. Reliability also increases in the appraisal process, if the involved teachers agree upon if a learner did/did not attain the specific objectives. Independent of the teacher or observer involved, the evaluator should be able to ascertain if an objective has or has not been achieved.

Humanism emphasizes students engage in decision-making to select objectives and learning activities. A learner might then choose handwriting activities involving the use of penmanship textbooks. Or, a different choice made may emphasize practicing handwriting skills within functional situations. These practical occasions can involve writing business and friendly letters, announcements, poems, plays and stories. As the need arises within the functional situation, the pupil is provided assistance as needed to achieve legibility in handwriting.

Humanists do not advocate giving physical prizes, badges, and certificates for quality achievement by individual pupils. Operant conditioning is involved when rewards are provided for successful achievement. (The success inherent in learning stresses rewarding the response in S—R theory of learning). Rather, humanism emphasizes the whole person (gestalt) being involved in learning. The late A. H. Maslow advocated meeting needs of the whole person in learning. Dr. Maslow then believed the following needs should be met on the part of students:

1. physiological needs—ample nutrition, rest, shelter, clothing, and water;
2. safety needs—security and lack of want;
3. loving and belonging—being wanted and accepted by others;
4. esteem needs—feeling prized for what can be done well (acknowledgment);
5. self-actualization (becoming the kind of person one desires to become);
6. knowledge needs (desire to learn subject-matter and necessary skills).

Miller wrote:

Below are some key assumptions and criteria of humanistic programmes:

- Humans have a tendency to realize their positive inner potential. Students are capable of a range of behaviours, and if the right conditions are provided they will move toward higher levels of functioning.
- Individuals have the capacity to direct their own behaviour. Although young children need the teacher's assistance, as they mature they are increasingly able to carry out their own learning.
- Values play an essential role in the learning process. It is important that students understand and develop a coherent value system that gives meaning to their lives and provides inner direction to their actions.
- Self-concept is integral to how a student learns and develops. Humanists cite evidence correlating positive self-concept with student learning and achievement. Thus they try to develop a classroom climate and curricula that are conducive to developing a positive self-concept.
- Cognitive, affective, and psychomotor learning are interrelated. Humanistic educators see these aspects of learning as interconnected, and thus cognitive learning is viewed in relation to affective and psychomotor development.

- Teachers should be facilitators of learning. Although at times the teacher may be directive, the main task is to develop a trusting and open classroom climate and then help students achieve their learning goals.
- In the humanistic classroom the students' concerns are accepted as valid content. Although the teacher may not be able to respond to all the concerns, at least he or she can create a climate so that the concerns can be acknowledged.
- Self-evaluation is central to humanistic education. Kirschenbaum states, "Humanistic education tends to move away from teacher controlled evaluation and shift to the student as he learns to evaluate his own progress toward his goals."

Gestalt psychology is highly significant in emphasizing humanism in teaching and learning situations. The needs of the total person must be fulfilled if optimal achievement is to take place.

Gestalt psychology is also inherent in the utilization of learning centres. As ample number of centres and tasks at each centre need to be in evidence so that students may sequentially select activities to pursue. Undesirable tasks as perceived by the involved student might then be omitted. A psychological curriculum is in evidence when students individually choose sequential tasks. The following are examples of titles of learning centres which also emphasize handwriting skills:

1. Writing business and friendly letters
2. Writing announcement
3. Writing plays
4. Writing poems
5. Writing stories
6. Writing notes of sympathy
7. Writing thank you notes
8. Writing experience charts
9. Practicing handwriting skills
10. Taking notes

Based on personal needs and interests, the pupil may sequentially select from any of the above named centres. Each centre will have several tasks or learning activities from which students may select.

Experimentalism as a Philosophy of Teaching

Experimentals believe that students solve real problems in school. The problematic situations must relate to life and living in society. The school curriculum then must not be separated from that which exists in society. Committees in society are involved in identifying and solving problems. In school, committees also need to be in evidence.

The handwriting curriculum needs to reflect what is useful in society. Functional situations then need to be in evidence for students. Ideally, the problematic situations should be identified by students. Learners might then perceive purpose in what they identified as being relevant to learn. Which situations existing in society may become relevant for students in handwriting?

1. writing a business letter on school stationery to order free materials relating to a social studies unit being studied;
2. writing a friendly letter to exchange with a friend or mailed to a relative;
3. writing a thank you note for a favour received;
4. writing a sympathy note to a friend who is ill;
5. writing an announcement for parents pertaining to a school function;
6. writing an invitation inviting friends to a birthday party;
7. writing a letter of recognition to a classmate who has achieved in an outstanding manner.

Each of the above named experiences is:

(a) functional in society;
(b) useful to the involved learner;
(c) practical and has utilitarian values.

Pertaining to experimentalism as a philosophy of education, Morris and Pai wrote:

> We must consider also a much more authentic strain of Experimentalist theory: the problem-solving curriculum. The more resolute Experimentalists, since they consider fundamentally wrong-headed the "subject-matter-set-out-to-be-learned" approach to learning, would favour scrapping the whole traditional curriculum. If we are really serious about inducting the young into a "cosmos of process," then working with the old order and compromising with a basically static substantive curriculum will only weaken our efforts

> and blunt the force of our argument. We must rid ourselves, they say, of the fundamental notion that learning goes on in compartments, that learning is essentially the mastery of preordered materials, organised and systematized into study-able form and set, like so much pastry, before the learner.
>
> Learning is essentially growing. And growing, in Experimentalist language, means the increase of intelligence in the management of life. This in turn means the expansion of reflective thinking and the consequent application of thought to action in the wide reach of affairs we honour with the name 'human.' If we are to produce growth effectively we must turn the whole learning process, as traditionally conceived, upside down! That is, we must start with the affairs of life, wherever we may meet them, and let those affairs dictate what should be learned and known in order to manage them properly. Hence the entire curriculum will be inverted from subject matter intended to be applied later to life situations to the life situations themselves that provoke the kinds of learning in or between subject-matter areas that intelligent living calls for.

Teaching Handwriting: Art versus Science

A perennial issue involving handwriting instruction pertains to the artist as compared to the technologist concept. If teaching is an art, creative endeavours are highly significant. The teacher then being an artist thinks of unique objectives, learning activities, and evaluation procedures. Previously utilized plans of instruction are no longer useful. New methods of teaching need emphasis to provide for individual differences among learners in handwriting.

The creative teacher does not like the concept of routine in teaching. Nor are the terms drill and practice important. Rather novel means of instruction are stressed in ongoing lessons and units. Students crave variety in activities. The teacher also prefers originality of strategies of teaching. Uniqueness in legibility for pupils to exhibit is important to the teacher as an artist concept. Tiedt in summarizing research wrote the following characteristics of a creative person:

> Because identifying creativity is not easy, we often fail to recognize this type of giftedness. The commonly used IQ test, it has been found, does not indicate creativeness. Although most researchers find a positive correlation between intelligence and creativity, the high scorer on the intelligence test may not score high on tests of creativity. Nor is the student who receives the highest grades necessarily the most creative child.

MacKinnon studied more than 500 famous writers, architects, composers—who were judged by their peers to be creative. He found that in general these artists had disliked school, did not identify with teachers, and had in many cases dropped out of school.

This study and others which followed resulted in a body of generalizations about the creative person which may prove helpful as we attempt to identify and to understand the creative student. The creative person has been found to possess the following traits:

1. Nonconformity of ideas, but not necessarily of dress and behaviour
2. Egotism and feelings of destiny
3. Great curiosity, desire to discover the answer
4. Sense of humour and playfulness
5. Preservance on self-started projects
6. Intense emotions, sincerity
7. Tendency to be shy
8. Lack of rigidity

The teacher as a technician concept of instruction advocates predetermining prior to teaching what students will be learning. The objectives then need to be stated precisely and in behavioural terms. A committee of teachers with supervisory guidance needs to select vital ends. The chosen objectives must be arranged from the simple to the complex in ascending order of difficulty.

Next, each teacher selects learning activities for his/her students to attain. The activities must assist students to achieve precisely what is stated in each measurable objective. Only then might a teacher measure to determine if a learner has been successful in goal attainment.

The teacher emphasizing handwriting instruction as a science advocates:

1. specific objectives for student attainment;
2. observable, measurable results from each student;
3. objective results from learners independent of who does the evaluating;
4. precise means of diagnosing learner progress as to letter formation, correct spacing of letters and words, proper slant of letters, right proportion of letters, as well as consistent legible slant in the written product.

An issue then exists pertaining to the artist versus the technician approach in the teaching of handwriting.

Self-Evaluation versus Teacher Appraisal

Who should be involved in appraising student achievement? The learner himself/herself might assess personal progress in handwriting. The teacher then needs to guide the learner in self appraisal. Specific or general items for improvement may be identified. Precise items to evaluate include proper letter formation, slant, alignment, proportion of letters, and spacing. After self diagnosis has been emphasized, the student with teacher leadership may develop lessons and methodology to overcome the identified deficiencies. To overcome weaknesses, the pupil with instructor guidance may work on remedial activities. The activities might include writing business and friendly letters, announcements, poems, plays, stories, as well as thank you letters for favours received.

Toward the other end of the continuum, the teacher largely may appraise student progress in handwriting. The teacher might then diagnose highly specific items. Items such as in manuscript writing, start the lines at the top only and pull downward. For circles or parts of circles in letters, the teacher guides students to write from left to right in formation of the abstract symbols. The fingers are to be utilized in forming the delicate parts of the letters, while the arm is used in moving progressively from left to right.

Myers wrote the following for diagnosing and remediating precise difficulties in handwriting involving the research of Frank Freeman, a specialist in the teaching of handwriting:

1. "The writer should face the desk squarely"—a side position causes spinal curvature.
2. "Both forearms should rest on the desk for approximately three quarters of their length"—if one elbow is unsupported spinal curvature is produced.
3. "The paper should be directly in front of the writer"—the paper on one side of the middle line requires a different adjustment of the two eyes causing eye strain and a twisting of the head and body which produces curvature.
4. "Place the paper with a tilt to the left for right-handers and a tilt to the right for left-handers so that the forearm

forms a right angle with the base line of the letters"—this position was found to be more common among good writers than poor writers.

5. "The hand should be held with the palm down"—good writers do not incline the hand with more than a 45 degree slope to the wrist. Poor writers tend to rest the hand on its side. Wrist action produces strain.
6. "The hand should rest upon the third and fourth fingers."
7. "The forefinger should rest lower down on the pen or pencil than the thumb." The end of the thumb should be against the pen or pencil.
8. "The pen or pencil should be grasped loosely, with the fingers moderately curved."
9. "The writing movement should be a combination of arm and fingers; the arm for the forward progress and the fingers for the delicate parts of the letters that the arm muscles are too large and powerful to control."
10. "The writing movement, particularly in the early stages, should be divided into a series of units of movement which are separated by slight pauses. This movement or rhythm is not continuous and uniform in speed.

Planned Curriculum versus Needs in Handwriting

There are educators emphasizing a preplanned curriculum for students. The objectives, learning activities, and appraisal procedures then would be developed by teachers and supervisors, prior to the beginning of a new school year. In achieving a preplanned handwriting course of study, involved teachers and supervisors would attend carefully to the following criteria:

1. quality sequence needs to be in evidence so that each student may gradually move from the easiest to that which is increasingly more difficult;
2. the scope of handwriting experiences would receive careful attention. Thus, breadth of content for learners would assist in attaining legibility in handwriting;
3. essential, core learnings need to be mastered by pupils. A basics curriculum is then in evidence;
4. an appraisal programme needs developing which assesses achievement of each student;

5. objectives need to be precise (not general) in handwriting;
6. learning activities should guide students to achieve objectives;
7. adequate stress needs to be placed upon diagnosis and remediation of handwriting errors;
8. one or more reputable handwriting textbooks should provide the majority of experiences for students;
9. transfer of learning needs to be emphasized in that quality in the formal period of time devoted to the teaching of handwriting is utilized in functional situations in writing;
10. a separate period of time needs to be set aside for the teaching of handwriting. Time on task is emphasized for each lesson taught. Definite goals need to be attained by students during the allotted time.

A needs approach in the teaching of handwriting would emphasize diagnostic and remedial work as the involved student reveals specific errors. For example, if a student is writing a business letter with teacher guidance to order free and expensive materials for a science or social studies unit, he/she may need help in forming the upper case letter 'B' correctly. Or, the student has incorrect proportion of the upper case 'C' and the lower case 'c'. The learner with the assistance of the teacher would then diagnose and work on overcoming the difficulty.

In a needs approach, within the functional writing situation, the student's personal errors in handwriting would be pinpointed and remedial work provided as individual errors made. The following would not be emphasized:

1. separating handwriting instruction from the everyday writing situations inherent in life;
2. specific remedial errors remedied outside the framework of functional writing;
3. eliminating students in planning objectives, learning activities, and appraisal procedures in the handwriting curriculum;
4. a logical curriculum in which preplanned goals have been selected in handwriting for student attainment. Rather, a psychological curriculum needs to be in evidence whereby teacher-pupil planning is utilized to develop the curriculum;

5. separate time during the day involved in the teaching of handwriting unrelated to other curriculum areas in the school setting;
6. a limited scope in the curriculum in which handwriting is taught as a separate subject, rather than emphasizing the correlated, fused, or integrated curricula;
7. a formal sequence preplanned by teachers and supervisors;
8. evaluation procedures determined and implemented solely by teachers and supervisors;
9. inadequate emphasis of transfer of learning from one situation to another, such as specific techniques acquired in handwriting lessons to functional writing situations;
10. lack of emphasis placed upon learner interests and purposes in handwriting.

Rewarding Handwriting Proficiency

How should pupils individually be rewarded for improved proficiency in handwriting? Behaviourists would recommend the use of success in learning, verbal praise, or prizes if students achieve well in handwriting. The teacher needs to ascertain how many precise objectives any learner can achieve realistically in order to receive a physical prize such as a certificate, badge, candy, or gum. The learner is aware of the exact number of measurable goals which need attainment in order to achieve one or more prizes.

Success in learning should be the lot of all students regardless of present achievement levels. If a student is able to perform better in handwriting presently compared to earliest attempts, he/she is successful, provided it is individual optimal achievement. Students being successful in attainment is recommended by all schools of educational psychology. Verbal praise is important to reinforce quality learning, in terms of behaviourism as an educational psychology.

Humanist educators also utilize verbal praise for work well done, but not to the extent advocated by behaviourism. Behaviourists advocate shaping and successive approximations as concepts in teaching. Shaping means to continually reinforce quantitative (measurable) achievement each step of teaching and learning. Behaviour of students in an acceptable direction might then be shaped. Successive approximations indicate that with shaping each student will continually aspire upward in goal attainment.

Behaviourism then advocates concepts of reinforcement, shaping, and successive approximations in guiding students to attain precise ends. External rewards tend to motivate student accomplishment.

Pertaining to reinforcing student progress in learning, Bowyer wrote:

> B.F. Skinner's programmed learning, in sharp contrast to branching, is linear where reinforcement is the primary basis of learning. Here the subject matter is developed in small steps and the pupil is rewarded by each success. At the same time, his knowledge is reinforced. The pupil is motivated by the reward for correct answers, and the sequence of questions is tight and carefully constructed in order to minimize incorrect responses. This type of programming is especially suited for drill and practice teaching.
>
> Crowder's approach is associated with intrinsic programming, and like Pressey, he relies upon multiple choice items. The pupil answers a question, and when he makes an error he is referred to correct sources of information. He can proceed only when the mistake has been eliminated. This, too, is a branching procedure, but when the student meets an obstacle he is helped by a specific direction. The method of programming necessitates an insight into how the pupil can be expected to think and to respond. The anticipated incorrect answers are used to help build knowledge and skill. All teachers who use cogent reasoning and well-conceived questions to encourage student answers utilize the branching technique, but the use of the machine enables the student to receive more individual instruction than is possible otherwise.

Toward the other end of the continuum, selected educators recommend that learning in and of itself is its own reward. Intrinsic motivation is then in evidence. No prizes, certificates, or badges should be given to learners to stimulate learning. Rather with stimulating learning activities, students from within perceive purpose, motivation, and joy in learning. Learning is prized for its own sake. The student is not achieving for reasons of securing extrinsic rewards. But, inside the learner, satisfaction exists for accomplishing and attaining.

Jerome Bruner, a leading educational psychologist, advocates intrinsic motivation or learning is its own reward. Morris and Pai wrote:

> ...Children often learn knowledge or skills as a result of rewards coming from the outside; extrinsic rewards are likely to conform to what is expected of them. Hence, a child who engages in learning activities for grades alone is likely to be docile and obedient to the teacher rather than spontaneous and creative on his or her own. This child becomes primarily 'other-directed.' Bruner hypothesizes that approaching learning as discovering something rather than as learning about something will lead children to act in terms of self-reward, intrinsic reward, that is, to be rewarded by discovery itself. Learning for instrinsic reward eventually frees children from immediate stimulus control, and they become competence-oriented, so that each child can be more of an 'inner-directed person.'

Somewhat opposite of behaviourism, selected educators then recommend that learning is its own reward. These educators believe that external prizes are unrelated to learning and may actually hinder the process of acquiring and attaining of understandings, skills, and attitudes. If learning is its own reward, students learn because an inward desire to do so is inherent in the student. Intrinsic rather than extrinsic motivation is significant.

Students learn due to wanting to learn. From within, the conditions of the student are such that positive feelings toward achievement are in evidence.

The Word Processor in the Curriculum

Relevant objectives need selecting for learners to attain. Numerous changes occur in society. Seemingly, situations in life are not stable nor static. Rather, change is a key concept. Changing societal situations need to be incorporated into the curriculum. The word processor, when more numerous in number than presently, may well provide vital goals in teaching-learning situations.

Objectives in ongoing Lessons and Units

There are selected criteria which need to be followed in choosing objectives. Thus, outcomes for student achievement must be:

1. purposeful so that reasons for learning are inherent;
2. meaningful in that what is being learned is understood;
3. interesting to stimulate intrinsic learner attention;
4. attainable in a manner which provides for diverse levels of achievement.

To translate the above-named criteria into goals for learners to realize, relevant ends need choosing reflecting the utilization of the word processor. The following concepts might well provide direction for selecting objectives, learning activities, and evaluation procedures in using word processors:

1. control card—a magnetic card containing instructions for the central processing unit;
2. electronic typewriter—electronic in nature and not mechanical in operation. The number of moving parts is few and operates in a silent manner;
3. automatic carrier return—the operator does not need to return the carriage at the end of a line of type. Automatically, the carrier is returned by the machine. Automatic centering is completed with a keystroke command to the central processing unit (CPU);
4. central dictation system—direct wiring of a system to a central location whereby direction from others is received;
5. input—content which goes into a computer;
6. K (kilo)—represented by 1000 characters, approximately. Thus, 30K equals 30,000 characters;
7. keyboarding—the actual operation of a typewriter;
8. log sheet—a document which is used by supervisors to record cost efficiency as to incoming/outgoing work of computer service;
9. magnetic diskette—diskette which has a magnetic coat on which 130 pages, approximately, of typed content may be recorded;
10. magnetic tape—tape which has magnetic coat and is used for recording of information;
11. memory—within the central processing unit, an internal device in which subject-matter can be stored and retrieved upon demand;
12. printer—a facet of the output device which prints content on paper;
13. record—storing typed content on a magnetic medium for use in the future;
14. search—a command to the word processor which causes the location of a specific section;
15. shared logic—two or more terminals can utilize the memory of the same central processing unit (CPU);

16. software—includes manuals, programmes, and flowcharts to assist in making optimal use of the computer. Software then are materials used to operate and control the hardware (computers).

Learning Activities to Achieve Objectives

Experiences for students should guide in achieving relevant objectives. Each student is at a different level of achievement compared to other learners. Thus, students individually will progress at different rates of speed in attaining objectives.

A variety of activities should be utilized in teaching and learning. Hands on approaches in utilizing the word processor should predominate as a learning activity. However, illustrations, slides, films, tapes, excursions, and filmstrips may also be utilized to provide for individual differences. Success in learning is important in order that each student might optimalize learning.

Sequence in learning is vital. If learnings are sequential, students individually have excellent opportunities to achieve objectives. A lack of learner progress may well be due to improper order of content and skills presented.

Ultimately, student achievement needs to be evaluated. A variety of evaluation techniques may be utilized. These include:

1. teacher observation of learner progress in operating a word processor;
2. teacher written test items, such as true-false, multiple choice, matching, essay, and completion;
3. discussions to notice learner progress;
4. checklists and rating scales to notice if objectives are being attained by learners;
5. anecdotal statements. Thus, the instructor records random behaviour of each student in learning to utilize the word processor.

The school curriculum should not be separated from trends in society. The use of word processors in the societal arena has tremendous implications in selecting objectives, learning activities, and appraisal procedures in curriculum development.

In Summary

Selected issues were identified in the handwriting curriculum. These include:

1. a separate subjectives versus a correlated curriculum;
2. behaviourism versus humanism;
3. experimentalism as a philosophy of education;
4. teaching handwriting: art versus science;
5. planned curriculum versus needs in handwriting;
6. rewarding handwriting: extrinsic versus intrinsic motivation;
7. the use of the word processor in the language arts.

Teachers and supervisors need to study, analyze, and attempt to synthesize diverse issues, in the teaching of handwriting. Ultimately, relevant goals, learning activities, and evaluation procedures need selecting to provide for individual levels of student achievement.

Barbe, Walter B. *et al*. (Eds.) wrote:

> Handwriting is a necessary skill that it is too often taken for granted. It has been the medium through which the history of humankind has been recorded for thousands of years. The role of handwriting in the development and growth of the human race is incalculable.
>
> The constituents of handwriting are the abilities that make humans unique among animal species: cognition, complex hand-eye movements, language competence, and aesthetics. These abilities are blended together to produce a visual communication system that is functional and beautiful. Through the simple act of applying a writing instrument to a smooth surface and creating a pattern of lines, a person can permanently record thoughts, opinions, interests, and emotions so that others might know them. Representing internal and external reality through graphic symbols interpretable by others is a distinct human talent rivaled only by the power of speech.
>
> The cry in education is no longer for relevance, but for competence. Schools, it is now recognized, must provide children with the basic skills they will need in order to continue their education.or to move into adulthood as workers. Handwriting is among the basic skills that have received more attention from the change in philosophy. Sales of handwriting materials have increased each year since 1975, and the amount of time spent on handwriting instruction has increased proportionately. Educators and parents are realizing that good handwriting is not a frill, but an essential ability that relates to success in school and in later life.

REFERENCES

Barbe, Walter B., *et al*. (Eds.), *Handwriting*. Columbus, Ohio: James Bloser, Inc., 1984.

Bowyer, Carlton H. *Philosophical Perspectives for Education*. Glenview, Illinois: Scott, Foresman and Company, 1970.

McNeil, John D. *Curriculum*. Boston: Little, Brown and Company, 1985.

Miller, John P. *The Educational Spectrum*. New York: Longman Inc., 1983.

Morris, Van Cleve and Pai, Young. *Philosophy and the American School*. Boston: Houghton-Mifflin Company, 1976.

Myers, Emma Harrison. *The Whys and Hows of Teaching Handwriting*. Columbus, Ohio: Zaner Bloser Company, 1963.

Tiedt, Iris M. *The Language Arts Handbook*. Englewood Cliffs, New Jersey, 1983.

12

Teaching Mathematics in the Elementary School

There are certain key ideas that pupils should develop in elementary school mathematics. These key ideas may be called structural properties which are basic to understanding mathematics in the elementary school.

In the kindergarten or first grade level, depending upon the achievement levels of learners, pupils can develop understandings pertaining to the commutative property of addition. For example, the teacher can show pupils three books in one set and two books in a second set. Pupils can, of course, be asked to tell how many books there are in each set. The two sets can then be joined together. Learners can then respond with how many members there are in the new set. Once pupils have responded correctly to these questions, the order of the two sets can be changed. The teacher can ask pupils how many members there are in the first set of books. Pupils would respond with 'two' if a correct answer is given. Now, learners would be shown the second set of books consisting of three members. They would tell how many books are in the second set. Again, the two sets can be joined together to form a new set, and pupils could then state orally how many members make up the new set of books. Thus, pupils can understand that $3 + 2 = 2 + 3$. The order of the sets did not affect the sum. The concept "commutative property of addition" would not be mentioned by the teacher in teaching these early primary grade pupils. The teacher could use the term "changing the order of sets" instead. It is difficult for young children to pronounce the word 'commutative' properly. Intermediate grade pupils should utilize the concept "commutative property" when communicating ideas to others. The commutative property of addition is a very valuable concept for pupils to understand. In the study of basic addition facts, the number of learning needed by pupils is cut in half as a result of developing understandings pertaining to the commutative property. Thus, if a pupil understands and attaches meaning to 5 + 4 = 9, he also realizes that 4 + 5 = 9. The commutative property of addition can be used again and again in the elementary school mathematics programme. In dealing with larger values, pupils can understand that 45 + 32 = 32 + 45 or 116 + 235 = 235 + 116.

It is important to have an ample number of learning activities for pupils at the appropriate stage of development to develop understandings pertaining to the commutative property of multiplication. In introductory learnings pertaining to this area, for example, pupils could be shown a set of four marbles. They could be asked how many marbles they would have if two of these sets were in their possession. The number sentence could be written on the chalkboard which would correspond with the set or sets of marbles shown to pupils, such as 2 x 4 = 8. Next, pupils could be shown a set of two marbles; they could be asked how many marbles there would be if 4 sets of marbles existed with two members in each set. A number sentence could be written on the chalkboard which could correspond to the concrete situation, such as 4 x 2 = 8. Materials should be changed frequently to maintain pupil interest in learning, such as using crayons, markers, children, pencils, chairs, candles, and other objects. The mathematics teacher must use a variety of objects and items within an ample number of learning activities to assist pupils in thoroughly understanding the commutative property of addition and multiplication.

A second major understanding pertaining to structural ideas in elementary school mathematics is the associative property of addition and multiplication. In the associative property of addition, the teacher can again have pupils develop important understandings using concrete materials and eventually have pupils progress to utilizing the abstract. For example, the teacher could call the names of three pupils who come to the front of the classroom. The names of two other learners can be called who would also come to the front of the room representing a second set. Finally, the names of four other pupils can be called and they would come to the front of the room. The teacher can ask now many members make up each of the three sets of pupils. A pupil can volunteer to write the corresponding number sentence on the chalkboard as it is given by pupils. The teacher can ask questions of learners as to how many pupils are in all three sets with the resulting information becoming a part in writing the number sentence, such as 3 + 2 + 4 = 9. All pupils in the front of the classroom can be asked to take their seats. The teacher then calls the names of four pupils who come to the front of the classroom. This is followed by the teacher calling the names of two other pupils for the second set and three pupils for the third set. A different pupil can volunteer to write the number sentence pertaining to pupils in the front of the classroom prior to and with joining together the members of the three sets to form a new set. Thus, learners will notice that 4 + 2 + 3 = 9. The teacher can also call pupils to the front of the room whereby the corresponding number sentence when writing the numerals on the chalkboard for each set and the total number of members in all three sets would be the following: 2 + 3 + 4. Pupils should receive ample practice using a variety of materials whereby they can develop a meaningful generalization pertaining to the associative property of addition. Thus learners will realize that three or more addends can be arranged in any crder and it does not affect the sum in addition.

At the appropriate stage of development, learners should also realize the associative property of multiplication. Thus learners in their own words would understand that the order of three (or more) factors does not affect the product in multiplication. For example, in introductory learnings pertaining to the associative property of multiplication, pupils could look at two chairs representing the number of members or elements in a specific set. Pupils could be asked a question pertaining to how many members would exist in a new set if three sets of chairs would be considered with two members in each set. To give the student additional assistance in determining the product, a comparison could be made between multiplication and addition. Three sets of chairs could be placed in the room with two members in each set. Pupils could conclude that 2 + 2 + 2 = 6 or 3 × 2 = 6. The pupil should understand the relationship of addition to multiplication. Learnings should be meaningful and make sense to the learner. It generally is very unpleasant to learn that which is not understood or lacks meaning. To proceed with pupils understanding associative property of multiplication, the six chairs can be taken as members of one set; pupils can then think of 4 sets, for example, each set having six members. To have pupils now enhance their thinking pertaining to the associative property of multiplication, pupils should think in terms of four chairs in a set with six of these specific sets. Chairs in the room could be arranged to have pupils see six sets of chairs with four members in each set. Thus pupils can see and understand that $(3 \times 2) \times 4 = 24$. The order of factors does not affect the product in multiplication. Ample number of experiences using a variety of objects and children should be utilized in guiding learners to understand in a meaningful way the associative property of multiplication. Thus, learners, for example, should realize that $(2 \times 3) \times 4 = (3 \times 2) \times 4 = (4 \times 3) \times 2 = (4 \times 2) \times 3$ by using concrete materials in learning activities which are interesting, understandable and purposeful.

It is important also for learners to understand identify elements. For example, pupils can develop the generalization at a very early age that any counting number plus zero equals that counting number. Seven objects plus zero objects equals the original seven objects. Learning activities which would assist pupils to realize this generalization could include the following:

1. Have six small toys, for example, in a box and ask pupils how many members there are in this set. In a separate box which has no toys, let pupils respond with the number of members in this set. Then have learners join the two sets together and state how many members there are in the new set. Change the order of the two sets so that pupils can generalize that $6 + 0 = 0 + 6$ (commutative property of addition) and that any counting number plus zero equals that counting number.
2. Three pupils can come to the front of the room; learners can be asked to state how many members there are in this set. A circle can be drawn on the floor which would encircle members of this set. A second circle can be drawn and pupils can tell how many members are in the empty set. Then members of both sets can be joined together to form a new set; learners can then state how many members make up the new set. Thus, the generalization can be

developed again that adding zero to a counting number results in a sum which is equal to the counting number.

3. The teacher can state orally a certain counting number; pupils at their desks would then place the corresponding number of members in a set using crayons, chalk, checkers, pencils, books, beads, corn, and other kinds of markers. String or yarn could be used to encircle the members of this set. Next the teacher could have pupils use string or yarn to encircle the set which has no members (if pupils placed six seeds of corn in the first set, then the second set would be any empty set with no corn seeds). The two sets could be joined together and again encircled with yean or string. Thus, pupils could develop meaningful understandings pertaining to the identity element in addition.

Learners at the appropriate stage of development should also attach meaning to the identity element in multiplication. The teacher, for example, could call the names of four pupils to come to the front of the room. Pupils, of course, could state how many members there are in this set. Learners could then be asked, "If we have one set of four pupils, how many pupils are there?" The basic multiplication fact '1 x 4' can be written on the chalkboard to guide learners to associate the abstract with the concrete situation where children are involved. Pupils should also, of course, notice the commutative property in that $1 \times 4 = 4 \times 1$. The teacher can ask for a volunteer to come to the front of the room. Pupils can now be challenged and encouraged to think of four sets with one member in each set. Learners can also notice how the number sentence written $4 \times 1 = 4$ can also be thought of as addition, $1 + 1 + 1 + 1 = 4$. In this learning activity, of course, primary emphasis is placed upon pupils realizing that any counting number times one equals that counting number. Too frequently, learners have thought in terms of $8 \times 1 = 9$; in this situation, pupils are confusing 8×1 (or 1×8) with $8 + 1$ (or $1 + 8$). Pupils must attach meaning to what is being learned so they realize that 1×8 means one set with eight members in the set, whereas, 8×1 pertains to eight sets with one member in each set. Once learners understand the identity element in multiplication, they can quickly respond with the counting number being the product if one of the factors is the numberal 'one'.

4. *The distributive property* of multiplication over addition is also important for elementary school pupils to realize at the appropriate stage of development. Thus, in the problem 6 (2 + 3) = ——, the six serving as a factor would distribute itself equally over the '2' and the '3'. Hence, (6 × 2) + (6 × 3) = 30. The same results would be obtained if the operation of addition were performed first such as 2 + 3 = 5; then six sets of five or 6 × 5 = 30. The distributive property of multiplication over addition is utilized very frequently by pupils when working problems pertaining to multiplication. In the problem 21 × 3 = —— the individual who thinks 3 × 1 = 3 and 3 × 2 tens = 6 tens resulting in a final product of 6 tens plus 3 ones or 63 is using the distributive property of multiplication over addition. Twenty-one times three can be written in the following way illustrating this property more clearly: 3 (20 +1) resulting in distributing the three equally over the 20 and the 1 or (3 × 20) + (3 × 1) = 63. Pupils need numerous opportunities to understand and apply key ideas pertaining to the distributive property of multiplication over addition.

Providing for Individual Differences

Pupils differ much from each other in mathematics achievement. In a heterogeneously grouped classroom, the range of achievement will be greater in mathematics achievement as compared to homogeneous grouping. In any plan of grouping, however, individual differences in mathematics will be a reality and must be provided for. Too frequently, teachers want to teach all pupils in a class at the same time and keep all learners at the same time place using a mathematics textbook. This certainly violates a very important rule of providing for individual differences.

There are numerous approaches to use in providing for individual differences within a class in elementary school mathematics. One approach is to state objectives behaviourally and have learners realize these at different rates of speed. Thus, in a class of second grade pupils, learners at different achievement levels could realize the following objectives (only attainable objectives should be stated):

1. Pupils will add correctly nine out of ten problems in addition with each problem having two 2 digit addends and no regrouping involved.
2. Pupils will add correctly nine out of ten problems in addition, regrouping involved, with each problem having two 2 digit addends.

It is quite obvious that the first objective is easier to achieve as compared to the second objective. In mathematical learnings for pupils, proper sequence is of utmost importance. Pupils should be accepted where they are presently and assisted in making continuous progress. With appropriate learning activities which are carefully selected, sequential learnings should become a definite experience for each pupil. Thus, one way of providing for individual pupils within a class is to use behaviourally stated objectives whereby each learner is at a different level of achievement as compared to other children.

A second approach to individualizing instruction in elementary school mathematics could pertain to pupils working at their own optimum rate of speed when utilizing a carefully selected series of elementary school mathematics textbooks. Through teacher observation and evaluation, pupils individually would be started at a specific place in the mathematics textbook where learner achievement is presently. A variety of learning activities would be provided to help pupils gain needed mathematical concepts, generalizations, and facts. Adequate guidance must be given to each learner as he progresses on a continuum when realizing optimum achievement. The teacher must assist each pupil individually when help is needed to solve problems, to understand structural properties, to understand basic facts, and to stimulate pupils in wanting to achieve. Adequate help must be given to teachers in checking papers and other pupil products in elementary school mathematics so that the teacher can devote his time to planning and teaching which is truly a professional responsibility.

To individualize instruction, the teacher of mathematics in a homogeneously grouped classroom could have learners work on the same or similar problem but at varying levels of complexity. With proper readiness activities, let us assume that pupils are working on the following operation: $31\overline{)684}$. Pupils can be asked how many 31's there are in 684. Practical application, of course, can be made of learning activities such as these. For example, if a boy had 684 marbles and he wanted to divide them equally among 31 boys, how many marbles would each boy receive? In receiving answers to the question, many responses basically would be correct. If a pupil would say there are ten sets of 31 in 684, this would be correct:

```
31)684
   310  10
   ---
   374
```

There are still 374 marbles then which have not been placed into the various sets. Pupils then could be asked how many 31's there are in 374. There are 374 marbles that still need to be divided among the 31 boys. If a pupil responds with 5, the teacher can continue writing the division problem in the following way:

```
31) 684
    310  10
    ---
    374
    155  5
    ---
    219
```

There are still 219 marbles that need to be divided equally among the 31 boys. The teacher can continually ask questions of learners until all marbles have been accounted for. Finally, the quotient figures can be added on the right hand side; a remainder will be a part of this problem. It generally is not long before pupils notice that it is tedious to work these kinds of division problems in the way presented. Learners individually will give the largest correct quotient figure ultimately with the first response such as in the following problem:

```
21) 857
    840  40
    ---
     17
```

Pupils can, of course, also notice that there are not enough left over in the remainder to do further dividing. Ultimately, individual learners can progress to the point of placing the quotient figures correctly above the dividend, such as in the following:

```
      40
21) 857
    840
     17
```

At different rates of speed then individuals can achieve to more mature levels of work that is done in working toward optimum achievement in elementary school mathematics. Thus, the teacher is helping to provide for individual differences in elementary school mathematics.

There are many ways which can be utilized to provide for individual differences in elementary school mathematics. The reader needs to study these many approaches carefully and evaluate each thoroughly in terms of acceptable criteria.

Learning By Discovery

Elementary school pupils need to have many opportunities to learn inductively or through discovery. Pupils have turned off frequently when the lecture or explanation approach to teaching is used largely. Educational psychologists have long advocated the pupils do better if they are actively involved in ongoing learning activities as compared to being passive individuals. When pupils learn by discovery, the teacher becomes a good asker of questions rather than a lecturer. Questions asked of pupils should follow good sequence; otherwise the teacher may jump too far ahead of pupils or questions are asked which do not challenge the thinking of learners. The teacher must have a good knowledge of mathematics so that important questions can be asked which will help learners make important discoveries and thus learn inductively.

On any grade level in the elementary school, pupils can develop important learnings in mathematics inductively.

If a first grade teacher wants to have pupils discover the commutative property of addition, the teacher could start with having pupils state orally how many blocks there are in a given set. Let us assume there were two blocks in the set. A second set, of blocks could be shown to learners, and pupils could tell how many members there are in the second set. In this second set, for example, there were three blocks. If learners responded incorrectly to how many members there were in either set, time may need to be spent in having pupils engage in rational counting (that is learn to count the number of blocks in each set). The two sets of blocks could be joined together to form a new set and learners could now be asked to state orally how many members there are in the resulting set.

The teacher could now place three blocks in the first set and two blocks in the second set. Pupils could be asked to tell how many members there are in each set. Following this, learners could tell how many members there are in the new set which joins together the previously mentioned two sets. Pupils can then realize inductively that the order of the two sets can be changed and yet the sum is not affected. Learners should state the generalization in their very own words which is meaningful to them. Materials need to be changed so that pupils have enough experiences to realize that the commutative property holds true in addition. The teacher, of course, may do some explaining when helping pupils develop learnings inductively.

Drill and the Mathematics Curriculum

The concept 'drill' has almost become a bad word in modern educational practices. With the beginning of the 1900's in the United States, drill was being deemphasized more and more in teaching-learning situations. Prior to that time, teachers in many cases would have pupils develop learnings in arithmetic using the drill procedure largely. To be sure, most learners must not have understood what they were learning, and, no doubt, interest was lacking in what was being presented. Once learners lost interest in learning, means were utilized to 'motivate' students through ways that, of course, would be considered undesirable today. Prior to the 1900's when many faculty members believed that the human mind operated like a muscle, teachers would drill pupils so that the mind would become strong. It was felt that exercising the mind would make it strong. Since then, of course, it has been discovered again and again that pupils may give up in trying if the learning activities are too difficult to be meaningful. Pupils may then develop feelings of inadequacy due to a lack of success in learning.

One would certainly advocate that pupils thoroughly understand and attach meaning to what is being learned in elementary school mathematics. Teachers should also vary learning activities to develop and/or maintain pupil interest in mathematics. The textbook should not be the sole determiner of content and methods. Learners should also 'see' purpose in what they are learning. Certainly, it is important to sense reasons for learning something. In initial learnings pertaining to a new process in mathematics, drill does not meet the criterion of helping pupils develop understandings or attach meaning to what is being learned, nor does it meet the criterion of providing interesting learning activities. The chances are in this learning situations, pupils will not see value in drill either.

If pupils are developing introductory learnings pertaining to division as in the following: 2$\overline{)4}$, the teacher should use various learning activities to assist learners in developing meaningful learnings. For example, four cookies could be taken to represent the dividend in the previously mentioned division fact. These four cookies could be divided equally between two children. This represents a concrete learning situation since real objects are being used. Social usage is involved in the ongoing learning activity since the cookies need to be divided equally between two pupils. These cookies can then be eaten by pupils. There should be ample cookies so that all pupils in the class can have the same satisfying learning experience. Most pupils then will sense that purpose is involved in learning since the cookies needed to be divided equally before they could be eaten. Much interest and enthusiasm can be generated within pupils when learning activities are varied. The teacher can also use, among other things, the abacus, sticks, crayons, and pupils when having learners develop understandings pertaining to basic division facts and other operations in elementary school mathematics.

Many pupils, for example, will recall basic addition, subtraction, multiplication, and division facts when appropriate principles of learning have been used in teaching. Most pupils find it too time consuming to continually find what 2$\overline{)4}$ is with the use of concrete objects. They realize that being able to recall previously developed learnings quickly is an asset and saves time in computation and in solving problems. There are some pupils who need drill to fix learnings in the mind. However, even in this case, drill procedures should be varied. Flash cards, for example, can be used to help pupils retain learnings previously achieved.

To give another example of pupils engaging in drill pertaining to elementary school mathematics, the teacher could draw and cut pictures of fish on construction paper of different colours. On each of these fish, a paper clip needs to be placed where the mouth is located. A 'fishing pole' consisting of a small stick together with the attached string and a magnet can then be used to 'catch' the fish contained in a small paper box. The student that catches a fish must respond correctly to the addition, subtraction, multiplication and division fact written on the fish in order to make claims to his success as a fisherman. Once pupils have developed learnings in a meaningful, interesting, and purposeful way, learners should be able to respond quickly to basic facts in addition, subtraction, multiplication, and division. The rate of achievement in this direction will depend upon the pupil's capacity, skill, motivation, and feelings. Each pupil, of course, will realize objectives at a different rate of speed. Learning activities involving drill should be varied to develop and maintain interest as well as provide for individual differences.

The concept 'practice' must be treated separately from 'drill'. It is very important that pupils have ample opportunities to practice that which has been learned previously. Learnings must be transferred from one situation to another. If pupils do not practice what has been learned previously, much forgetting, of course, can occur. Thus, once learners have understood a new process in mathematics, practice needs to be provided to fix learnings in the minds of pupils. There are certain criteria to follow in having pupils engage in practice in elementary school mathematics.

1. The textbook should not be the only source to use in having pupils practice what has been learned previously; activities need to be varied.
2. Periods of time devoted to practice should not be excessively long; time devoted to practice must be in harmony with child growth and development characteristics.
3. Not every pupil needs the same amount of practice after understandings have been developed pertaining to a new process in mathematics.
4. Practice sessions definitely must not destroy interest in learning.
5. Pupils should definitely understand and attach meaning to what is being practiced in elementary mathematics.

6. Learners must sense reasons for engaging in learning activities involving practice.
7. Application of work performed in practice sessions must be related to life outside of school and society in general.
8. Learners must have opportunities to evaluate their own achievement in practice sessions.
9. Pupils with teacher guidance need to diagnose weaknesses in practice sessions devoted to elementary school mathematics and work in the direction of remedying deficiencies.
10. Learners should be accepted by the teacher as human beings having worth regardless of present achievement levels in mathematics.
11. The teacher must work in the direction of having each pupil be successful and thus develop feelings within learners of an adequate self.
12. It is important that pupils enjoy practice sessions devoted to mathematics so that positive attitudes are developed.

Relationship of Knowledge

Elementary school mathematics strongly emphasizes the importance of the relationship of knowledge. Educational psychologists have long stressed the importance of learners sensing that knowledge is related rather than fragmented. It is difficult to recall many isolated bits of information. Content that is perceived as being interrelated can be recalled easier. Thus, mathematics teachers should think in terms of pupils developing appropriate attitudes which would view knowledge as being related.

The modern programme of elementary school mathematics stresses the importance of pupils realizing that subtraction undoes addition. In other words, subtraction is the inverse operation of addition. On the kindergarten or first grade level, depending upon the present stage of development of each learner, individuals can understand that subtraction undoes addition. At their desks, individual pupils can be asked to place four markers in a set. Learners then can be asked to place two markers in a second set. They can write the addition fact that would be $4 + 2 = 6$. Learners can then be asked to take two markers away from the six markers and indicate how many markers are left by writing a number sentence pertaining to the original six markers followed by two markers being taken away leaving four markers: 6 - 2 = 4. Thus, pupils can understand that originally there are four markers in a set in the addition problem with two markers representing a second set being joined together to form a new set of six markers. Six markers in a set with two markers being taken away left the original four markers. In their own words pupils can develop a generalization pertaining to subtraction undoing addition. Thus 4 + 2 = 6 and 6 - 2 = 4.

On the kindergarten or first grade level, pupils should study the subtraction undoes addition as soon as a basic addition fact is understood in a meaningful way using a variety of learning activities. Many learning activities should be utilized to help learners thoroughly understand that subtraction undoes addition. Pupils become frustrated in learning if they do not understand or cannot attach meaning to what has been learned. Much forgetting also will occur if learners do not understand what has been learned.

In proper sequence, pupils can attach meaning to the relationship of addition to multiplication. For example, pupils could be asked how much money they would have if three nickels were owned. The nickels should be shown to pupils. Learners should also be asked to state how many pennies there are in a nickel. They can change each nickel representing a set into pennies. The question can be raised as to how much is 3 × 5. Pupils can also be led to think in terms of adding 5 + 5 + 5 in addition. Thus 3 × 5 means three sets with five members in each set, hence 3 × 5 = 5 + 5 + 5.

Arithmetic, Algebra, and Geometry

The traditional elementary school curriculum placed much emphasis upon arithmetic and had a tendency to minimize algebra and geometry. The concept of "arithmetic in the elementary school" had to be changed to "mathematics in the elementary school" which included not only arithmetic but also geometry and algebra. In the modern mathematics programme, computation and social usage of arithmetic is not adequate to prepare individuals to live in the latter part of the twentieth century and the twenty-first century.

What was formerly reserved in geometry for the intermediate grade and junior high years has now been brought down, in many cases, to the primary grades. If taught in a meaningful way, first and second graders, for example, can develop understandings in geometry pertaining to lines, line segments, rays, points, closed and open curves, simple and non-simple curves, squares, rectangles, triangles, and circles. Better methods of teaching plus better teaching materials have made it possible to bring learnings down to a lower grade level than was formerly thought possible. No doubt, most elementary school pupils have also had a richer background of past experiences as compared to learners a generation ago. Pre-school and public school pupils experience the world of geometry all around them. They see squares and rectangles in buildings when looking at window panes, doors, and the sides of bricks. Squares and rectangles can also be observed in sidewalks. Circles can be noticed in certain window panes in buildings as well as in circle drives or circular gardens. Headlights on cars are also circular in appearance. Thus pre-scholars, as well as elementary school pupils, have rich opportunities in building background experiences from their environment pertaining to the world of geometry. The geometry curriculum in the elementary school mathematics programme must be successful in achievement so that an adequate self concept is developed as well as an appreciation and liking for geometry.

Pupils on the first grade level, for example, can develop many understandings pertaining to algebra in the mathematics curriculum. Once, these pupils have developed understandings in a meaningful, purposeful, and interesting way in a specific learning situation, to cite an example, that 4 + 3 = 7 and 3 + 4 = 7, the mathematics teacher can have learners think of solution sets to the following open sentences: 4 + _ = 7 and _ + 3 = 7. The number line can guide pupils in finding the solution set to state a true sentence. Number lines can be purchased commercially; they can also be made for teacher and pupil usage. Modern mathematics textbooks contain many number lines. In the above example of 4 + _ = 7, the number line can be used in the following way:

⟵⟶
0 1 2 3 4 5 6 7 8

The child can point to the value of '4' on the number line. The pupil can now reason in terms of how many jumps need to be made to reach '7'. The child, of course, discovers that the correct answer is 3. Thus 4 + 3 = 7. The sentence can no longer be classified as an open sentence; it is now classified as a true sentence. Markers such as beads, and other manipulative materials can also be used by learners to find the solution set. In this case, pupils can place four beads in a set to represent the first addend in the equation 4 + _ = 7. Seven markers can be placed in a set to represent the sum. Thus, individual pupils inductively can determine how many markers should be placed in the place so that a true sentence results. The answer, of course, would be three. If a pupil had decided incorrectly that four markers go into the space, the teacher should merely ask what the sum of 4 + 4 is. Learners could use crayons, sheets of paper, and chalk, for example, to determine the correct answer. At this point pupils could also generalize that 4 + 4 = 7 is false in terms of being a number sentence. Thus, learners would experience true, false, and open sentences.

Pupils should develop meaningful learnings pertaining to relationships between and among numbers. Thus, the concepts of 'less than,' 'greater than,' and 'equal to,' become important. A set of six members is greater than a set of four members. A set of three toys is less than a set of five toys. A set of four balls is equal to a set of four balls. With the use of manipulative materials, pupils should develop these understandings in an interesting, meaningful, and purposeful way.

Thus, a modern programme of elementary school mathematics places much emphasis upon some kind of rational balance among arithmetic, geometry, and algebra.

Rational Counting

From the previous discussion, it is quite obvious that young pupils can master and apply the concept of rational counting. Kindergarten and first grade pupils need much assistance in this area from teachers of mathematics. Too frequently, faulty methods and materials have been used, and thus learners have not been able to use what has been learned. The teacher can ask questions like the following pertaining to functional situations in life:

1. How many books do you have on your desk (let us assume a library book and a textbook are on the desk of each learner.)
2. How many pupils want milk in the first row? The number of pupils wanting milk in each row can then be counted.
3. How many pupils are in school today in the first row? Second row? Third row? Fourth row?
4. How many pupils are on the committee to feed the fish in the aquarium?

5. How many pupils are on the committee to take care of the plants in the classroom?

The teacher needs to think of numerous learning activities whereby pupils can engage in rational counting. If pupils want to say more numbers than there are members within a set, the teacher could have pupils point to each member as the appropriate number is spoken orally. For example, the learner would point to a book on his desk and say 'one'; then he would point to the next book and say 'two,' and so on. Thus, the pupil will be developing basic understandings pertaining to one-to-one correspondence. The correct number then is said orally as the child points to a particular member of a set.

A kindergarten or first grade pupil may not have mastered the sequence of numbers when counting. These pupils, of course, would be working at a lower level of maturity than those that have mastered the proper sequence of numbers through ten, for example. Generally, many pupils in the preschool years become fascinated with numbers; they, in many cases, can say the correct sequence of numbers up to a point when entering the first grade. In a good kindergarten mathematics programme, learners can engage in rational counting. The teacher does not want to frustrate learners when readiness cannot be developed for rational counting. Much harm is done in teaching when pupils are forced to learn that which is not attainable. Emotional problems may then set in where pupils learn to dislike elementary school mathematics.

Evaluating Pupil Achievement in Mathematics

It is essential that proper procedures be utilized to evaluate pupil achievement in mathematics. Evaluation should be a continuous process. Learner achievement must be assessed in terms of objectives. Teacher effectiveness in teaching is thus evaluated. There are certain questions the teacher can ask of herself pertaining to teaching elementary school mathematics. Among these questions could be the following:

1. Did I provide for each pupil in the classroom?
2. Did pupils thoroughly understand what was thought?
3. Was there proper sequence for each pupil in making continuous progress?
4. Did pupils learn to enjoy mathematics more than formerly?

5. Did each pupil achieve at his own unique optimum rate?
6. Are pupils developing more proficiency in computational skills?
7. Do learners volunteer to do additional work in mathematics?
8. Do pupils appear to like mathematics as well as other curriculum areas in the elementary school?

The teacher can also evaluate pupil achievement in elementary school mathematics with the use of behaviourally stated objectives. These objectives must be reasonable for learners to achieve. The following are examples:

1. The pupil will add correctly nine out of ten addition problems.
2. Ninety per cent of the class will multiply correctly eight out of ten multiplication problems.

It is possible to measure if learners have or have not achieved the above stated objectives.

For the first objective, the teacher would select addition problems which would be representative of those that pupils have had ample meaningful practice on. The results of solving these problems would reveal to the teacher what pupils have and have not learned. Additional learning experiences would need to be provided for pupils where mastery has not been in evidence. Learners reveal if they have or have achieved the stated objective. In the second objective the same procedure would be followed as in the first objective; however, a class minimal achievement level is also stated such as "90 per cent of the class will multiply correctly eight out of ten multiplication problems." In both objectives, the teacher has standards to gauge his or her effectiveness in teaching. If the objectives were too complex for pupils to achieve, necessary adjustments need to be made so the curriculum is adjusted to the learner. The teacher also needs to be aware of teaching that which learners have already mastered. Objectives need to be adjusted which are attainable for learners.

Diagnostic tests can also be administered to determine what pupils do and do not understand. The results of diagnostic tests should pinpoint specifically what difficulties and errors learners are making in elementary school mathematics. The diagnostic test may pinpoint a lack of understanding on the part of the learners in areas such as the following:

1. structural properties of numbers, such as the commutative, associative, and distributive laws pertaining to addition and multiplication;
2. the union and intersection of sets;
3. other bases, than base ten;
4. the Roman and Egyptian system of numeration;
5. Venn diagrams;
6. use of the number line;
7. addition, subtraction, multiplication, and division;
8. true, false, and open sentences in elementary school mathematics;
9. perimeters and areas of squares, rectangles, triangles, etc.;
10. equations and relationships between numbers.

In evaluating pupil achievement in elementary school mathematics, the teacher can develop a teacher-made test. This can be a pretest to assess pupil achievement prior to beginning a new unit of mathematics. The teacher-made test can also be developed and given at various intervals when a unit is being taught to assess how well pupils are achieving objectives. The teacher-made test can also be given at the end of a unit to determine achievement from the time the pretest was given. In the post-test the mathematics teacher can evaluate how well learners achieved the objectives at the close of the unit. The teacher's effectiveness as a teacher is thus being evaluated. During the time the unit is taught or at the end of the unit, the teacher-made test must be valid in terms of covering what has been taught. Thus, if learners have had ample opportunity in meaningful, interesting, and purposeful ways to develop learnings pertaining to the following: 32)640 22)440 21)630 12)480 11)550 23)690 41)820, teacher-made tests should contain representative problems pertaining to what pupils have learned previously. It would, of course, not be valid to test pupils in this case pertaining to the following problems in division: 317)6491 81)7284 69)4947 76)8123 47)9205 and others. Pupils have not had the opportunities to develop understandings pertaining to division problems of this level of complexity. The teacher-made test should also be reliable in that learner's results when taking the test again would be consistent, all things basically being equal or equivalent. If the child is ill physically or emotionally upset, consistency of results on the part of a learner is then not possible.

The Metric System

It is important for elementary school mathematics teachers to teach an ample number of units on the metric system. Pupils, no doubt, will be using the metric system of measurement in functional situations in life in the near future. Thus, the traditional system of measurement using such measures as inches, feet, yards, miles, quarts, gallons, and bushels may be greatly minimized or become obsolete in the near future. Units of study on the metric system should stress the following criteria:

1. learnings are relevant for pupils;
2. functional use can be made of learnings gained;
3. concrete objects are used in teaching-learning situations;
4. purpose and interest in learning on the part of pupils is inherent.

Faculty Meetings, and Computer Inservice Education

Teachers and administrators need to study change in society. Changes occurring in society have significant implications in the school curriculum. One change, among others, in the societal arena involves the rather heavy use of computers in the business world, as well as in the personal lives of individuals in home setting. Computer use in society has been increasingly significant in the last twenty years, in particular. Rather rapidly, computers are coming into thorough use in the classroom.

We might a school emphasize to assist administrators and teachers to utilize computers in developing quality objectives, learning activities, and evaluation procedures?

Agendas and Faculty Meetings

School administrators must provide leadership in implementing purposeful faculty meetings. There needs to be adequate input from both administrators and faculty members in developing a relevant agenda. The agenda needs to be in the hands of participants at least two to three days prior to the meeting. Which agenda items might be emphasized in a series of faculty meetings involving computer usage in the curriculum?

Certainly, participants need to study and select quality software involving the curriculum. Unless the concept of quality is emphasized in selecting software, students will not benefit from computerized instruction. Thus, relevant standards need to be developed involving the selection of appropriate software.

A second agenda item might involve inservice education with faculty members learning to operate a computer at increasing levels of proficiency. A hands on approach is recommended. Thus, participants need to achieve relevant learnings involving the keyboard, the monitor or screen, and the printer. Selected faculty members may wish to develop their own programme(s) using BASIC language.

Thirdly, administrators and teachers may wish to learn which commercially developed programmes are available in the different curriculum areas. A very relevant criterion to emphasize in programmed learning is to provide for optimal achievement on the part of each learner. Thus, adequate attention needs to be given to provide for individual differences among learners.

A fourth agenda item might well involve a study of possibilities and limitations of computer usage. Certainly, a vital learning for administrators and teachers involves understanding the potential for computer use at the present time.

Fifthly, school personnel may desire to pursue the diverse programmes of instruction available in the computer field. These involve computer assisted instructions (CAI) with programmed learning, simulation and games, problem solving, as well as drill and practice. Each participant needs to understand the previously named concepts and their inherent philosophies.

After an adequate number of relevant agenda items have been developed, teachers and administrators at the faculty meeting may then discuss which items to discuss initially. Agenda items need clarifying and possess adequate specificity. Problem areas to be discussed involving a series of planned meetings is vital and should assist in developing an improved curriculum for students. Teachers with administrative leadership should then discuss the following additional items:

1. When to have the sequential faculty meetings in terms of dates and time factors.

2. Which reference materials to have in order to secure needed information on identified problem areas. The resources should include books, pamphlets, journal articles, slides, films, filmstrips, transparencies, illustrations, and persons possessing specialized skills in computer usage. Reference materials need to be utilized in a place and area in which administrators and teachers can benefit optimally.

Administrators and teachers should volunteer to serve on one or more committees to obtain adequate information pertaining to agreed upon agenda items. Perhaps, each participant will desire to serve on one committee only, initially. Adequate content needs to be obtained pertaining to the agenda item being pursued within a committee. Progress reports should be given by each committee to the entire faculty. The reports can be presented throughout the school year, as salient data is being obtained. Faculty members need to be informed as to progress being made by each committee. Also, participants learn from each other, as relevant information is being presented in terms of progress reports from diverse committees.

Criteria for Committee Endeavours

There are recommendable criteria or standards that committee members need to follow when gathering and appraising information. These include:

1. All should actively participate and no one dominate committee endeavours.
2. Ideas presented need to be respected. Hopefully, greater efforts will come forth from individuals within a committee setting. Developing a wholesome self-concept is important.
3. Content discussed needs to circulate among committee members and not between selected individuals only.
4. Committee members should stay on the topic being pursued and not pursue unrelated areas.
5. Higher levels of cognition (thinking) need emphasis in order to achieve quality curriculum content.

Hardly, might committees achieve relevant ideas unless the above named criteria are adhered to.

In Summary

Learners must develop understandings pertaining to structural properties in mathematics such as the commutative property of addition and multiplication, the associative property of addition and multiplication, the distributive property of multiplication over addition, the additive identity, and the multiplicative identity. It is very important to provide for individual differences in the class. Numerous approaches can be used to provide for individual pupils in the class. Learning by discovery or the inductive approach is important to use when providing learning activities for pupils. To fix learnings in the minds of pupils after meaningful, interesting, and purposeful learning activities have been provided, appropriate practice must be provided for learners. Pupils should have ample opportunities to sense the relationship of knowledge. Isolated bits of information, in many cases, may soon be forgotten. The mathematics curriculum must emphasize some kind of rational balance among arithmetic, geometry, and algebra. Algebra and geometry must receive their fair share of emphasis in the total mathematics curriculum. It is important that early primary grade pupils understand the concept of set and develop appropriate skills to be able to engage in rational counting. A variety of approaches should be utilized to evaluate pupil achievement in elementary school mathematics. Evaluation should be continuous and in terms of stated objectives. Thus teacher observation of learner achievement is important as well as the use of standardized achievement and diagnostic tests, and teacher made tests. The computer curriculum needs to be planned carefully. Relevant objectives need to be chosen for students to achieve. Learning activities should be purposeful, meaningful, and interesting to guide students to achieve worthwhile goals. Ultimately student achievement needs to be evaluated to notice sequential progress in computer understandings, skills, and attitudes.

REFERENCES

Ediger, Marlow and Digumarti Bhaskara Rao. *Teaching Mathematics Successfully*. New Delhi: Discovery Publishing House, 2001.

Ediger, Marlow and Digumarti Bhaskara Rao. *Elementary Curriculum*. New Delhi, India: Discovery Publishing House, 2003.

Ediger, Marlow and Digumarti Bhaskara Rao. *Teaching Mathematics in Elementary Schools*. New Delhi. Discovery Publishing House, 2004.

Psychology of Learning in the Mathematics Curriculum

There are numerous psychologies which teachers and supervisors need to study, evaluate, and ultimately implement selected tenets aiding individuals to achieve in an optimal manner. Each psychology of learning needs to be appraised in terms of guiding students to:

1. perceive meaning and understanding in learning;
2. reflect purpose or accept reasons for participating in ongoing lessons and units;
3. achieve increased levels of motivation for achieving and accomplishing;
4. develop interest in the mathematics curriculum.

Humanism and the Psychology of Learning

Humanists believe that students should be involved in determining what to learn (the objectives), as well as the means (activities and experiences) of learning. A psychological curriculum is then in evidence in the classroom. Each learner might then select which station and task to pursue sequentially. Each centre or station can have a list of activities typed on a task card. The involved student must choose which tasks to pursue and which to omit. A humane mathematics curriculum may then be in evidence.

Humanism emphasizes strongly that individuals attempt to achieve self-actualization. Self-actualization stresses that each person desires to attain what he/she believes to be optimal achievement intellectually, socially, emotionally, and physically. To attain self-actualization, intermediary goals need achievement. A.H. Maslow (late humanist psychologist) emphasized the following levels that individuals must achieve to ultimately realize self-actualization:

> On the basis of data gathered over many years of study and research, Maslow identifies man's basic psychological needs, in order of prepotency, as: *(i)* safety, *(ii)* love and belongingness, and *(iii)* respect and self-esteem. It should be emphasized that these basic needs are essentially unconscious, and when they are not filled, man's behaviour is more or less dominated by the drive to fill them. Maslow calls this behaviour *deficiency-motivated* (or coping) behaviour. To the extent that the environment does not permit basic needs to be filled, psychopathology occurs: The individual becomes 'starved' for safety, love, or esteem; he perceives himself and the world around him from an extremely limited narrow, and distorted perspective; and he behaves (to a greater or lesser degree) neurotically. At the risk of great oversimplification, we might say that according to this theory, paranoia, for example, results from extreme deprivation of the safety need.
>
> In contrast to the neurotics described above, psychologically healthy people have more or less gratified their basic needs for safety, love, and esteem. When these needs are satisfied, Maslow hypothesizes that individuals tend to be motivated... This behaviour of self actualizing individuals is called *growth-motivated* (or expressive) behaviour. Because growth-motivated individuals are less encapsulated (by unconscious basic needs), they interpret environment situations in more objective terms.

Humanism does not emphasize that:

1. teachers alone select objectives, learning activities, and evaluation procedures;
2. what is measurable in terms of student learning represents the most relevant goals to attain. Rather, the interests, purposes, and personal meanings that a learner brings to any situation is vital. These basically are intrinsic and not subject to measuring;
3. a logical mathematics curriculum for students which stresses a teacher ordered sequence of objectives for student attainment. In contrast, the involved student chooses sequential activities from among alternatives. Thus, a psychological, not logical, set of learnings is emphasized.

Instructional Management Systems (IMS)

Advocates of IMS believe in students achieving precise, behaviourally stated objectives. After instruction, the mathematics teacher may measure if a student has or has not achieved a measurable objective. The objectives are arranged sequentially by the teacher or a committee of teachers. A logical, not a psychological curriculum in mathematics is then in evidence. The instructor has arranged the objectives from those which are easier to attain to an increasing level of complexity. Arrangement of these goals is made so that ideally students will be successful in achievement. For example, objective number one is a prerequisite to achieving goal number two. Goal number two needs to be attained prior to objective three, and so on. The mathematics teacher has then ascertained which the proper or appropriate sequence of objectives should be. The involved learner does not decide individually or through student-teacher planning which objective needs to be achieved first, second, third, fourth, and so on. The teacher is the key person in determining and ordering objectives for learners to achieve.

A comprehensive system of recording of achievement for each learner may be implemented. Since each objective is measurable if a student has/has not been successful in goal attainment, records may be kept to determine precisely which ends have been attained by any one learner. Also, the student and the teacher can notice which objectives still need to be achieved. The objectives are arranged in an ordered sequential arrangement to optimize learner achievement.

Pertaining to the utilization of measurable objectives in teaching, Morris and Pai wrote:

> In establishing behaviours that will be beneficial to the learner and to society, behaviour engineers are most concerned with reaching target behaviours (aims of education) by gradually and systematically modifying 'old' behaviours and/or shaping new responses. In other words, overall aims of education are first translated into specific objectives involving competencies in various disciplines and other areas of the learner's life, such as learning the three R's, responsible citizenship, and so on. These objectives in turn are formulated into specific programmes, courses, and learning activities, the purposes of which are also defined in terms of specific behavioural changes. Each of these competencies are then analyzed into still smaller and simpler behaviours, so that by learning them the child can eventually

read the target behaviour. Hence, educational goals must be stated in terms of specific and directly observable behaviours.

It is for this reason that the use of behavioural objectives in instructional and curricular planning is indispensable to education as behaviour engineering, because these objectives serve not only as clear guides to learning activities but also as standards by which the teaching-learning processes can be evaluated.

IMS advocates do not stress:

1. the use of open-ended general objectives in the mathematics curriculum. Precise objectives provide more direction and guidance in terms of what students are to learn. In fact, clarity of intent as to what pupils are to learn is inherent in measurably stated objectives;
2. teacher-pupil planning in developing the mathematics curriculum. Rather, the math teacher determines what students are to learn (the objectives), as well as the means of learning (activities and experiences);
3. a psychological mathematics curriculum in which pupils with teacher guidance sequence their own learning. The teacher selects and logically arranges objectives for students to achieve, according to IMS advocates.

Structure of Knowledge

Structure of knowledge advocates believe that students should achieve structural ideas (major generalizations) identified by professional mathematicians. The structure of mathematics emphasizes learners acquire key ideas that held true again and again when progressing through the formal years of schooling. These might well include the:

1. commutative properties of addition and multiplication;
2. associative properties of addition and multiplication;
3. distributive property of multiplication over addition;
4. identify elements of addition and multiplication;
5. property of closure for addition and multiplication;
6. inverse properties of subtraction and division.

Those emphasizing structural ideas psychology believe that students should acquire content inductively. To learn inductively, the student with teacher guidance needs to discover these main ideas as determined by professors of mathematics on the higher education level. Reputable, quality textbooks in mathematics generally emphasize the six above named key generalizations, among other structural ideas. Main ideas, such as the structure of knowledge can be emphasized again again as learners progress through the diverse sequential years of schooling. For example, a first grade learner discovering that 3 + 2 = 2 + 3 (commutative property of addition) or the fourth grade student realizing that 4623 + 3641 = 3641 + 4623 reflects a spiral curriculum. Thus, structural content provides a framework to the learner in continually perceiving relationships, as well as methods of learning-inductive procedures. The mathematics teacher must be a good asker of questions, rather than a lecturer or explainer in utilizing induction as an approach in guiding pupil learning.

Sequence in learning activities is important. Manipulative (enactive) materials should be used first when appropriate. Thus, an abacus, markers and objects are used as concrete materials to aid student discovery of structural ideas. Secondly, iconic materials, in sequence, need adequate emphasis. These include pictures, slides, filmstrips, films, and drawings to illustrate objectives reflecting structural ideas. Ultimately, symbolic learnings need to be stressed. The symbolic represents abstract phases in learning, such as the use of numerals and letters in the mathematics curriculum.

Woolfolk and Nicolich wrote the following comparing Jerome Bruner's structure of knowledge psychology with that of Jean Piaget.

> At the *enactive* stage, which corresponds roughly to Piaget's sensorimotor stage, children learn to represent objects by acting on them. These early years are filled with solving problems of how to crawl, walk, play with toys, and generally use the body to be effective in the world. Children at this stage learn by doing and by seeing what others do. Telling is helpful only if the child can also act it out or see someone else act it out. It is the action that will be represented internally.
>
> At the *iconic* stage, which corresponds to the early years of Piaget's preoperational stage, children begin to form pictures or images to represent what is going on in their world. At this point, they can remember events from the past and imagine the future in terms of visions of what might happen again. These images are much like photographs in that they are highly realistic and closely tied to actual physical experience.
>
> At the *symbolic* stage, which corresponds roughly to the later years in Piaget's preoperationally stage and to the other years as well,

children are able to represent their world through symbols, the most important of which is language. These symbols need not copy physical reality but can be abstractions. With such abstract symbols, people can ultimately hypothesize about possibilities, people, places and things they have never experienced.

Programmed Learning

Programmed learning, whether in textbook or micro-computer software form, emphasizes precise, measurable ends in the mathematics curriculum. Programmers determine the sequential objectives for students to attain. Pilot studies are run to ascertain the best order of presenting a set of programmed items. Basically, if a student is ready to pursue a given programme, he/she should be highly successful in its completion. Perhaps, a ninety per cent rate of success should be in evidence for a student in completing any specific programme.

In the utilization of programmed materials, the involved student reads a few sentences or a very short selection, responds to a multiple choice or completion item, and receives immediate feedback as to which the correct response is. If a response is correct, in a computerized item, the learner may be given a second chance to respond. Should be student have still responded incorrectly, the correct answer is shown on the screen. In using programmed textbooks, the correct answer is uncovered by the student as given by the programmer, the learner also knows immediately if he/she is correct or incorrect in responding. In linear programming, the student sees the correct answer and is ready for the next sequential item. Read, respond, and check are concepts that are used continuously, in using programmed textbooks or software and the microcomputer.

The programmer selects the subject-matter, order of learning content, and the correct response for each item in programmed learning.

Preston and Hermann wrote the following pertaining to programmed instruction:

> The pupils read one frame at a time and respond to it. It may call on them to answer a multiple-choice question by pushing a key on a machine (a minority of available programmes is presented by teaching machines) or by making their choice in a programmed textbook. Or they may be directed to construct an answer.

After the child responds, he or she is informed of the correctness or incorrectness of the response by a light or some other signal in a machine or by an answer appearing at a designated place in the programmed book. This information is known as 'feedback.' If the response is false, he or she is given either the correct information that can be advantageously utilized in making another choice. This feedback feature is a central element in programmed instruction. It informs the child of his or her progress and indicates the next step—whether to repeat an exercise, respond to a similar exercise, or go on to the next step. In any case whatever, he or she is directed to do next is designed to reinforce learning—to increase his or her chances of responding correctly to the question or task the next time it is encountered. It is evident that the programme performs two functions that a busy teacher handling an entire class cannot accomplish: *(i)* it presents the subject-matter to each child at a rate appropriate to his or her needs, and *(ii)* each child responds overtly to each presentation and receives, without delay, reinforcement for every response he or she makes.

Programmed learning does not advocate:

1. student-teacher planning in determining objectives, learning activities, and appraisal procedures;
2. learners acquiring much content before feedback is given on the correctness/incorrectness of each step of learning;
3. pupils practicing what is incorrect in terms of subject matter learning. Rather, immediate knowledge of results is provided to students after having acquired a small amount of subject-matter in each sequential step of learning;
4. internal processes being important in instruction. Instead, that which is observable and measurable is important.

The Basics

Much has been written pertaining to students learning the basics—reading, writing, and arithmetic. Proponents of the basics believe there is an essential body of knowledge that all students should master in mathematics, as well as in other organised bodies of knowledge. Frills and fads are to be eliminated in the curriculum. Basic, essential learnings can then be identified. The chosen subject-matter can be ordered properly for students to achieve on each grade level. Mastery in acquiring subject-matter in mathematics is important.

General or behaviourally stated objectives may be utilized in teaching. To achieve objectives on the part of students, the teacher may assign work to be completed by learners using reputable basal mathematics textbooks, workbooks, and worksheets. A deductive method of teaching involving lecture, explanations, and demonstrations by the teacher might well be emphasized heavily. A comprehensive programme of evaluation using teacher written tests, standardized tests, instructive observation of student progress, anecdotal statements, checklist, and rating scales can be used in the mathematics curriculum. Remedial work biased on diagnosis of specific problems in learning must also be stressed in teaching situations:

Shepherd and Regan wrote:

> Each disequilibrium and its companion, accommodation by society, has had its impact upon the school as an institution of that society. Therefore, the schools and their curriculum vehicles have also experienced a testing of mission and purpose, a programme, and of product, as well as a critical appraisal of service and spirit. The tensions of the school and its curriculum vehicles seem to originate from three sources: the potential displacement of the family through the school as an agency of a nation-state; the movement from a industrial culture to a yet, unrealized future culture; and the accommodations to the constitutional conditions of independence and dependence, individuality of conformity, and inclusion and exclusion. In general, the functioning of the curriculum in the socialization of individuals is the prime source of the powerful tensions being experienced by the schools.
>
> During this period of tension and disequilibrium, the number and variety of curriculum alternatives available have rapidly multipled. The alternatives range from "back to the basics," to "forward to the future." In unsettled times, alternatives are apt to be presented as dichotomies. Although it is most unlikely that a movement can go backward and forward in the same instant; it is possible that the continuity involved in the development of an individual and an institution can be maintained and furthered.

A subject-matter curriculum in mathematics does not emphasize:

1. learning by discovery by students. Rather the teacher through lecture and explanations provides essential content to learners;
2. variety in learning activities. Basically, the use of the textbook, workbook, and worksheets, contain what is necessary for pupils to acquire;

3. planning the objectives, activities to achieve goals, and appraisal procedures with students. The mathematics teacher is in the best position, due to training and experience, in determining what pupils are to attain.

In Summary

There are numerous psychologies available to provide guidance in assisting learners to achieve in an optimal manner.

1. Humanism emphasizes that students become proficient decision makers to achieve sequence in learning.
2. IMS advocates that teachers of mathematics arrange order of goals for pupils to achieve.
3. Structure of knowledge psychology stresses an inductive procedure to assist students to progress sequentially in acquiring major generalizations.
4. Programmed learning proponents believe that a programmer is in the best position, through field testing, to order precise objectives for pupils to achieve.
5. Advocates of the basics believe there is a core of essential knowledge in mathematics for each and every student to acquire.

Hopefully, teachers will select those psychologies in an integrated whole to assist each student to learn as much as possible in ongoing lessons and units in mathematics.

REFERENCES

Morris, Val Cleve, and Young Pai. *Philosophy and the American School*. Boston: Houghton Mifflin Company, 1976.

Preston, Ralph C., and Wayne L. Hermann, Jr. *Teaching Social Studies in the Elementary School*. Fifth Edition. New York: Holt, Rinehart and Winston, 1981.

Shepherd, Gene, and William Ragan. *Modern Elementary Curriculum*. Sixth Edition. New York: Holt, Rinehart and Winston, 1982.

Woolfolk, Anita, and Lorraine McCune Nicholich. *Educational Psychology for Teachers*. Englewood Cliffs, New Jersey: Prentice-Hall, Incorporated, 1980.

Zais, Robert. *Curriculum, Principles, and Foundations*. New York: Thomsas Y. Crowell Company, 1976.

Designing the Mathematics Curriculum

Teachers, principals, and supervisors need to study, evaluate and implement in the public school setting selected accepted ideas pertaining to an effective design in the elementary school mathematics curriculum. Thus, concepts such as scope and sequence become important when an appropriate design is developed for a relevant elementary school mathematics curriculum.

Scope in the Mathematics Curriculum

The question frequently arises as to "what should be taught in elementary school mathematics." Which understandings, skills, and attributes should pupils develop to become proficient and contributing members in American society? There are no clear-cut, easy answers to this question. There are, however, selected individuals and groups of individuals whose studies and/or statements of thought and philosophy may provide relevant guidelines:

1. Writers of reputable mathematics textbooks can provide a guide in determining 'what' (scope) pupils are to learn in an up-to-date curriculum. There are advantages as well as disadvantages in using this approach rather exclusively. Advantages could be the following:
   - *(a)* Recognized writers and involved publishing companies in the field have spent much time and money in developing and evaluating content in mathematics textbooks for pupils.

(b) The teachers' manual related to the elementary school mathematics textbooks for pupils can have excellent teaching suggestions to utilize in ongoing units of study.

(c) The textbook for pupils on any grade level clearly indicates the inherent unit titles for learner interaction in teaching-learning situations.

(d) Learning activities for pupils within each unit of study are clear and sequentially presented.

(e) The contents of the textbook can be utilized to provide for individual differences in the class setting by having pupils work at different present achievement levels.

(f) Much of the work of the teacher has been done in developing the mathematics curriculum when utilizing a reputable mathematics textbook to select objectives, learning experiences, and appraisal techniques in ongoing units of study.

(g) Pupil interest and purpose can be developed within specific units of study when effectively utilizing a relevant series of elementary school mathematics textbooks. Carefully selected experiences for pupils can aid in stimulating interest and purpose for learning.

Disadvantages in using mathematics textbooks almost exclusively would be the following:

(a) Sameness in kinds of learning experiences provided for pupils may become rather boring to learners. Pupils generally like to experience a variety of learning experiences including the use of reputable elementary school mathematics textbooks.

(b) The heavy use of textbooks in the mathematics curriculum may not meet the needs, interests, and abilities of selected pupils.

(c) Pupils differ from each other in terms of learning styles possessed. Thus, the learning style of a few pupils may not harmonize with the heavy use of textbooks in providing content for the mathematics curriculum.

(d) Teachers need to be creative in selecting objectives, learning activities, and appraisal techniques in ongoing units of study. Heavy use of mathematics textbooks in teaching-learning situations can deemphasize creative efforts of teachers.

(e) There is a tendency to keep an entire class of pupils together at the same place at the same time when textbooks are emphasized heavily in teaching-learning situations. Thus, individual differences are not adequately provided for in the class setting.

(f) Units of study in a series of mathematics textbooks may overemphasize selected facts, concepts, and generalizations and deemphasize other relevant learnings for pupils. For example, the structure of mathematics may be overly stressed to the point where computation skills are deemphasized.

It appears desirable to utilize reputable elementary school mathematics textbooks along with other carefully chosen learning activities to provide for the needs, interests, and abilities of individual learners.

Emphasis upon the use of selected elementary school mathematics textbooks to determine the scope (what is taught) in ongoing units of study for a specific school year may reveal the following content, for example, for the fifth grade level:

(a) Sets, numerations, and number

(b) Properties and patterns of addition and subtraction

(c) Properties of multiplication and division

(d) Fractional numbers and their operations

(e) Decimals, ratio and proportion

(f) Nonmetric geometry

(g) The metric system

(h) Metric geometry—Finding perimeter, area, and volume

(i) Measurement in today's society

(j) Line, bar, and picture graphs; probability

(k) Numeration systems (other than base ten)

Thus, in utilizing a reputable elementary school mathematics textbook as a basis for providing content in teaching/learning situations, it appears that the following would be viable criteria to follow:

(a) Use of variety of learning activities—such as markers of different kinds, films, filmstrips, transparencies and the overhead projector—to enrich experiences of pupils and to provide for individual differences.

(b) Preassess pupils to determine where each should begin at the beginning of a specific school year within a given unit of study, and guide each learner to experience continuous progress.

(c) The scope of the mathematics curriculum should include those learning experiences which will guide learners to become contributing members in society.

2. The teacher may write measurable behaviourally stated objectives when determining scope in the elementary school mathematics curriculum.

The following are examples of behaviourally stated objectives in a unit of "Addition and Subtraction of Whole Numbers."

(a) The pupil will add correctly nine of the ten problems; each addition problem contains two one-digit addends

(b) The pupil will subtract correctly nine out of ten problems containing a one-digit minuend and one-digit subtrahend

(c) The pupil will solve correctly five out of six word problems containing two one-digit addends to be added

(d) The pupil will subtract correctly five out of six word problems containing a one-digit minuend and a one-digit subtrahend.

For each of the above behaviourally stated objectives, the teacher needs to select interesting, purposeful, and meaningful learning experiences in order that learners may achieve these desired needs sequentially. Pupil achievement may then be measured if each objective has or has not been attained. If an objective is not realized by a learner, the teacher would need to diagnose to determine the cause or causes for this happening. Additional learning experiences then need to be provided for these learners so that they may also be successful in attaining stated measurable objectives.

Thus, behaviourally stated objectives written by the teacher (or teachers) pertaining to diverse units of study in mathematics can pertain to what is taught or the scope of the curriculum area.

3. Pupils should achieve structural ideas in elementary school mathematics. Jerome Bruner, psychologist from Harvard University, has been very instrumental in stressing the importance of pupils perceiving properties or the structure of a curriculum area. Pupils would continually understand these structural ideas in greater depth as they progress through the public school years. Jerome Bruner in the book, *The Process of Education*, writes the following:

> We begin with the hypothesis that any subject can be taught effectively in some intellectually honest form to any child at any stage of development.

Important structural ideas that pupils may achieve in mathematics could include the following:

(a) the commutative property of addition and multiplication;

(b) the associative property of addition and multiplication;

(c) the distributive property of multiplication over addition;

(d) the identity elements for addition and multiplication;

(e) the property of closure for addition and multiplication.

Jerome Bruner would stress the importance of pupils developing structural ideas inductively. Thus, the teacher must:

(a) select relevant learning experiences which would guide pupils to discover structural ideas in mathematics. (The teacher definitely would not lecture or present long explanations to pupils on the meaning or meanings attached to these key ideas);

(b) assist learners to continually discover these structural ideas as they progress through the public school years. (These key ideas cannot be mastered on any one grade level in the elementary school);

(c) guide pupils to realize these structural or key ideas on increased levels of complexity as learners achieve continuous progress in the school and class setting. (For example, on the first grade level, most pupils learn that "5 + 7 = 7 + 5." On higher grade levels pupils learn that "13 + 18 = 18 + 13; 145 + 258 = 258 + 145; 3296 + 1835 = 1835 + 3296," and so on—the commutative property of addition.)

Reasons for emphasizing the structure of knowledge in teaching pupils include the following:

(a) Subject matter specialists can do a better job of selecting what is important for pupils to learn as compared to teachers, principals, and supervisors in the class setting.

(b) It is the teacher's role to choose learning experiences which will guide pupils to achieve inductively the identified structural or key ideas as determined by content specialists.

(c) Subject-matter specialists and educators must work together to improve the public school curriculum.

(d) Public school pupils should utilize methods of study emphasized by subject-matter specialists such as that used by mathematicians.

4. Pupils may experience the use of programmed learning in the mathematics curriculum.

Programmed learning follows selected ideas pertaining to how pupils learn. The following are major generalizations pertaining to programmed learning:

(a) Pupils progress in very small steps in learning.

(b) Each small step of learning is sequentially arranged.

(c) In the use of programmed materials, the pupil generally looks at a picture, reads related content, responds to an item, and then checks the correctness of the response. The first step of learning indicated above (looking at a picture) may be omitted in some programmed materials. The sequence of these steps in learning is repeated again and again as far as pupil learning is concerned.

(d) The learner knows almost immediately if he/she is right or wrong in terms of responses given. If the pupil was correct in the response given, reinforcement in learning is involved. If an incorrect response was given by the learner, he/she now knows the correct answer after checking with the correct answer indicated by the programmer.

(e) The pupil may progress at his own optimal rate of learning when programmed materials are used.

(f) Rarely does a learner respond incorrectly to an item in sequence since the progressive steps in learning are small enough generally to prevent incorrect responses.

Disadvantages in utilizing programmed materials include the following:

(a) Problem solving is generally not stressed in programmed materials.

(b) The sequential steps in learning may be too small for certain pupils. Gifted and talented students may, of course, not need these small sequential steps in learning to be successful achievers.

(c) If programmed materials were used exclusively in learning, boredom may set in on the part of individual learners. Human beings seemingly crave a variety of experiences in the school and class setting as well as in life.

(d) The learning styles of selected pupils may not harmonize with the philosophy inherent in programmed learning in the class setting.

Programmed materials emphasize the Stimulus-Response school of thought in terms of how pupils learn. Thus, pupils in the mathematics curriculum using programmed learning materials must experience a Stimulus, such as seeing a picture of three boys and being asked to tell how many members are in this set. The pupil gives a Response to this item by writing the numeral '3' or the word 'three.' Next, the learner may check the correctness of his response with the answer given by the programmer in the programmed mathematics textbook. Similar, small sequential steps in learning then follow for the individual pupil utilizing programmed materials.

The teacher of mathematics could programme content for pupils pertaining to arithmetic, algebra, and geometry. These resulting materials must

(a) present learnings in small steps to pupils (Stimulus);
(b) give pupils an opportunity to respond to each item (Response);
(c) be arranged sequentially to insure pupil success in responding to each item;
(d) give learners an opportunity to check the correctness of each response made before going on to the next sequentially developed item.

5. Pupils should experience problem-solving activities in the class and school setting. The Gestalt school of thought in terms of how pupils learn would emphasize the following conditions for pupils:
   (a) The whole child is involved in learning such as the emotional, intellectual, social and physical facets of an individual's development.
   (b) The pupil perceives situations as wholes first rather than parts.
   (c) The wholeness of a situation can be analyzed in terms of parts.

Pupils in a stimulating learning environment should have ample opportunities to identify problem areas. Learners, for example, may identify problem areas in the mathematics curriculum from the following learning activities:

(a) Viewing a bulletin board display emphasizing four cookies to be divided among eight pupils. Division of a counting number by a counting number resulting in a fraction may be emphasized in an ongoing unit of study. A pupil may think of related situations in life that he/she is facing, a situation whereby a counting number is to be divided by a counting number resulting in a fractional value.
(b) Viewing a filmstrip on sets. Thus, the pupil is noticing in this presentation how two sets which are disjoint may be joined together to form a new set. An involved pupil may have wanted to find out how many marbles he/she now

has after originally having a set of eight, and six additional marbles were added to the set as a gift from a peer.

(c) Watching a demonstration by the teacher using markers to show the meaning of a subtraction problem involving a single digit minuend and a single digit subtrahend. The involved learner now thinks of a related problem in subtraction which needs solving as far as his/her own personal experiences in everyday living are concerned.

(d) Noticing situations in the class setting which require problem-solving skills. Thus, from the class and school environment, pupils notice a problem or problems which need solving pertaining to the use of arithmetic, algebra, and geometry. Pupils may then measure, weigh, or find the volume of a container in a real-life situation. For example, selected pupils may need to find how many cups (can substitute metric measurements) are in a pint when following directions in developing a food product in the class setting.

In daily situations outside the school and class setting, pupils, of course, detect problems needing solutions involving the use of mathematics:

An eight-year-old has saved $6.75 (use currency of nation involved) from allowance money received, he desires to buy a baseball glove costing $12.98. The child attempts to determine how much more money is needed to make the purchase. The eight-year old thinks about different approaches to use in coming up with a solution to the problem. The child brings to bear related knowledge in attempting to solve the problem. Ultimately, the eight-year-old may count by fives or tens from $6.75 to $12.98 to determine how much additional money will be needed to buy the baseball glove.

The Gestalt approach in learning emphasizes:

(a) wholistic situations in life from which a problem or problem areas are identified.

(b) previously gained related knowledge is brought to bear upon the solution of the problem;

(c) insight is gained by individuals in obtaining a needed solution;

(d) solutions to problems are held tentative. Thus, the new problems are identified for existing situations.

In Summary

There are numerous schools of thought in psychology and philosophy attempting to explain how individuals learn. Teachers, principals, and supervisors must study and appraise diverse schools of thought in education pertaining to how human beings gain learnings. Ultimately, educators in the public school setting must develop a philosophy and psychology of their own to implement in teaching-learning situations. Teachers, principals, and supervisors may develop a rather consistent school of thought such as Stimulus-Response or the Gestalt approach. Other public school educators may be eclectic in teaching-learning situations selecting that which is deemed relevant and viable from diverse schools of thought explaining how individuals learn.

Whichever school of thought is selected, the following principles of learning should be accepted by all teachers, principals, and supervisors in the school setting pertaining to teaching mathematics and other curriculum areas:

1. Learning activities must capture the interests of pupils
2. Pupils must understand what is learned
3. Balance among understandings, skills, and attitudinal goals must be emphasized in ongoing units of study
4. Good sequence in learning must be inherent on the part of learners
5. Pupils need to feel successful in learning
6. Learners must develop feelings of an adequate self-concept
7. Each pupil must experience adequate readiness activities prior to experiencing new learnings.

REFERENCES

Duke, Daniel Linden and Adrienne Maravich Meckel, *Teacher's Guide to Classroom Management*. New York: Random House, 1984.

Ediger, Marlow and Digumarti Bhaskara Rao. *Teaching Mathematics Successfully*. New Delhi, India: Discovery Publishing House, 2001.

Ediger, Marlow and Digumarti Bhaskara Rao. *Relevancy in Elementary Curriculum*. New Delhi: Discovery Publishing House, 2004.

Kramer, Klaas, *Teaching Elementary School Mathematics*. Second Edition. Boston: Allyn and Bacon, Inc., 1970.

Mahaffey, Michael L., and Alex F. Perrodin. *Teaching Elementary School Mathematics* Itasco, Illinois: F.E. Peacock Publishers, Inc., 1973.

Millar, John P. *The Educational Spectrum*. New York: Longman, 1983.

Schminke, C.W., *et al*. *Teaching the Child Mathematics*. Hinsdale, Illinois: The Dryden Press, Inc., 1973.

Issues in the Mathematics Curriculum

There are basic, essential learnings which all pupils need to achieve in mathematics, according to selected educators and most parents. No doubt, all pupils need to develop adequate proficiency in addition, subtraction, multiplication, and division. The essentials are relevant for pupils presently, as well as in the adult world. Practical use can then be made of learnings involving the basics in the school curriculum. What has been acquired as essential subject matter in ongoing units of study is used to solve personal and social problems involving mathematics.

Issues and Mathematics

There are teachers emphasizing that pupils achieve proficiency in bases other than base ten. For example, a pupil may achieve understandings of base five numeration. With meaning and interest attached, a pupil might then understand five symbols used in base five. These are 0, 1, 2, 3, and 4. Understanding of place value is very significant. Thus in 213 base five, there are three ones, one five, and two twenty-fives (3 + 5 + 50 = 58 in base ten). Concrete, semi-concrete, and abstract materials may be utilized as learning activities to assist pupils to understand place value in base five.

To practice application of base five learnings, pupils may utilize toy money to buy selected items in a miniature supermarket in the classroom setting. Empty cereal boxes, fruit and vegetable containers, and flour sacks, among other items, may have prices stamped in base five values. Base five toy money is then utilized to 'buy' chosen items. Adding the prices of a given set of items and determining change are then emphasized in base five learnings.

Advantages given for emphasizing base five learnings include:

1. learners obtain new experiences pertaining to place value and digits used in base five;
2. enrichment experiences are available for gifted and talented pupils, especially on higher grade levels;
3. pupils may expand mathematical thinking in going beyond a single base (base ten) and incorporate experiences involving base five, along with other bases.

Disadvantages given for pupils studying other bases than base ten include the following:

1. learners need to understand and attach meaning to base ten due to its highly functional use in society. Other bases generally do not have a functional value in society;
2. pupils experience frustration in attempting to understand a different base than base ten;
3. time is valuable in the mathematics curriculum. Available time must be given to guide pupils to understand base ten.

A second issue in the mathematics curriculum involves the degree of specificity necessary to state useful objectives. Behaviourists believe that objectives for pupils to achieve should be written in measurable terms. The teacher may then select learning activities for pupils to achieve the chosen ends. After instruction, the teacher may measure if a pupil has or has not attained the measurable objective. A new teaching strategy may need to be chosen to help the unsuccessful learner achieve the objective. Successful learners may work on achieving the next sequential end. Pupils individually may achieve optimally in attaining the specific ends.

Humanists believe in an open-ended mathematics curriculum in which each pupil may choose sequential tasks. The teacher may structure the learning environment. Pupil-teacher planning of objectives, experiences, and appraisal procedures might also be utilized. Pupils, however, decide which tasks to pursue, as well as which to omit. Learners generally choose tasks based on inherent terests, purposes and personal meaning.

Advantages given for emphasizing behaviourism in the mathematics curriculum include the following:

1. The teacher is certain as to what will be taught in mathematics based on precise objectives selected for pupil attainment.
2. The teacher may measure if a pupil has or has not achieved an objective. A teacher might then be certain if an objective has been attained before a pupil moves on to the next sequential goal. Proper sequence in experiences may then be in evidence for each learner.

Advantages given for humanism, as a psychology of learning, might involve the following:

1. pupils are more interested in learning if choices may be made as to what to learn sequentially;
2. life in society requires that pupils choose and make choices. The school curriculum presently must also emphasize decision making by pupils;
3. a humane curriculum may well be in evidence if input from learners is an end result in curriculum development.

A third issue pertains to the degree hand held calculators should be utilized in the mathematics curriculum. The conservative element is with us in advocating that little or no use be made of calculators. Advocates of minimizing the utilization of calculators in the mathematics curriculum believe in the following statements:

1. pupils need to develop proficiency in addition, subtraction, multiplication, and division using paper and pencil in the basic four operations. Audio-visual aids may be utilized to make learnings meaningful to pupils. However, computation skills must be developed using paper and pencil;
2. mastery learning in addition, subtraction, multiplication, and division prepares to become problem solvers in the adult world. Drill and practice are important in committing to memory basic facts in addition, subtraction, multiplication, and division. Using hand held calculators hinders pupils in developing proficiency in arithmetic.

Those advocating rather heavy use of hand held calculators by pupils in arithmetic believe the following:

1. much drudgery can be eliminated in the arithmetic curriculum. For example, once pupils understand a new process in a meaningful manner, learners may then use hand held calculators in problem solving experiences. If pupils understand how to check a long division computation, interest in learning is destroyed if paper and pencil procedures are continually used in checking procedures;
2. pupils may experience drill and practice in responding to basic number pairs using hand held calculators. For example, if a pupil is practicing adding 3 + 5, 5 + 3, 6 + 4, and 4 + 6, among others, he/she may respond orally to 3 + 5 = □ and 5 + 3 = □ before pressing the equals sign on the hand held calculator. In sequence, with more complex learnings involved, learners may again and again meet up with the commutative property of addition A + B = B + A, e.g. (3698 + 4347 = 4347 + 3698).

Advantages given for utilizing hand held calculators rather heavily in the mathematics curriculum include the following:

1. technology is with us and will increasingly influence methods of teaching and means of arriving at specific decisions;
2. pupil motivation for learning may well increase with the utilization of calculators;
3. learners' interest in achieving objectives in mathematics might well increase when learning activities are more enjoyable involving the use of technology.

A fourth issue in the mathematics curriculum pertains to the degree geometry should be emphasized in the mathematics curriculum. Lay people in society feel heavy emphasis needs to be placed on the three R's (reading, writing, and arithmetic) in the curriculum. There are selected educators who agree on the rather heavy implementation of a three R's curriculum. What then might be the role of geometry in the mathematics curriculum? During the 1960's 'modern' mathematics was emphasized. Mathematicians on the college/university level had much input into the mathematics curriculum for elementary, junior high or middle school, as well as secondary levels of instruction. Numerous mathematicians advocated geometry receiving somewhat equal emphasis as compared to arithmetic in the mathematics curriculum. Reasons given for advocating a strong geometry curriculum include the following:

1. geometry is in evidence continually in the natural and human made environment. For example, in diverse buildings, there are square, rectangular, and circular windows. Line segments, points, planes, solid figures, and angles are inherent in geometric figures;
2. the concept of *balance* needs to be emphasized in the mathematics curriculum. Thus, geometry, as well as arithmetic, statistics, probability, and algebra need to comprise the total programme of instruction in mathematics;
3. there may be no conflict between metric geometry and arithmetic in the mathematics curriculum. For example, in metric geometry, considerable arithmetic is utilized to determine perimeters and areas of geometric figures.

A fifth issue involves inductive-deductive controversies in teaching. In inductive teaching, the teacher needs to guide pupils to make discoveries. Lecture and lengthly explanations are not desired in inductive methods of teaching. Rather, the teacher uses a variety of materials to set the stage for inductive learning. For example, if pupils are to learn regrouping and renaming in subtraction (borrowing), the teacher might utilize a concrete situation in which the temperature reading dropped from 35° to 19° Fahrenheit. Pupils with teacher guidance may actually read and record the temperature readings. How might the problem be solved as to how many degrees the temperature reading dropped? One pupil may respond with the need to count from 19 to 35 to determine the difference. Another learner may respond with showing 35 sticks and taking 19 away. Thus 35 – 19 = 16. The temperature reading then dropped 16 degrees. A learner might also show a more sophisticated way of operating to determine the difference between 35 and 19 degrees using a place value chart. Each learner may then understand what is involved when regrouping 35 in terms of 2 tens and 15 ones in a place value chart. Nine ones may then be removed from 15 ones, and one ten from two tens. The remainder is 16.

In a deductive method in having pupils understand how many degrees in temperature readings were involved in dropping from

35 to 19, the teacher may use concrete (manipulative materials), semi-concrete (pictures, filmstrips, slides, and study prints), as well as abstract materials. Along with these materials, the teacher in a meaningful way may explain to learners what is involved in regrouping and renaming to determine the difference between 35 and 19. Communicating content moves from the teacher to the pupil. Later pupils, with teacher guidance, need to apply what has been learned.

Additional Issues in the Mathematics Curriculum

There are other relevant issues needing resolving in ongoing units of study in mathematics. These include:

1. an activity centred versus a subject centred mathematics curriculum;
2. subject-matter learned by pupils as a means to an end versus subject-matter learned as an end in and of itself;
3. an integrated versus a separate subject mathematics curriculum;
4. utilitarian goals versus a basics mathematics curriculum stressing essentials for all learners.

In Conclusion

Teachers, principals, and supervisors need to study vital issues in the mathematics curriculum. After careful analysis of the issues, solutions need to be developed. Ultimately, pupils need to experience relevant objectives, learning activities, and appraisal procedures. Each pupil needs to achieve optimally in mathematics.

REFERENCES

Ediger, Marlow and Digumarti Bhaskara Rao. *Teaching Mathematics in Elementary Schools*. New Delhi, India: Discovery Publishing House, 2004.

Ediger, Marlow and Digumarti Bhaskara Rao. *Relevancy in Elementary Curriculum*. New Delhi: Discovery Publishing House, 2004.

Science in the Curriculum

A quality science curriculum needs to be in evidence in the school/class setting. Each person lives in a world of science. The natural environment with its plants and animals reflects subject-matter in science. Inventions and technology to improve the lot of each person truly emphasize the methods and content of science.

To live effectively in society, students individually need to experience the wonders and contributions of science and scientists. A vital programme of science instruction should be the lot of each student.

The Use of Experiments

A modern programme of elementary school science will have much in the area of experiments that pupils will perform with teacher guidance. This will mean that learners should actually be involved in conducting these experiments whenever possible. Almost all units taught in elementary school science can emphasize experimentation. For example, if pupils are studying a unit on "Magnetism and Electricity," the following objects and items can be placed on a learning centre to initiate the unit:

1. containers which contain shreds of paper, pieces of wood, a piece of plastic, and different kinds of cloth;
2. nails, paper clips, different size coins, a piece of copper, and other kinds of metals;

Pupils can notice which objects and items on the learning centre are attracted and which are not attracted by the use of magnets.

Scientists engage in conducting many experiments. This is a way of gaining new knowledge. It is a way of identifying new problem areas. Once these problem areas have been clearly defined; information can be gathered to solve these problems. A hypothesis or hypotheses are then developed which pertain to an answer or a solution to the problem. The hypothesis or hypotheses are tentative and not final or fixed. Only through testing can elementary school pupils develop some degree of certainty as to the correctness or accuracy of the hypothesis. Too frequently when science experiments are conducted, pupils want to jump to hasty conclusions as to the outcomes. An experiment or experiments are conducted to test a hypothesis or several hypotheses. In the preceding example pertaining to the unit "Magnetism and Electricity," pupils could hypothesize as to which kinds of objects and items will be attracted by the magnets. This is only a hypothesis and not a fact. The hypothesis, of course, is based on knowledge. Pupils could then test the hypothesis with the actual using of the magnets. Different kinds of magnets should be utilized to test the hypothesis. Hypotheses are substantiated, modified, or refuted based on testing. As time goes on, with the further study and thought, new concepts and generalizations may be developed pertaining to previously held conclusions.

Very early in the experiences of elementary school pupils, the concepts of 'experimental' and 'control groups' should be emphasized. Pupils on the kindergarten level, for example, may be studying a unit on "Plants in Our Community." The questions may arise as to what plants need in order to grow well. On a learning centre, two potted plants can be placed. It is important to have these plants as alike as possible in terms of quality. The soil should be as comparable as possible for the two potted plants. The amount of moisture that each potted plant is to receive should be held constant also. In other words, both potted plants should receive the same treatment except for one variable which will be tested. This variable will be that one of these potted plants has a cardboard box placed over it. This plant will represent the experimental group whereas the other potted plant will be the control group. Pupils can then test their hypothesis as to what will happen to the plant in the experimental group if it receives no sunshine. The plant in the experimental group can be compared with the plant in the control group at selected intervals. Experiments such as these should be conducted using a variety of kinds of plants. In each case there should be an experimental group as well as a control group. If the outcomes are always the same in this experiment, pupils can achieve accurate generalizations.

In the unit previously mentioned pertaining to "Plants in Our Community," other variables can be tested also as to what plants need in order to grow. Let us again assume for purposes of discussion that the two potted plants are as similar as possible in terms of quality. They receive the same amount of sunshine due to their location. The soil of these potted plants is similar. The one variable that will now be tested will pertain to the amount of moisture that one plant will receive as compared to the other plant. Desert plants would not be involved in this experiment. One of the potted plants will receive no moisture while the other receives a proper amount. Pupils can observe what happens at different intervals when the experiment is being conducted. The plant receiving no moisture for a period of time would be in the experimental group whereas the plant which is receiving the normal treatment is in the control group. Again, pupils should have ample opportunities to observe what actually happens when the one variable is tested. Another variable that could be tested in the experiment would be the soil that is used in the potted plant. All other variables would remain the same. Pupils could use three kinds of soil; sandy soil, clay and loam. Thus, with several experiments such as these, pupils could generalize as to which kind of soil is most beneficial to plants.

Pupils must have opportunities to identify problems and questions; secondly, information or data needs to be gathered; thirdly, a hypothesis or hypotheses are developed; and finally, the hypothesis or hypotheses are tested and subject to revision and modification. These steps may not necessarily be followed rigidly. However, pupils should use the methods of science in conducting experiments so that results are unbiased and objective.

The Importance of Science

More time, no doubt, is devoted to teaching elementary school science than ever before. One of the writers can well remember attending a five teacher rural elementary school when science was taught once a week on the intermediate and upper grade levels in the later 1930's and early 1940's. The science curriculum then consisted largely of reading about science from a specific series of textbooks. The reading was generally done orally with each pupil taking his turn. Many students in graduate and undergraduate classes of one of the writers attending the elementary school years in the 1930's and 1940's mention similar learning experiences. The use of experiments in elementary school science has been discussed previously; experimentation should be central in a modern programme of science. The time, of course, devoted to the teachings of science has increased much.

There is much for pupils to learn in science in a scientific age. The space age, jet planes, cars, trucks, buses, ships, refrigerators, ranges, washers, and driers—to mention a few of man's achievements—require that pupils understand and develop major concepts, principles, and generalizations of science. This means that adequate time needs to be given to the teaching of science.

Many elementary schools have adequate time devoted each day to the teaching of science. To be sure, ample time given to teaching a specific curriculum area will not automatically make for optimum achievement on the part of pupils. However, if pupils are to realize carefully selected objectives, the proper amount of time needs to be given to provide for quality learning activities in elementary school science and evaluate if stated goals have been achieved.

Thus, society has realized the importance of science for pupils in the elementary school. If learners are to do well in science on the secondary level, they need to experience an excellent science programme on the elementary level. Young children are curious about their natural environment. Selected pupils have come to school late on the kindergarten and first grade levels due to being curious about insects, rocks, plants, snow, puddles of water, and other natural phenomenon while walking to school.

Teachers have been amazed about the items children will bring to school for a science learning centre. Little or no coaxing needs to be done here. Pupils voluntarily want to bring objects to school pertaining to the curriculum area of science. They may bring rocks, insects in containers, tadpoles in jars, plants, magnets of different kinds, and other items related to science. Pupils can raise many important questions on what has been brought for the science learning centre. Pupils may reveal their interests by asking questions such as the following:

1. What do insects feed on?
2. How are rocks formed?
3. How do tadpoles change into frogs?
4. What do plants need in order to grow?
5. Why do magnets "pick up" certain things but not other materials?

Pupils with teacher leadership can discuss possible answers to these questions. Research also will need to be done to get needed information in solving problem areas. The area of science offers many occasions for pupils to develop interest in and become curious about natural phenomena. It almost appears that pupils are naturally interested in science. Thus, it is no wonder that elementary school science is receiving more emphasis than ever before in the elementary curriculum. Also, in an industrial, automated society, pupils must understand contributions that science has made to improve the quality of living for human beings.

Inservice Education in Science

With more science taught in the elementary school curriculum than ever before, it has become very important to conduct an adequate number of workshops and hold an ample number of faculty meetings to update science in the elementary school.

An elementary school or several elementary schools conducting workshops in the teaching of science must, first of all, determine what facet or facets of the science curriculum need to be emphasized in this approach to inservice education. Cooperatively, then, faculty members should decide upon the theme of the workshop. The theme can be decided upon only by studying trends in elementary school science and evaluating where one's school is presently in this important curriculum area. Thus, a gap will generally exist between where the school is presently and where it should be in elementary school science. The following areas may represent some of these gaps:

1. objectives of elementary school science;
2. selection of unit titles;
3. proper sequence in the science curriculum;
4. conducting experiments;
5. using science equipment effectively;

6. using a variety of learning activities;
7. assessing pupil achievement effectively;
8. developing a philosophy for teaching science;
9. assisting pupils in reading science content;
10. identifying the scope of the science curriculum;
11. learning by discovery in science.

Committees can be developed based on decisions made in the general session pertaining to problem areas that need solution in the area of elementary school science. It is excellent if each participant in the general session can select the committee he or she wishes most to participate in. Committee members need to sense purpose in work that is done. In other words, if participants can voluntarily select the committee they wish to serve in and sense that purpose is involved in solving problem areas, energy levels should be high for optimum achievement. The following resources should be available for all committee members:

1. knowledge resource personnel who can work effectively with people;
2. a professional library from which participants can get needed information.

Thus, members of the different committees involved in working to gain more insight into an effective elementary school science programme should have resources available which will help in gaining quality results from effort put forth.

It is necessary for participants in a workshop to work on problems and areas of interest of their very own choosing. This would then provide for individual differences among committee members. It may be that one participant alone has the following problem pertaining to the teaching of elementary school science: assisting pupils in working on committees where responsibility of each member commensurate with ability is in evidence (this teacher may have had difficulty in getting certain committee members to do their share of the work). Thus, the individual participant in the science workshop can work in the direction of solving a relevant problem in the teaching of science. Consultant help and resource materials would be available to help participants on an individual basis.

Faculty meetings in an elementary school should also be devoted to improving the elementary science curriculum. An agenda committee composed of three or four faculty members can arrange items for discussion at the next faculty meeting. It is good to rotate the members of this committee to provide for a broad base of participation on the part of faculty members of an elementary school. Every faculty member should have equal rights to present items to the agenda committee for discussion at faculty meetings. The agenda should be in the hands of participants two to three days before the meeting is held. This should give all participants ample opportunities to think about the various alternatives and possibilities when discussing solutions to questions and problem areas. Individuals can volunteer or be assigned to serve on committees to solve selected problem areas. Some of the problem areas that may be identified in faculty meetings pertaining to the teaching of elementary school science could be the following:

1. How can the inquiry approach be utilized when teaching science?
2. How does one write objectives which are behaviourally stated?
3. How can pupil achievement be effectively evaluated when using the problem solving approach?

Much thought, research, and discussion can go into the solving of each of these questions or problems. Some faculty members, no doubt, will need to visit other schools and observe teachers, for example, using the inquiry approach in teaching, as well as observe other innovations.

Developing Curriculum Guides

Each public school system should develop curriculum guides which can be utilized by teachers in teaching the different curriculum areas of the elementary school. Curriculum guides should be used in terms of providing suggestions for teaching. They should definitely not be prescriptive. In the early history of curriculum guides, it was felt that these were to be followed rigidly. Today, the emphasis definitely is upon selection, in terms of good criteria or standards, as to what will be utilized from a curriculum guide. The curriculum guide, along with other reference sources, can assist the science teacher to do a better job of planning for teaching elementary school pupils.

The question arises as to what are the salient parts of a good curriculum guide. The format followed in developing these guides may vary from school system to school system. However, there will be some basic agreements as to which essential parts to include in a curriculum guide. The following are important parts of a curriculum guide in terms of the section devoted to elementary school science:

1. statements pertaining to a philosophy of teaching science;
2. suggestions for using the guide;
3. general and specific objectives for teaching different units of study;
4. scope and sequence of science units for each grade in the elementary school;
5. suggested learning activities for each science unit;
6. suggested evaluation techniques to use in evaluating pupil achievement;
7. a listing of child growth and development characteristics;
8. suggestions for implementing committee work, and teacher-pupil planning;
9. suggestions for helping pupils learn inductively, use the problem solving approach, and learn through the inquiry approach;
10. a good bibliography listing teacher references and pupil references.

From the preceding parts that could go into the developing of a curriculum guide, it is quite obvious that the teacher can have a valuable source of ideas to use in planning the science curriculum. For example, the teacher can evaluate and select objectives which pupils should achieve in a specific unit. The teacher also has numerous opportunities to select learning activities, from the curriculum guide which should help a given set of learners achieve to their optimum. The evaluation section of the guide should give the science teacher some new approaches to utilize in effectively evaluating pupil achievement. Again, curriculum guides must be used as guides and not as a holy book which must be followed precisely.

Use of Television in Science

Educational television has made many important contributions in upgrading the science curriculum. Elementary schools that have access to closed-circuit television generally will have listings of programmes which teachers will have well in advance of their showing. These programmes will relate directly to ongoing units being taught in science. For each unit of study, guides have been or should be developed pertaining to the different telecasts. For each broadcast, a listing of objectives for pupils to achieve is important. The teacher can sense then what each broadcast will emphasize in terms of objectives. Suggestions for learning activities are presented in the guide which will provide readiness within learners for viewing the telecast. The teacher can then select which activities would do the best job of providing readiness for learning so that adequate background knowledge will be developed within pupils. If pupils do not have the needed concepts, facts, terms, and generalizations necessary for understanding the telecast, optimum achievement cannot result. The readiness activities should also assist pupils in developing interest in the broadcast. An inward desire should exist on the part of the learner in wanting to watch the telecast. Certainly, learners should have identified some questions which they would want to have answered when viewing the broadcast.

After the telecast, follow-up activities are necessary so that pupils can use what has been learned. Answers to questions raised before the broadcast can be discussed. Experiments may need to be performed in order that pupils can get needed data in answer to questions. Pupils may volunteer to develop reports on selected topics which relate to the broadcast using science encyclopedias or regular encyclopedias. Taking an excursion may help to answer additional questions raised after the telecast. In other words, there are many learning activities for pupils which will assist them to 'branch out' in broadening their thinking and interests after having viewed a telecast.

Using Knowledge of Children

Science teachers who do a poor job of teaching may not be using knowledge pertaining to important child growth and development characteristics. Teachers need to study each of their pupils carefully so that the best quality of learning activities can be provided. Educational psychologists have long emphasized the importance of providing for individual differences in a class. Too frequently, however, little has been done in this area by practitioners. A very clear violation of providing for individual differences exists when science teachers want to keep all pupils 'together' by having the whole group study the same thing at the same time. Perhaps, science has become a reading course where pupils spend much time in reading content from a series of elementary school science textbooks. As educators should be well aware of, this activity will be too difficult for some pupils; for others it is too easy. Very few pupils will find that the content is written on their reading level. Pupils also desire new experiences and want variety in learning activities they are participating in.

Many statements have been written on child growth and development characteristics. Faculty members of an elementary school need to study these contributions written by psychologists and educators realizing that pupils differ from each other in many ways within a class, such as interest, intelligence, abilities, past experiences, motivation, appearance, height, and weight.

Variety in Learning Activities

It is important for the science teacher to provide a variety of learning activities for pupils. This would be important for the following reasons:

1. pupils have different learning styles;
2. different levels of achievement in science exist within any class of pupils;
3. not all pupils, of course, benefit equally from the same activity;
4. teachers have different teaching styles;
5. selected learning activities capture the interests of pupils more than do other kinds of experiences;
6. individuals desire new experiences;
7. monotony in activities hinders pupils in developing proper motivation toward learning.

There are many learning activities in elementary school science which would assist pupils in gaining needed concepts, main ideas, facts, and generalizations. These learning activities could help pupils in the area of problem solving. The following, among others, could become purposeful learning activities for pupils in elementary school science: conducting experiments and demonstrations, taking excursions, reading from a series or several series of elementary school science textbooks, getting information from a set or several sets of general encyclopedias and/or science encyclopedias, reading from library books, working at learning centres, using pictures, using transparencies and the overhead projector, constructing objects, making models, utilizing filmstrips and films, listening to tape recordings, interviewing resource personnel, viewing slides, visiting museums, having discussions, giving oral reports to the class, writing reports, engaging in dramatic activities, making dioramas, developing friezes, completing murals, making graphs and charts, developing illustrations, and participating in panel discussions. There are many, many kinds of learning activities for pupils in elementary school science; there should basically be no boredom on the part of pupils when this curriculum area is being taught. It is important to select those learning activities which will help pupils to do the very best possible in elementary school science.

Approaches to teaching science can also be varied in terms of using the inductive versus the deductive approach to learning. Much has been written about the advantages of using the inductive approach as compared to the deductive approach. Some of these advantages are the following:

1. pupils have to do much responding so that generalizations and conclusions can truly be discovered;
2. learners reveal where they are presently in achievement when learning by discovery;
3. pupils can become actively involved in ongoing learning activities;
4. it keeps learners "on their toes" when doing much responding in ongoing learning activities;
5. pupils have many opportunities to do critical and creative thinking;
6. a variety of learning activities can be utilized in the inductive approach;
7. pupils can become more self-directed with less reliance on the teacher dominating the classroom situation;

8. teachers become more flexible in their thinking when less reliance can be placed upon how pupils will respond;
9. learners can work more in the direction of using the methods and approaches of scientists; scientists gain much knowledge and information through discovery.

The science teacher can have pupils develop generalizations deductively. For example, in a unit on "Liquids, Solids, and Gases," the teacher could perform an experiment whereby a bottle with a narrow opening would be filled with a few inches of water a narrow opening would be filled with a few inches of water and placed on a hot plate. A balloon would be stretched over the narrow opening of the bottle before it is placed on the hot plate. Pupils would be encouraged to see what will happen. The balloon, of course, becomes larger. The teacher then proceeds to explain to the class why the balloon became larger and what happens when air is heated.

In the inductive approach utilizing the same experiment, the teacher could have pupils hypothesize freely as to what will happen when this same bottle, containing a few inches of water, with the attached balloon is placed on the hot plate. Reasons for the hypotheses can also be discussed thus giving the teacher much information on where learners are presently in achievement pertaining to the area now being taught in the unit "Liquids, Solids, and Gases." Following the discussion, the hypotheses need to be tested using the experiment. The experiment can be performed more than once so that pupils can sense that the outcomes in the experiment will have the same results. The size of the openings of the bottles as well as the size of the balloons can vary when having pupils view the same kind or type of experiment when noticing that the results are similar in terms of generalizations or conclusions realized. Further research can be done using elementary science textbooks, encyclopedias, films, filmstrips, and other resources to explain conclusions realized from conducting the experiment. In using the inductive approach, the teacher does a very small amount of explaining or lecturing. The teacher sets the stage for learning. Pupils identify problems, gather information, develop hypotheses, test hypotheses, and revise them when necessary. Active involvement on the part of pupils is of utmost importance in ongoing learning activities.

A science teacher could tape record his own teaching and evaluate the quality of experiences pertaining to pupils learning by discovery or using the inductive approach. If a portable video-tape machine is available in the elementary school, teaching performance in science could also observe non-verbal facets of communication such as gestures, facial expressions, and body movements in the teaching-learning situation. Valuable feed-back from learners can come from viewing different facets of teaching on video-tape. The teacher can notice such factors as the following:

1. Do pupils appear interested or bored in the ongoing learning activities?
2. Are all learners actively involved in the lesson being presented?
3. Do a few pupils dominate the discussion while others refrain from participating?
4. Do pupils feel free to hypothesize pertaining to possible outcomes of science experiments?
5. Are pupils using a variety of reference sources in gathering data to develop and/or test hypotheses?
6. Do pupils reveal curiosity in wanting to learn more about any unit of study in elementary school science?

If the teacher has access to video-taping teaching performance, of if a tape recorder is used only, he can analyze what kind of verbal interaction occurred between pupils and the teacher in a classroom situation. The teacher, for example, can notice the following in teaching-learning situations:

1. Do pupils have ample opportunities to hypothesize?
2. Does the teacher ask many relevant questions of learners pertaining to ongoing units of study in science?
3. Are these questions on the present achievement level of pupils?
4. Do pupils have needed background information to develop meaningful hypotheses?
5. Is lecturing minimized much in ongoing learning activities?
6. Is the teacher praising pupils in achieving desired objectives in elementary school science?
7. Do learners identify relevant problem areas?

8. Does it appear that pupils individually are being challenged in developing in inward desire to learn?
9. Does the teacher give pupils adequate time to engage in hypothesizing when being involved in problem solving activities?
10. Does the teacher refrain from scolding or minimizing pupils in the class setting?

Behavioural Objectives in Elementary Science

Elementary school science lends itself very well to having teachers state their objectives behaviourally. Selected educators advocate that objectives be stated precisely. Advantages of behaviourally stated objectives are the following:

1. These objectives very clearly state what learners are to learn.
2. It can definitely be measured if pupils have achieved these objectives.
3. Learning activities can be selected carefully which will guide learners to realize the objectives.
4. Teachers can be held accountable for pupils realizing the objectives.
5. Learners can achieve these objectives at different rates of speed thus providing for individual differences.
6. Parents can notice specifically what their pupils have learned.
7. Principals and supervisors can have a better basis for evaluating teacher performance.
8. Teachers could even be paid on the basis of achievement or lack of it in terms of learner performance (this could be a motivating factor for some teachers).
9. Objective criteria are used to assess pupil achievement; these criteria are the behaviourally stated objectives.

As in almost any innovation, there are also disadvantages to behaviourally stated objectives. The following, among others, are some of the disadvantages:

1. Too frequently, the trivial or unimportant is taught since the lowest level of cognitive objectives are easiest to write.

2. No one can definitely be sure what pupils actually should learn when stating all objectives precisely prior to teaching.
3. Objectives should come from the learner also and not the teacher only.
4. Affective domain objectives may become minimized if all objectives need to be stated so that it can be measured precisely if pupils have achieved them.
5. Learners become rather passive individuals if all objectives are stated by the teacher prior to teaching.
6. By stating objectives in advance prior to teaching, the teacher is assuming that proper sequence in learning will be in evidence.
7. The teacher should focus more on the learning activity rather than the objectives since it is in this framework that interest and meaning is developed.
8. Behavioural objectives are very time consuming in writing.

The science teacher, the elementary school principal, and the supervisor need to study behavioural objectives carefully to determine if this plan of teaching is really wanted in elementary school science. Workshops and faculty meetings can be devoted to the study and implementation of behavioural objectives. Objectives which pupils are then to achieve should meet the following criteria:

1. they are important or relevant;
2. they stress key ideas or generalizations emphasized by specialists in the different areas of science such as in biology, chemistry, physics, zoology, botany, geology, and astronomy;
3. there is balance among understandings, skills, and attitudinal objectives.

All behaviourally stated objectives should follow the following standards:

1. the objectives should be clearly written so that little or no room exits in their interpretation;
2. it can definitely be measured if the objectives have been achieved;

3. it states what learners will learn as a result of teaching.

If pupils are studying a unit on "The Solar System," the following objectives may have been identified for pupils to realize:

1. The pupils will list in writing the nine planets in proper sequence from the sun.
2. The pupil will recite orally the names of the largest and the smallest planet.
3. The pupil will write a fifty word paper on the possibility of life as we know it on a planet of his own choice (excluding the planet earth).
4. Pupils in their own words will define the meaning of the following concepts; solar system; universe; planet; satellite; asteroids; theory; hypothesis; magnetic pole; constellation; rotation; and revolution.
5. The pupil will demonstrate and discuss the causes of the different seasons of the year.
6. Learners will predict what will happen in the future in space exploration.
7. A model of the solar system will be made in committees of three; the model will be evaluated in terms of criteria discussed in class.

The first and second behaviourally stated objectives require recall of information which is the lowest level of cognition. Pupils would recall the names of the nine known planets in proper order, and be able to name the largest and smallest of these planets. The third objective may also involve simple recall of what has been learned previously by pupils. Pupils could recall from a discussion if there is or is not life as we know it on one of the planets and write on the selected topic. Pupils individually, however, could also be quite creative when writing a paper of at least fifty words pertaining to the possibilities of life existing on a planet which he chooses to write on. The paper could involve unique, novel, original, and constructive ideas which would involve synthesizing of knowledge. The fourth objective goes beyond recall of knowledge. It is true that the child would need to think of definitions he has heard of previously pertaining to such words as solar system, universe, planet, satellite, asteroids, theory, hypothesis, magnetic pole, constellation, rotation, and revolution. The learner, however, would need to reveal his understanding of these concepts by giving definitions in his own words. Comprehension of the meaning of these concepts would be important to pupils when achieving this objective. The fifth objective would generally involve applying what has been learned previously. The knowledge and information the child has developed previously is now utilized in demonstrating the cause of the different seasons of the year. The pupil could use a large globe to represent the earth and a flashlight to represent the sun. The learner could also make drawings on the chalkboard and/or use pictures in clarifying the various causes for the different seasons of the year. In the sixth objective, creative thinking based on much knowledge is involved. Pupils would need to have considerable background information to make predictions as to what will happen in the future as far as space exploration is concerned. The last objective involves a psychomotor domain objective in that a construction activity is involved requiring the use of the muscles. To be sure, much thought and research will go into the making of an accurate model of the solar system. Pupils will need to check the accuracy of their model in terms of standards or criterial developed in class. The latter part of this objective (objective number seven) can involve a very complex level of thinking. Definite criteria will need to be developed in class so that the model of the solar system can be effectively evaluated in terms of these guidelines.

Thus, behaviourally stated objectives can be used effectively in a modern programme of elementary school science. It is important when emphasizing these kinds of objectives that teachers have pupils go beyond the level of recall of information. The science teacher also needs to think in terms of some kind of rational balance among cognitive, psychomotor, and affective domain objectives. Never should one category of objectives dominate teaching-learning situations. One category of objectives does affect the other category or categories.

Adjusting the Science Curriculum to the Child

Too frequently, the teacher has objectives for pupils to achieve which are excessively complex. The science teacher may have felt that this is a way of setting high standards in a specific curriculum area. Many pupils then cannot achieve these objectives and develop feelings of an inadequate self. Pupil achievement goes downhill in situations such as these. Learners think and feel that they cannot do well in elementary school science and this becomes a reality. If pupils perceive that they cannot do well in science, this is the way that learners will behave. The teacher needs to have some kind of pretest in a new science unit to determine where learners are presently in achievement. Once this has been determined, objectives can be developed which are attainable. If objectives are attainable, learners can feel successful and develop feelings of an adequate self. The curriculum is then adjusted to where pupils are presently in achievement in different units of study in elementary school science.

Certainly, there is danger, too, in teaching pupils what they already know in a new unit of study. A pretest can give elementary science teachers data if objectives need to be made more complex. Again, the objectives should be attainable for learners. The science curriculum in this case is again adjusted to present achievement levels of learners.

In Summary

Conducting experiments is a very important type or kind of learning activity in a modern elementary school science programme. Balance among the different curriculum areas in the elementary school must be stressed in teaching-learning situations. Inservice education for teachers, principals, and supervisors is important to update the science curriculum. Curriculum guides can be a valuable source to utilize when selecting objectives, learning experiences, and evaluation techniques in a modern programme of elementary school science. A variety of learning experiences should be provided for pupils in the elementary school. The science curriculum must be adjusted to the present achievement level of each learner. Inductive approaches should be emphasized by the teacher in teacher-learning situations; critical and creative thinking as well as problem solving should be emphasized. Attitudinal objectives are important for pupils to achieve. There must be proper balance among the following kinds of objectives for pupils to achieve:

1. understandings, skills, and attitudes or
2. cognitive, affective, and psychomotor domains.

Adequate emphasis needs to be placed upon microcomputer instruction in the curriculum. Wright and Forcier list the following general criteria in selecting computer courseware:

1. Content is accurate
2. Content is appropriate
3. Presentation is clear.
4. Screen display is highly readable
5. The computer's capabilities are effectively employed
6. Programme executes reliably
7. Programme is cost effective
8. Programme is easy to use
9. Support materials are effective
10. No racial or sexual discrimination implied.

REFERENCES

Ediger, Marlow and Digumarti Bhaskara Rao. *Teaching Science Successfully*. New Delhi, India: Discovery Publishing House, 2001.

Wright, Edward B. and Forcier, Richard E. *The Computer: A Tool for the Teacher*. Belmont, California: Wadsworth Publishing Company, 1985, page, 158.

Trends in Elementary School Science

Teachers, principals, and supervisors need to study relevant trends in the science curriculum and thus update the objectives, learning activities, and evaluation procedures utilized presently in the elementary school science programme. Which are selected relevant trends in elementary school science that could be implemented?

Experimenting in the Science Curriculum

Each unit of study should stress the importance of using related science experiments. In fact, experimentation should be a major way of obtaining concepts and generalizations for pupils in the curriculum area of science. This is true for the following reasons:

1. Scientists in a laboratory setting perform experiments as a means of gathering information.
2. Problem solving can be emphasized in ongoing units of study in science such as identifying a problem, gathering information pertaining to the problem, developing a hypothesis (or hypotheses), testing the hypothesis (or hypotheses), and developing needed modifications and revisions of the stated hypothesis, if necessary. Problem solving needs to be stressed in all curriculum areas in the elementary school as well as in life.
3. Pupils must develop skills relating to critical thinking when content is evaluated pertaining to ultimately developing a hypothesis. Critical thinking is important

in all curriculum areas in the elementary school as well as in life.

4. Pupils need to become careful observers in ongoing learning activities involving science. Too frequently, learners want to jump to hasty conclusions pertaining to the outcome or outcomes of a science experiment. Pupils, however, should carefully observe what is happening during an experiment and base their conclusions on what has been observed. In units of study in elementary school science and in the natural environment, pupils may be guided to observe facets of the following:
   (a) leaves, twigs, rocks and minerals, different kinds of soil, trees, grass, and clouds;
   (b) birds, fish, turtles, frogs, and diverse animals included in the category of mammals;
   (c) animals without backbones such as worms, grasshoppers, bees, oysters, crabs, spiders, and ants;
   (d) the effect of heating selected liquids, solids, and gases;
   (e) the hardness of different kinds of rocks and minerals;
   (f) objects and items attracted or repelled by magnets;
   (g) the effects of a grass covering on soil having a hilly contour.

Reading Content in Science

Pupils gain much valuable content in ongoing units of study in science through reading of ideas. Reading sources in elementary school science may include the following:

1. elementary school science textbooks;
2. general encyclopedias as well as science encyclopedias;
3. library books containing science content;
4. content from basal readers containing information pertaining to science;
5. pamphlets, leaflets, and related sources containing content in the area of science.

When reading content in science, pupils need to read for a variety of purposes such as:

1. gaining relevant concepts, e.g. liquids, solids, gases, magnetism, electricity, electromagnets, electrons, protons, neutrons, compounds, and elements;
2. acquiring generalizations, e.g. liquids, solids, and gases basically expand when heated. There are exceptions, such as water, a liquid turning to ice, a solid;
3. gaining facts, e.g. stegosaurus, allosaurus, tyrannosaurus rex, and the brontosaurus were dinosaurs that lived during the Mesozoic era;
4. obtaining directions, e.g. reading directions to make science equipment in ongoing units of study, e.g. magnets, electromagnets, and develop a complete circuit through parallel and series wiring;
5. gaining sequential ideas, e.g. reading content to notice the order of relative durations of geological eras—Precambrian, Paleozoic, Mesozoic, and Cenozoic;
6. thinking critically about content read, e.g., noticing factual statements as contrasted with statements of opinion or accurate statements from those which are inaccurate;
7. thinking creatively pertaining to ideas gained from reading, e.g. stating a hypothesis pertaining to a problem area prior to conducting a related experiment. Thus, the learner presents a unique original hypothesis before a science experiment is performed relating to an ongoing unit of study.

Conducting Excursions

Pupils with teacher guidance need to experience reality. Too frequently, the science curriculum has presented abstract learnings to pupils largely. It is important for pupils to experience reality for the following reasons:

1. Pupils may then gain accurate concepts, generalizations, and main ideas.
2. Learners desire a variety of learning activities rather than sameness in experiences.
3. Concrete situations, such as the taking of excursions, are a way of learning for pupils.
4. Pupils may be guided to sequence their own learnings in concrete situations.

Excursions should be taken under the following circumstances only:

1. The place to be visited is free from danger for learners.
2. No reasonable substitution can be made for the excursion in terms of other learning experiences.
3. Parental or guardian permission has been given in writing for taking the excursion. Duplicated forms can be developed readily for obtaining permission for pupils to go on excursions.
4. Adequate guide service is available to aid learners in achieving optimal development during the excursion.
5. The excursion helps pupils achieve relevant objectives in an ongoing science unit.
6. Pupils perceive purpose or reasons for taking the excursion.
7. Content presented during the excursion is meaningful and understandable to pupils.

There are many units of study in elementary school science in which related meaningful excursions may be appropriate for pupils:

1. If pupils are studying a unit on "The Pond Community," they may actually visit a pond site with teacher guidance. Prior to visiting a pond community, the teacher should guide pupils to perceive purpose for the excursion. A set of pictures or a filmstrip presentation may set the stage for pupils participating in the excursion. From these learning experiences, pupils may be stimulated to ask questions such as:
   (a) What kind of life generally is in evidence in a pond?
   (b) What is the surrounding environment like adjacent to a specific pond?
   (c) How can pond communities be kept clean?
   (d) How does a contaminated pond affect human beings?

The identification of problem areas by pupils provides readiness activities prior to pupils visiting a pond community. The actual excursion can provide answers to pupils related to the identified problem areas.

2. If pupils are studying a unit of "Preventing Soil Erosion," they may visit an area where:
   (a) gully erosion or sheet erosion has occurred;
   (b) steps have been taken to prevent erosion, e.g., grass has been seeded, terraces have been built, strip-cropping is in evidence, and trees have been planted.

Observations made by pupils need to be discussed to reinforce and clarify learnings.

Using Construction Activities

Pupils with teacher leadership should have ample opportunities to engage in construction activities in ongoing units of study in science. The following are selected values pupils may attain from participating in construction activities:

1. Eye-hand coordination may be developed by pupils. Thus, psychomotor skills (use of the finer or larger muscles) are being emphasized in units of study pertaining to science.
2. The actual making of science equipment can be psychologically sound for learners in that creativity is being emphasized in the science curriculum.
3. There needs to be balance between and among cognitive, psychomotor, and affective objectives since life itself consists of activities in these three domains.
4. Pupils can actually use science equipment made in ongoing units of study. Not all equipment used in science experiments should, of course, be commercially purchased. Active involvement rather than passive learning is involved when pupils plan, develop, and evaluate what has been constructed in terms of science equipment and materials. Feelings of participation on the part of pupils are important in the elementary curriculum.
5. Pupils participating in construction activities can open future doors to vocational and avocational interests. Each pupil should have opportunities to discover his/her interests and develop these talents to the maximum possible.

Using Films, Filmstrips, and Slides

The teacher should make ample use of audio-visual aids such as films, filmstrips, and slides. Pupils can see movement and reality in motion picture film presentations. It is difficult, however, to stop a film presentation at a given point for discussion purposes. The use of slides and filmstrips, of course, provides ample opportunities to stop presentation and discuss the contents when needed. In fact, it is highly recommended that pupils raise questions and present related ideas pertaining to any frame in a filmstrip or any one slide. Clarification of ideas is important in any learning experience. The following experiences are important for pupils prior to viewing an audio-visual presentation:

1. Introductory activities. Pupils must experience selected learning activities prior to the audio-visual presentation in order that interest, motivation, and purpose are developed and maintained. If pupils, for example, are to view an audio-visual presentation on "The Human Body," they may, as introductory activities, participate in:
   (a) discussing how to develop and maintain good health;
   (b) using a microscope to look at onion cells;
   (c) developing standards for safe living in the environment;
   (d) discussing foods to be eaten to maintain good health.
2. Follow-up activities. After the audio-visual presentation has been completed, pupils with teacher guidance may participate in:
   (a) doing research from a variety of reference sources on developing and maintaining good health. Pupils may divide into committees for this activity and report their findings to members of other committees;
   (b) drawing pictures of different kinds of cells, e.g., bone, skin, and blood cells. Various reference sources need investigation to provide background information;
   (c) evaluating the home and school environment in terms of safety standards developed during the introductory activities;
   (d) planning and serving a meal which would stress proper nutrition for pupils.

Using Writing Activities in the Science Curriculum

The language arts skills of writing should receive adequate emphasis in the elementary school science programme. If pupils, for example, are studying a unit on "Plants, Animals, and the Seasons," they many engage in diverse kinds of writing experiences.

1. develop an outline. Each pupil with teacher direction may develop an outline pertaining to content that has been read relating to an ongoing unit of study. The outline should contain a title. Main divisions should include Roman numerals. Subdivisions may be represented with capital letters in sequence. Details may present the finer points of each subdivision. Hindu-Arabic numerals should represent each detail. The accuracy of an outline can be checked in terms of criteria such as the following:
   - *(a)* Does the title cover the contents of the outlines comprehensively?
   - *(b)* Does each main division (represented by Roman numerals) relate directly to the title?
   - *(c)* does each item in the subdivision relate to the intended main division in the outline?
   - *(d)* Do the details (represented by Hindu-Arabic numerals) relate directly to the intended subdivision?

A correctly developed outline should generally follow this format:

Title

I. Main Division

A. Subdivision

B. Subdivision

C. Subdivision

1. Detail

2. Detail

II. Main Division

A. Subdivision

B. Subdivision

1. Detail

2. Detail

To have consistency in an outline, all parts should contain either sentences or phrases. Generally, if Roman numeral I is inherent in the outline, Roman numeral II must also be present. Additional main divisions may be added as needed. If subdivision A is utilized in the outline, subdivision B should also be inherent. Additional subdivisions may be added as needed. The same pattern would follow when utilizing details.

2. develop a written report. The content of the outline may be utilized to develop a written report. Written reports may deal with:
   (a) summaries of experiments conducted in ongoing units of study in science;
   (b) diary entries kept by pupils on a daily basis pertaining to understandings, skills, and attitudes acquired. Members on a committee should be rotated in writing these diary entries;
   (c) logs kept on a sequential basis relating directly to what pupils have achieved in an ongoing unit of study in science. Content in a log would pertain to learnings acquired during a longer period of time than on a daily basis, such as ideas recorded once a week;
   (d) content written on a particular topic chosen by a child or a committee of learners. Thus, in a unit on "Weather and How It Affects Us," reports may be written on the following areas:
   what causes rain to fall.
   different kinds of clouds, e.g., cumulus, cirrus, *et al.*
   weather forecasting.
   tornadoes, cyclones, and hail.
   sleet, snow, and forest.
   the monsoon climate, Mediterranean climate, desert areas, and jungle regions.

   In developing written reports, the following concepts should be emphasized by pupils as readiness would permit:
   unity of ideas in a paragraph.
   appropriate sequence of paragraphs.
   thorough development of content within a paragraph.

creative and critical thinking inherent in the written product.

correct spelling of words.

legible handwriting.

proper capitalization, punctuation, and usage.

Ideas must come first in any written product. The mechanics of writing such as correct spelling of words, legible handwriting, and proper capitalization, punctuation, and usage are of secondary importance.

3. write poetry. Pupils can reveal previously gained learning in science by writing poems. Thus, learners may reveal acquired understanding, skills, and attitudinal objectives in ongoing units of study as a result of engaging in the writing of diverse kinds and forms of poetry. Creative thinking is emphasized thoroughly when pupils exhibit spontaneous, unique ideas as a result of writing selected poems. The following kinds of poems may be written by learners:

(a) haiku poetry. Pupils should possess needed prerequisite learnings before participating in the writing of haiku poems, or any other kind of learning activity. Haiku poems contain three lines—five syllables, seven syllables, and five syllables in sequence. Generally, haiku poems contain content dealing with the natural environment. Selected units of study in elementary school science may then provide relevant content. Illustrations may be drawn by learners related to the written content.

The learning environment needs to be arranged so that pupils are intrinsically motivated in wanting to write haiku poetry. Content in selected slides, pictures, filmstrips, films, and the outdoor environment may aid in setting the stage for learners in desiring to write hakiu poetry. If pupils, for example, are studying a unit on "Wildlife of Our Community," ultimately, from a rich learning environment, individual pupils may choose a topic to write about.

Cardinals
Happy Cardinals
Flying, hovering, gliding
Freshly out of sight.

This poem contains three lines following the five, seven, five sequence in terms of syllables per line. Pupils, inductively may learn to distinguish haiku from other forms of creative writing. The teacher may read selected haiku poems to pupils. These poems may be printed on the chalkboard. Learners may then be guided in developing relevant generalizations pertaining to what a haiku poem is.

(b) free verse. Pupils do not need to have ending words rhyme when writing free verse. The lines may vary from each other as to length when free verse is written. Free verse then is a very open-ended approach in the writing of poetry. From a stimulating learning environment, pupils may select a title for writing verse following tenets of free verse. If pupils are studying a unit on "Proper Nutrition and Diet," free verse may be written on:

Drinking Milk
Protein Foods
Carbohydrates
Starches
Staying Healthy

Pupils voluntarily may wish to share their written products with others, thus noticing how content may vary from free verse to free verse.

(c) couplets, triplets, and quatrains. Pupils should have ample opportunities to engage in writing verse where diverse patterns of rhyme are inherent. Couplets contain two lines of rhymed verse, whereas triplets have three lines with all ending words rhyming. Quatrains contain four lines; the first and second lines as well as the third and fourth lines may rhyme. There may be other lines which rhyme in a quatrain such as lines one and three as well as lines two and four. The lines in a couplet, a triplet, and a quatrain should be somewhat uniform in length.

Pupils should be stimulated through a variety of learning experiences to write verse creatively. If pupils, for example, are studying a unit on "The Use of Simple Machines," the stage may be set for creative writing of verse by having pupils:

(a) look at and discuss simple machines such as the lever, screw, wedge, pulley, wheel and axle, and the inclined plane;

(b) observe and evaluate pictures showing diverse simple machines;

(c) discuss the uses of simple machines observed in the surrounding environment of the school;

(d) read about and appraise the history of simple machines.

Ultimately, pupils may become stimulated to write creative verse. The following are examples of diverse kinds of rhyming verse:

(a) couplet The man was working with a wedge.
Nearby was a fence containing hedge.

(b) triplet He tried to use a lever.
The rock was moved, never.
Nonetheless, he moved objects ever.

4. Other forms of written work. There are many additional kinds of writing activities that pupils may participate in such as:

   (a) writing plays, announcements, and notices;

   (b) writing biographies of famous scientists.

Art Work in the Science Curriculum

Learning activities, involving art work can do much to enrich the elementary school science curriculum. Thus, the science teacher must provide a variety of learning experiences involving art in the science programme.

1. Developing murals. Pupils in a committee with teacher guidance may plan and develop a mural pertaining to an ongoing unit of study in science. Thus, if pupils for

example are studying a unit on "Animals with Backbones," they may decide upon scenes involving

(a) diverse kinds of fish;

(b) amphibians, e.g., toads and frogs;

(c) reptiles, e.g., snakes, turtles;

(d) various types of birds;

(e) mammals, e.g., human beings, monkis, chimpanzees, gorillas.

2. Developing friezes. A series of pictures developed by a committee of pupils is inherent in cooperatively planning and implementing the frieze concept in art work. A variety of media should be available to pupils when working on a frieze. Thus, crayons, coloured pencils, and finger paints should be readily accessible at the frieze centre. If pupils, for example, are studying a unit on "Animals Without Backbones," they may develop a series of illustrations (a Frieze) on:

(a) protozoans, e.g., the ameba, the paramecium, and the euglena;

(b) porifera (sponges);

(c) coelenteratas, e.g. hydras, jellyfish, coral, and sea anemones;

(d) plathyhelminthes (flatworms), e.g., planarian, flukes, and tapeworms;

(e) aschelminthes (roundworms) e.g., hookworm, ascaris, and the trichinella;

(f) annelida (segmented worms), e.g., earthworm and sandworm;

(g) echinodermata (spiny animals), e.g., starfish, the sea urchin, the sea cucumber, and the sand dollar;

(h) mollusca (shellfish), e.g., clams, scallops, mussels, oysters, slugs, and snails;

(i) arthropoda, e.g., shrimp, lobster, crayfish, and crabs.

Insects also are members of this phylum—praying mantis, grasshopper, walking stick, dragonflies, ladybugs, and potato bettles.

3. Developing individual pictures. To reveal what has been learned during and after the time a unit has been in

progress, pupils individually may complete an illustration pertaining to a relevant concept or generalization. If learners, for example, are studying a unit, "The Human Body and How It Works," each pupil may select to develop an illustration pertaining to:

(a) the digestive system, e.g. a carefully planned and prepared picture, using a variety of art media, may be developed on the stomach and digestion;

(b) the muscular system, e.g. an illustration may be completed pertaining to the heart, an involuntary muscle, which cannot be controlled by the human body, or to voluntary muscles which can be controlled by the human being;

(c) the circulatory system. The individual pupil may choose to complete a drawing on the heart, the blood vessels, and general circulation of the blood;

(d) the respiratory system, e.g., the lungs, bronchial tubes, the throat, the voice box, the nose, nasal passages, and the windpipe.

Dramatizations in the Science Curriculum

In selected units of study in science, pupils with teacher guidance may participate in dramatic activities. Thus, for example, in a unit entitled, "Biographies of Famous Scientists," pupils may engage in research from a variety of references to plan, develop, and implement selected dramatizations. Ultimately, pupils may reveal obtained learnings by dramatizing specific scenes from, among others, the lives of:

(a) Louis Pasteur

(b) Edward Jenner

(c) Enrico Fermi

(d) Albert Einstein

(e) Sir Isaac Newton

(f) Robert Oppenheimer

Creative dramatics would stress the use of words, spontaneously presented, as the need arises. This form of dramatic activity should follow the following standards:

1. The presentation should be accurate and reveal pupils' related understandings, skills, and attitudes.

2. The creative presentation should indicate comprehensiveness of content gained from research activities.
3. Each pupil must reveal that effort has gone into developing the final presentation.
4. Learners individually need to reveal that meaning and understanding are attached to what has been learned.
5. Each pupil should develop feelings of belonging and participation in the ongoing dramatic activity.
6. Pupils individually and within the group must develop feelings of satisfaction and success from creative dramatics learning experiences.
7. Each learner should be encouraged to identify and recognize new problems and questions requiring additional needed research.

Scope and Sequence in the Science Curriculum

There are important questions that teachers, supervisors, and principals need to identify and solve in the area of elementary school science. The concept of scope pertains to 'what' should be taught in diverse units of study in elementary school science. Thus, breadth of unit titles in a kindergarten through grade six continuum would pertain to the problem of 'what' should be taught in the elementary school science curriculum.

Directly related to the problem of scope (what is to be taught) in the elementary science curriculum is the concept of sequence. The concept of sequence pertains to 'when' specific units of study should be taught, such as on the kindergarten level, grade one, grade two, grade three, grade four, grade five, or grade six. The concept of sequence may be expanded to include generalizations pertaining to the order of units of study within any specific grade level.

When implementing desirable standards pertaining to the concepts of scope and sequence in the science curriculum, the following questions need ultimate solutions:

1. Which content in specific units of study is relevant for pupils to understand and attach meaning to in the elementary school science curriculum?
2. Which skills and attitudes should pupils gain in ongoing units of study science?

3. What is the best order (sequence) for learners to acquire these desired understandings, skills, and attitudes?
4. What criteria may be utilized to select relevant units of study in elementary school science?
5. What methods or approaches may be utilized to determine appropriate scope and sequence in diverse units of study in elementary school science?

The following units of study in elementary school science, among others, are commonly taught on the kindergarten level through grade six:

1. Our Pets
2. Insects—How they help and hinder us
3. Exploring space
4. Uses of Megnetism and electricity
5. Machines—How they help us
6. Ecology and a clean environment
7. Living things and prehistoric life
8. Our solar system
9. Air, Weather, and how it affects it
10. Plants and animals in our environment
11. The seasons—How they affect us
12. The changing surface on the earth
13. Stars, Constellations, and the Universe
14. Chemical changes, molecules, and atoms
15. How the human body works
16. Uses of sound and light
17. Heat and its many uses

There are significant questions that require careful consideration pertaining to the above-named unit titles:

1. Can well-developed criteria be formulated to determine on which grade level or grade levels each of the above units should be taught?
2. What are appropriate standards to utilize in determining the best order or sequence of these units of study within each grade level?

3. Should the scope of the science curriculum (breadth of unit titles) be broadened to incorporate more content from mathematics, social studies, language arts, and health?
4. Who should be involved in determining appropriate scope and sequence of units of instruction in elementary school science?

In Summary

A variety of interesting, purposeful, and meaningful learning experiences need to be provided for elementary school pupils in the science curriculum. The following learning activities are important for pupils in the science curriculum:

1. experimentation;
2. reading;
3. excursions;
4. construction activities;
5. educational television;
6. films, filmstrips, and slides;
7. written work;
8. art work;
9. dramatizations.

Teachers, principals, and supervisors must give careful considerations to scope (what is taught in science) and sequence (when pupils are to develop appropriate understandings, skills, and attitudes) in determining relevant units of study in elementary school science.

REFERENCES

Herman, Jerry J. *Developing an Effective Elementary Science Curriculum*. West Nyack,. New York: Parker Publishing Company, 1969.

Lewis, June E., and Irene C. Potter. *The Teaching of Science in the Elementary School*. Englewood Cliffs, New Jersey: Prentice-Hall, Inc., 1970.

Renner, John W., *et al*. *Teaching Science in the Elementary School*. Second Edition. New York: Harper and Row Publishers, Inc., 1973.

Rowe, Mary Budd. *Teaching Science as Continuous Inquiry*. New York: McGraw-Hill Book Company, 1973.

Victor, Edward. *Science for the Elementary School*. Fourth Edition. New York: The Macmillan Company, 1985. Chapters 6A and 6B.

Social Studies in the Elementary School

Since the world is 'shrinking' in size due to better transportation and communication, it is more important than ever before for pupils to study justifiable units in the social studies. The following problems on the world scene make it imperative that pupils have the needed understandings, skills, and attitudes to engage in problem solving activities in the classroom.

1. There are wars and threats of war between and among nations such as in the Middle East.
2. New nations are formed and the names of some countries no longer exist due to varying causes.
3. Friendships between and among nations change. Nations which formerly were friends become neutral toward each other; they also may become enemies. Friendship can be developed between countries which in the past had relations which were negative.
4. Selected countries may trade much with each other and engage in very little or no trade with other nations on the face of the world.
5. Certain countries have more of the necessary natural resources which make for a prosperous country as compared to other nations.
6. Technology and inventions change the ways of living of a particular subculture or country.

7. Languages that people speak in the world differ from each other thus making for difficulty in communicating ideas.
8. Differences in religious beliefs and doctrine in different countries of the world can make for misunderstandings among nations.
9. Countries of the world differ much from each other in military strength. Even a small country armed by a world power can become a threat to larger neighbouring countries which have less of the effective kinds of military hardware.
10. Leaders change in different nations of the world. Some of these changes come about through elections. Others come about through revolution and invasions.
11. Many changes occur on the local and state levels in such areas as education, welfare, housing, equality of opportunity, jobs, growth of cities, population changes, pollution, technology, and inventions.
12. There are nations of the world which have much influence over other less powerful countries. The more powerful nations of the world include the United States, the Soviet Union, Mainland China, France, Great Britain, and Japan.

Thus, it is important for pupils to have a good understanding of each person's relationships to others and of people interacting with their physical and cultural environment. Pupils must learn to get along well with classmates, school personnel, and others in their environment. Human beings in the world must understand others better, along with developing positive attitudes toward others, so that a better life can exist for all. Destroying property and lives through wars and other violent means hinders human beings from realizing their optimum. Too much time is spent destroying and ruining rather than building up and achieving within a nation as well as within the world. Elementary school pupils need to develop those understandings, skills, and attitudes which will assist them in becoming good citizens in a democratic society.

Objectives of the Social Studies

Each elementary school, as well as the entire school system, should spend an adequate amount of time in identifying important objectives for pupils to achieve in elementary school social studies.

There are numerous skills in the social studies which pupils should achieve to become more proficient citizens in a democracy. Among others, the following skills would be important for pupils to achieve:

1. **SKILLS OBJECTIVES**

1. Reading social studies content with understanding.
2. Using the card catalogue to locate needed reference surfaces.
3. Using appropriate word recognition techniques to identify new words.
4. Reading for a variety of purposes in the social studies.
5. Using the indes and table of contents to locate information.
6. Working effectively together with others in committees.
7. Dramatizing roles and events effectively from various units of study.
8. Using the problem solving approach effectively.
9. Evaluating content through the use of critical thinking.
10. Utilizing creative thinking in coming up with new solutions to problems.
11. Constructing and reading information from picture graphs, line graphs, bar graphs, and circle graphs.
12. Using a variety of reputable sources to gather information, such encyclopedias, almanacs, films, filmstrips, tapes, records, models, pictures, slides, and resource persons.
13. Presenting information clearly and effectively to classmates and other individuals in the environment.
14. Reading and comprehending current affairs items from recent newspapers and magazines.
15. Listening effectively to the contributions of others within committees as well as the class as a whole.
16. Comprehending the contents of news broadcasts and television reports pertaining to news items.
17. Being able to disagree politely with others and still present other points of view on a problem or question.
18. Making charts to convey information effectively in the social studies.

2. ATTITUDINAL OBJECTIVES

The quality of attitudes that pupils have certainly affects the number of understandings and skills that pupils will be developing. Negative attitudes hinder pupil achievement and a lack of optimum development will thus result. The following attitudes, among others, are important for pupils to achieve:

1. Working harmoniously with others in the environment.
2. Appreciating the problem solving approach in the social studies curriculum.
3. Appreciating the contributions of minority groups in developing the United States.
4. Valuing democracy as a form of government and as a way of life.
5. Appreciating creative ideas suggested by others in the solving of problems.
6. Valuing the inquiry approach and critical thinking in the social studies.
7. Wanting to develop important concepts and generalizations in the social studies.
8. Developing and/or maintaining a desire to read content for leisure time activities as it relates to ongoing units of study.
9. Wanting to utilize a variety of learning activities to solve problems.
10. Having a desire to identify and solve problems in society.
11. Feeling an obligation to participate effectively as a constructive member in society.
12. Respecting the thinking of others.
13. Appreciating the cultural products of people of other lands, such as art, music, architecture, language, and religious beliefs.
14. Wanting to develop the ability to present information clearly and accurately to others.
15. Desiring to keep up with current events and current issues as they happen in the world.
16. Wanting to utilize the card catalog, index, and table of contents to locate information.

17. Wanting to develop necessary skills to identify new words when reading social studies content.
18. Feeling the necessity of reading for a variety of purposes.
19. Wanting to attach meaning to social studies content through pantomiming, role playing, creative dramatics, the use of puppets, and other approaches.
20. Appreciating the use of graphs and charts in simplifying information in content pertaining to the social studies.
21. Wanting to listen carefully to the thinking of others.

3. UNDERSTANDINGS OBJECTIVES

Teachers, supervisors, and principals, cooperatively, should spend ample time in determining which objectives pupils are to achieve and realize. This is true not only of skills and attitudinal objectives but also of understanding objectives. Too frequently, no doubt, trivia has been taught pertaining to names, dates, and places in historical units in the social studies. These are vaguely remembered or forgotten by learners as time has moved on. Thus, it is important for understandings objectives to be carefully identified. The "explosion of knowledge" has made it doubly necessary to weed out that which is irrelevant and unimportant.

In many cases, understandings objectives which pupils are to realize will pertain to specific social studies units. A first grade unit on "The School" will have different understandings that pupils need to achieve as compared to a unit on "Visiting the Zoo" for that same age level of pupils. There are, however, major generalizations which pupils may achieve that cut across different units of study.

The following understandings objectives, among others, could be important for pupils to realize in a unit on Great Britain:

1. Great Britain is a leading manufacturing country in the world.
2. Many agricultural products are imported from other nations of the world to Great Britain.
3. Great Britain has exhibited much influence in world affairs.
4. This nation is a permanent member of the Security Council in the United Nations.

Trends in the Social Studies

Each elementary school should devote ample time to the study of trends in the teaching of elementary school social studies. Too often, social studies has consisted of pupils reading content from their textbooks. Social studies should not be a reading course. Reading social studies content is one learning activity, but it is not the only experience for pupils in the social studies curriculum. What can the elementary school do to keep up with recommendations for a modern programme of social studies?

Scope and Sequence

A modern programme of elementary school social studies places much emphasis upon good sequence among units of study. Too frequently, there has been little or no connection between and among units taught in sequence. One unit of study should be related to and lead harmoniously into the next unit of study. For example, if intermediate grade pupils are studying a unit on the age of discovery pertaining to the New World, a unit that would be related could be entitled "Colonization in the New World." An area of the world, of course, had to be discovered before it could be colonized. The two units would definitely be related to each other. Good sequence could then be a definite possibility between these two units in elementary school social studies. If first grade pupils are studying a unit on "Going to School" at the beginning of a school year, a unit on "Living in the Home" could come in proper sequence with good teaching. The school and its influence cannot be isolated from the home environment. The two environments interact; neither is an island unto itself.

For each grade level, cooperative efforts need to be put forth within an elementary school or several elementary schools to develop proper sequence in social studies units from kindergarten through grade twelve. Thus, the question arises as to which units should be taught first, second, third, fourth, and so forth for each of the grade levels in the elementary school.

Good teachers of social studies also need to think of proper sequence of learning activities within a unit. Generally, one would say that learning activities should progress from the simple to those which are more complex. This would be a gradual process. When thinking of sequence in learning within a specific social studies unit, which of the following learning activities should come first, second, third, fourth, fifth, and sixth pertaining to a unit entitled "Living on the Farm?"

1. Viewing and discussing a filmstrip entitled "Lets Visit the Farm."
2. Reading pages 110-115 from the textbook and discussing the contents.
3. Visiting a modern farm and discussing observations which were made.
4. Having the country agent present a set of slides and a talk relating to a modern farm.
5. Developing a frieze within a committee of four members; the frieze would pertain to selected scenes on modern farming practices and procedures.
6. Showing and discussing transparencies on farming using the overhead projector.

Each pupil has a different learning style just as teachers have different teaching styles. The teacher needs to select those learning activities which will help each learner achieve to his or her optimum. The following, among others, could help to provide for individual differences among pupils and also vary the kinds of learning activities that are provided:

1. making model villages, famous buildings, and toys;
2. constructing boats, cars, airplanes, and trucks;
3. making relief maps and globes relating to the area being studied in a unit;
4. developing books, scrolls, puppets, marionettes, and musical instruments;
5. making costumes pertaining to people of other lands;
6. making butter and a model dairy farm;
7. completing model circus scenes when studying the related unit;
8. making candles, dyeing cloth, and making an oxcart pertaining to units on "Colonization in the New World";
9. developing a pioneer kitchen and covered wagon when studying units on the westward movement;
10. developing dioramas, murals, models, friezes, cartoons, and illustrations pertaining to ongoing units of study;

11. making posters, booklets, and exhibits on important facets of the unit being studied;
12. reading from the textbook or textbooks, selected sections in the encyclopedia, and library books;
13. viewing films, filmstrips, slides, pictures, and other audio visual media;
14. listening to tapes and records;
15. taking an excursion;
16. interviewing competent resource personnel.

Readiness for Learning

There are several ways in which to think of readiness on the part of pupils to benefit from specific or given units of study in the social studies.

First of all, educators generally believe that pupils can benefit from more complex units of study than was thought possible a decade and longer ago. For many years, it was believed that pupils, for example, should study units on the home and school on the first grade level since these were 'close' to the pupil. Pupils experience the home and the school; thus, there is this closeness between the unit being studied and the personal experiences of pupils. On the second grade level, pupils would study units on the city, neighbourhood, or shopping centres as they exist in medium and large size cities. These units would branch out further from pupils' environment as compared to the home and school which were units of study for the first grade level. By the time pupils are in the fifth grade, they may be studying units on Canada, Mexico, and historical units pertaining to the United States. Thus, pupils on these grade levels would be studying units which would be located outside of the United States. Historical units on the United States would deal with the past which is removed in time from the everyday experiences that elementary school pupils have. On the sixth grade level, pupils could be studying units on The Common Market Countries, the Middle East, the Soviet Union, Australia, Japan, Southeast Asia, and Brazil. These areas would be further removed from the everyday experiences of pupils in the elementary school as compared to social studies units being studied on previous grade levels.

It may be rather arbitrary in some cases as to which grade level specific units in the social studies should be taught. The television set in the home has brought the faraway near to the child. In their homes and in school, pupils can view television programmes which deal with happenings in London, Paris, Moscow, Rio de Janeiro, Buenas Aires, Melbourne, Montreal, and other areas of the world. Thus, elementary school pupils today have much more opportunity to view reality on television screens pertaining to faraway places as compared to learners a generation ago or longer. More accurate, colourful, interesting illustrations in magazines pertaining to faraway places are available to learners than ever before. More pupils in the United States have had opportunities to travel in the United States and abroad to see scenes and sights than was true formerly. It is no wonder that pupils in the elementary school may be able to benefit from more complex units of study in the social studies than ever before. Many excellent social studies units on Mexico have been taught on the second grade level. These teachers may be very knowledgeable about Mexico and have the necessary materials and teaching skills to develop interest in this unit. Thus, the social studies curriculum can be adapted to the pupil rather than adjusting the child to the curriculum. Each child should attach meaning to what is being learned as well as have developed interest in the ongoing unit of study.

Teaching Units in Depth

Many teachers of social studies have a tendency to teach units utilizing the survey approach. Thus, for example, many units would be taught on the sixth grade level as would be indicated by the following unit titles which would need to be completed in a school year:

1. Visiting Japan
2. Living in Australia
3. The Common Market Nations
4. Canada—Our Neighbour to the North
5. Mexico—Our Neighbour to the South
6. The Soviet Union
7. Mainland China
8. Living in India and Pakistan

9. Islands of the Pacific
10. Brazil—The largest country in South America
11. Spanish Speaking countries of South America
12. Countries of Southeast Asia
13. The Antarctic and Its Future
14. Nations of Central Europe
15. The Middle East
16. Visiting Spain and Portugal

It is quite obvious from the many unit titles listed that the survey approach to teaching social studies would be utilized. Pupils would get a smattering of content from many units of study rather than developing learnings in depth from a few carefully selected units. The faculty members of an elementary school should rather select six or seven units to be taught in a specific school year. Thus pupils would be able to study in depth each unit that is taught. For example in a unit pertaining to Brazil, the following understanding could be achieved by pupils:

1. the art, architecture, and music of Brazil;
2. the political system of that country;
3. the geography of Brazil such as rivers, plateaus, valleys, and plains;
4. the past which lead to present day happenings (history);
5. the culture of various groups and subgroups of pupils;
6. different socio-economic levels and their effects upon group behaviour (sociology);
7. exports and imports of Brazil as well as goods and services produced in that country.

It is certain that pupils will understand various people of the world better if units are taught in depth. Limited understandings can be developed of any unit in social studies if a teacher needs to hurry through the teaching of many units in a school year. Pupils need to have opportunities to study human beings by viewing them from the different disciplines that make up the social sciences, namely, history, geography, political science, sociology, anthropology, and economics. It is certain that pupils won't understand the people of Brazil, for example, by studying the system of government of that country only. Pupils also need to understand the values, customs, religious beliefs, norms of society and subcultures, vocations and occupations, products and services produced and sold, imports and exports, the history, and geography of Brazil.

The Structure of Knowledge

Educators such as teacher, principals, and supervisors, alone should not determine what is to be taught in social studies. The content of the social sciences is too complex to be selected by educators alone when developing the social studies curriculum. Too frequently, social studies teachers have taught what is unimportant, trivial, and irrelevant. Social scientists should have an important role in selecting social studies content for pupils in the elementary school. This is not to say that social scientists alone would determine content in units of study in the social studies. Certainly, teachers, principals, and supervisors will have a voice in the selection. Elementary school pupils also have an important task in selecting content for different units of study. The social studies teacher must develop pupil interest and purpose in various units of study. Thus, the teacher will have interesting, appealing bulletin boards for pupils to view. If pupils are to begin a unit on Japan, perhaps the following pictures can be placed on the bulletin board with the interesting title or caption:

1. Japanese workers on an assembly line in a modern factory;
2. a home scene which is accurate and representative pertaining to a Japanese family;
3. men in fishing boats which clearly illustrates important facets of this industry;
4. a representative urban scene in Tokyo or other large city in Japan;
5. farmers in a rural area taking care of their crops and livestock.

The teacher's goal is to get pupils in wanting to ask many questions about Japan when viewing the bulletin board display. The following questions may be asked by pupils:

1. How are cars assembled on an assembly line in Japan?
2. What are some leading products manufactured in Japan;
3. Who buys these products?

4. How do Japanese and American homes differ from each other? How are they alike?
5. How important is the fishing industry to Japan's economy?
6. How does Tokyo differ from New York or Chicago? How are they alike?
7. What products are produced on Japanese farms and how are they sent to market?
8. How do farm products in Japan eventually get to the consumer?
9. How important are the following concepts to the Japanese economy?
   (a) imports;
   (b) exports.

If the social studies teacher is teaching this same unit on Japan, individually or cooperatively with pupils, interest centres can be developed. These items could be placed on a table or several tables in the classroom. As an example, the following objects pertaining to Japan could be placed on an interest centre:

1. toys representative of what Japanese children play with;
2. traditional dress of Japanese people;
3. models of Japanese made cars;
4. a relief map of Japan;
5. a model farm scene in rural Japan.

Pupils individually could ask questions of each other and of the teacher pertaining to these items on the interest centre. A good class discussion could follow the identification of these problem areas or questions. Pupils, as an example, may ask the following questions pertaining to the interest centre:

1. How are Japanese toys different from those that American children play with?
2. How have patterns of dress changed in Japan during the years?
3. How are Japanese cars assembled?
4. What is the land like in Japan and what kinds of crops are grown there?

5. How does farming in Japan differ from that in the United States?

Much research could be done by pupils using a variety of resources such as reference books, records, interviews, slides, filmstrips, maps, globes, and films to get needed information to answer these questions.

In the preceding examples, it is noticed that pupils should have ample opportunities to identify questions and problems for which information can be gathered. The interests of pupils are very important when thinking of learning activities which should be provided for learners in elementary school social studies. However, social scientists also have an important contribution to make in helping to determine key ideas or structural ideas which pupils should develop inductively pertaining to each social studies unit. These social scientists would specialize in their area of speciality from one of the following disciplines in the school sciences.

1. anthropology;
2. geography;
3. history;
4. sociology;
5. political science or civics;
6. economics.

Balance in Units Title

An important question that an elementary school must answer pertaining to the social studies curriculum in which unit titles should be taught in the different grade levels so that balance exists among the different areas of the world that pupils study. To be sure, pupils could devote most of their time in the social studies studying about the contributions and development of the Western world. This is important for pupils. However, pupils also need to become thoroughly familiar, among other areas, with the Middle East, the Far East, India, and Pakistan, and nations of Africa. In fact, many major important happenings are occurring in these areas. Thus, pupils need to have a thorough understanding of the Western world, but the changes, development, and contributions of the non-western world need also to be adequately emphasized in a modern elementary school social studies programme.

Faculty members in an elementary school and the total school system involved in teaching the social studies should make a thorough study as to units taught presently in the different grade levels of the elementary school. Do revisions need to be made so that some kind of rational balance exists in different units that are taught in the social studies? Based upon diagnosis as to the units presently taught in the social studies in the elementary school, faculty members can make rational decisions pertaining to pupils obtaining a world view which is comprehensive in the social studies.

Stating Objectives Precisely

There is a trend in elementary school social studies in stating objectives precisely. This means that observers generally would agree as to what is to be taught by looking at a statement of objectives. Thus pupil achievement can be measured if objectives are stated behaviourally. Objectives which are written behaviourally state what the learner is to do as a result of teaching. Consider the following objectives:

1. The pupil will write a fifty word paper on the Amazon river.
2. Pupils will develop democratic behaviour.

In the first objective pupils will, as a result of teaching, develop understanding, concepts, and generalizations pertaining to the Amazon river. Ultimately, pupils will be able to write a fifty word paper on the Amazon River. In the second objective, much vagueness exists as to what will be taught. There are various interpretations as to what democratic behaviour is. The objective does not state how much of this behaviour pupils are to develop. Thus, it cannot be measured if learners are achieving the objective.

Teachers must be precise in writing their objectives so that it can be determined what will be taught. In educational literature today much emphasis is placed upon teacher accountability. The teacher is then held accountable for what pupils are to learn. Principals and supervisors can then determine what will be taught to pupils. Also, it is easier to select learning activities which will guide learners in achieving objectives if each objective is clearly written. It is difficult to select appropriate learning activities if vague, ambiguous objectives are written. The final question arises as to how pupils are to be assessed if the objectives lack clarity. In situations like these it cannot be determined if objectives have been achieved.

A word of caution is necessary here. To be sure trivia and unimportant learnings can be stated precisely when writing specific objectives. The following objectives can be written precisely where no room exists in interpretation as to what will be taught:

1. The pupil will list in writing the capital city of each country in South America.
2. Pupils will recite orally five leading farm crops of each country of South America.
3. Pupils will list four leading manufactured products of each South American country.

In the above objectives pupils have used the lowest level of cognition only and that is recall of facts. To be sure, there are important facts for pupils to learn. These facts, however, must be selected very carefully since there is much content that needs to be learned in different disciplines of knowledge. The teacher needs to have pupils engage in critical thinking, creative thinking, and problem solving. To be sure pupils engage in recall of facts when engaging in critical and creative thinking as well as problem solving. However, pupils do something with the facets when engaging in higher levels of thinking. Comparing statement and evaluating them, coming up with unique, new, novel ideas, and the solving of problems is very important in a modern programme of elementary school social studies. A democratic society demands that pupils become proficient in higher levels of thinking so that individuals become more effective in decision-making.

Continuous Comprehensive Evaluation of Achievement

If teachers are to evaluate pupil achievement well, continuous evaluation needs to be in evidence. Pupils need to be evaluated comprehensively so that all facets of achievement are assessed.

A teacher who does not continuously evaluate pupil achievement will not know at what point or points pupils are not making continuous progress. One can think of pupil achievement as being represented by points on a line or line segment. For pupils to achieve continuously on this line, evaluation needs to be done continuously. Otherwise, the social studies teacher definitely cannot know if pupils are achieving well. If pupils have not developed a particular concept or generalization, they may not be successful in moving on to more complex learnings. Teachers of social studies must think of proper sequence for pupils in learning; otherwise continuous progress may not come about in learner achievement. Sequential learnings on the part of children can come about only when teachers assess learner progress continuously.

Too often, it has been thought and felt that paper-pencil tests alone can adequately assess pupil achievement. To be sure, in many situations, good evaluation can come about with the use of true-false, multiple-choice, completion, matching, and essay test items. This would be true, especially, of understandings or cognitive domain objectives. To evaluate skills objectives and attitudinal objectives, other forms of assessment need to be utilized. If a pupil is to develop skill in gathering information from using a set or several sets of reputable encyclopedias, hardly would a paper-pencil test alone evaluate pupils' achievement effectively in this area. It would be good to actually observe pupils to determine if they can do the following when looking up information from encyclopedias:

1. The pupils can identify the correct topic heading for the information he is to gather. For example, if the pupils is to gather information on opium in a unit on the harmful use of drugs, which heading would he look under in the appropriate reference books?
2. The pupil knows the letters of the alphabet and can find the appropriate place in the encyclopedia from which information is to be gathered.
3. The learner can comprehend the contents well when gathering information.
4. The child can take notes over what he reads and develop an outline in proper sequence when utilizing the notes.
5. The pupil can write a summary of the ideas read from the encyclopedia using topic sentences, proper sequence in paragraphs, unity within paragraphs, and the necessary skills in the mechanics of writing (capitalization, punctuation, spelling, handwriting, and sentence structure).
6. The learner can present ideas, gained from research, effectively to the class. Listeners then have an inward desire in wanting to get major concepts and generalizations presented by the speaker.

7. The presenter utilizes appropriate audio-visual materials, such as pictures, slides, drawings, and the overhead projector, when presenting his findings to the class.

When utilizing these guidelines to evaluate pupil achievement, the present level of achievement of each child must be assessed and then assist each learner to progress continuously to realize optimum achievement. The following is of utmost importance to remember: no two pupils will be at the same place in achievement when realizing these guidelines or standards. Each pupil is at a different level of achievement.

It is important also to think of comprehensive evaluation in the social studies. Too frequently, pupil achievement has been evaluated pertaining to understandings objectives only. To be sure, these are very important objectives to achieve. Secondly in frequency of evaluation in terms of objectives, assessing skills which pupils have developed has been given some considerations. The category of attitudinal objectives, no doubt, is least often evaluated.

It is indeed very difficult to write a paper-pencil test to evaluate pupils' attitudes. There are standardized tests which evaluate pupils in the area of attitudes of the affective domain. The social studies teacher must always observe pupils to notice changes in feelings, values, and beliefs. Is there a positive change in this area from day to day or for longer periods of time? Generally, longer periods of time are needed to see growth in the affective domain. It may, of course, take years to change some attitudes. The teacher needs to evaluate himself in terms of the following criteria when thinking of assisting pupils in attitude development:

1. Are pupils interested in learning activities provided for them? If not, what kinds of activities should be selected so that positive attitudes may develop toward learning?
2. Do pupils understand what is taught? If learnings are not meaningful for pupils, much turning off will occur by pupils in realizing objectives.
3. Does the teacher assist each learner to be successful in the school situation? It is no wonder that pupils develop negative attitudes if they feel unsuccessful.
4. Are pupils being guided in social development so that they like working with others in committees, the class as a whole, and others in the larger environment?

5. Is the pupil developing and/or maintaining feelings of an adequate self concept? If learners feel inadequate to the tasks at hand, they will generally lack in total school achievement.
6. Does the teacher respect all pupils regardless of socio-economic levels, colour of skin, religious beliefs, and status within the class setting?
7. Are pupils assisted in developing respect for each other? Too frequently, pupils call each other mean names which cause feelings of resentment and reprisal.
8. Are pupils realizing desired understandings and skills through carefully selected units which assist in developing positive attitudes? No doubt, some units in the social studies would be eliminated and others would be added when answering this question. More social studies units need to be taught which will guide learners in personal and social development.

Thus, it is necessary to evaluate pupils achievement in all facets of development using a variety of evaluation techniques. One very important evaluation technique to utilize is teacher observation. Teacher observation needs to become objective in evaluating pupil achievement. Through reading, study, thought, empathy, and understanding, teachers can guide pupils in personal and social adjustment as well as other facets of development.

Being A Democratic Human Being

In a society which emphasizes democracy as a form of government, it is important for schools to stress a philosophy of education which is in harmony with ideals of democratic living. American society and its schools should emphasize a consistent philosophy which would pertain to democracy as a form of government and also as a way of life. Teachers of social studies have gone to extremes when providing a psychological environment which was to assist pupils in developing to their optimum. Unfortunately these extremes did not harmonize with basic ideas of democratic living, nor did they help learners achieve to their highest possible capabilities. Consider the teacher on one end of the continuum who expects a pin-drop quiet classroom. Pupils are asked to speak only when the teacher asks the questions. The question asked at a given time may be directed to one pupil only.

The answer required is factual and a 'right' answer is wanted. Critical thinking, creative thinking, and problem solving would not be stressed. Each pupil would constantly face the front with little or no interaction with other pupils. Pupils would be reprimanded in front of others for 'infrastructure' of strict rules and regulations. The teacher may strictly play the role of a policeman and disciplinarian in the classroom.

Contrast the autocratic teacher described above with one who is anarchic. The anarchic teacher would represent the other extreme on the continuum. This teacher would permit pupils generally to do as they wish with few, or perhaps, no restraints. The anarchic teacher would be the leader in the class situation if requested by pupils. Pupils could roam around the room freely with little or no purpose involved in these movements. Pupils would visit with each other whenever and wherever they wished with little or no respect for others.

Democracy as a way of living in the class situation would stress that there is mutual respect between and among pupils and faculty members.

Using Maps and Globes in the Social Studies

Ample opportunities should be given to pupils in the use of maps and globes. With a 'shrinking world' due to better transportation and communication, it is more important than ever before for pupils to develop necessary skills to use maps and globes effectively. It is difficult to say in which country of the world a crisis will develop that would affect the interests of leading countries in the world such as the United States and the Soviet Union. India and Pakistan, Berlin, the Cuban missile crises, and the Middle East have been critical areas in the world which could have involved major world powers in a confrontation. It is important for pupils to have ample knowledge pertaining to place geography whereby areas of the world can be located on maps and globes. It is also important for pupils to develop more complex understandings such as how climate affects the kinds of crops grown in a given area, or how latitude affects the kind of temperature reading a given area of the world will have.

The following represent selected major understandings that pupils should develop pertaining to the use of maps and globes:

1. Pupils should realize that distances can be computed by using the scale given on the map or globe. Maps and globes vary as to the number of miles that would be represented by one inch as given in the scale of miles.
2. Specific places on the earth can be located using the concepts of 'latitude' and 'longitude.'
3. North latitude refers to distance in degrees north of the equator while south latitude refers to distance in degrees south of the equator.
4. East longitude has reference to distance in degrees east of the prime meridian while west longitude relates to distance in degrees west of the prime meridian.
5. Distances north and south of the equator are measured along a meridian while distances east or west of the prime meridian are measured along a parallel.
6. The earth rotates from a west to east direction once each 24 hours (causes for day and night can be shown by using a flashlight, a darkened room, and a globe which represents a model of the plant earth). The imaginary line on which the earth rotates is called its axis.
7. The earth revolves around the sun approximately once in 365¼ days. On March 21 and September 21, approximately, the sun is directly overhead at noon on the equator. Whereas on June 21, approximately, the sun is directly overhead at noon on the Tropic of Cancer located 23½ degrees north of the equator; on December 21, the sun is overhead at noon on the Tropic of Capricorn located 23½ degrees south of the equator. Other factors involved in determining temperature readings include elevation of land being considered, ocean currents, and nearness to bodies of water.
8. The axis of the earth on a globe points toward the north star. (On a bright day at noon each pupil can look directly at his shadow; he is facing north at this time. Pupils while facing north can be shown the position of the North Star as it would be at night).
9. Maps do not represent as accurately the surface of the earth as compared to globes. With the use of maps, however,

a certain continent, country, or area can be studied more conveniently than on a globe since it will be represented on a larger area.

10. Some of the symbols used in legends on maps and globes are standard symbols. For example, symbols on maps which represented hospitals, railroad tracks, and paved roads are standard symbols. There are also symbols which vary from legend to legend on different maps and globes that are used.
11. Any circle has 360 degrees. There are 24 time zones in the world thus making each time zone have an approximate value of 15 degrees of longitude.
12. A hemisphere is represented by half of the earth; four hemispheres can be referred to—southern, northern, western, and eastern.
13. The direction of north on a map pertains to going directly to the North Pole; whereas the direction of south means to go directly to the South Pole. There are different projections of maps so the direction of north may not always be 'up' on the map.
14. Low, middle, and high latituded refer to specific areas or parts of maps and globes, such as the low latitudes lying north and south of the equator while the high latitudes are located around the north and south poles. The middle latitudes refer to those parts lying between the low latitudes and the high latitudes.

Current Affairs in the Social Studies

To keep the social studies curriculum updated, each elementary school should have a good current affairs programme in all grades. Units which deal with history, geography, economics, sociology, anthropology, and political science may become outdated unless recent happenings, events, and issues are brought in to the social studies programme. If the teacher is teaching a unit on "The United States Today," certainly the unit can become somewhat obsolete unless current affairs are brought into the ongoing unit of study. Too frequently, social studies teachers in teaching historical units have delved too thoroughly, no doubt, in units that deal with early American history such as "The Age of Exploration," "Colonization in the New World," "The Beginning of the United States," and others. Units which deal with the present time then are slighted or, perhaps, even omitted. The present is very important in elementary school children since this is the world they live in now and understand better than any other period of time in American history. The pupil needs to understand present trends, issues, problems, and strengths in the United States if he is to become a participating member in society working toward identifying problems and solving them. Certainly, a democratic citizen is one who greatly appreciates the positive in American society and yet works for an even stronger democracy as a form of government as well as a way of life.

Boundaries of countries change. Only with keeping up with the news can be knowledgeable of new nations which arise and those which no longer exist. Witness the great number of new countries that have arisen on the continent of Africa after World War II. It is difficult for any individual to become thoroughly familiar with each country in Africa. Well educated people have discovered to their amazement that they didn't know the names of certain countries on that continent that came up on news broadcasts. The surface of the earth has also changed in terms of geographical features. Earthquakes, volcanoes, folds, and faults have altered the surface of the earth. Current affairs can help pupils keep up-to-date in terms of happenings in the field of geography. Certainly, space feats and explorations have done much to change our knowledge of the moon and Mars, in particular.

There are many important current issues and events in the field of economics. The rate of employment and unemployment varies in per cent from time to time within most countries. Many countries have problems in balancing imports with exports. This situation can change from time to time. Thus, much emphasis can be placed upon economics in a modern programme of current affairs instruction. The total amount of money involved in the gross national product (GNP) of any country can vary from year to year. Current affairs item could also assist learners to understand the meaning of inflation as it pertains to buying goods and services in any country.

In the area of sociology, many current affair items need to be studied to keep this area of the social science updated. Over-population, of course, has not always been a problem on the face of the earth. Today, it is a major problem in many countries of the world. Norms of a subculture change and are modified due to reevaluating of beliefs, values, and ideals. Norms also change as a result of borrowing ideas from other subcultures and societies. New inventions also help bring on changes within any group of people.

In the area of anthropology, current events and issues can and do become a part of news broadcasts. A subculture is discovered for the first time and this group is in the stone age. New excavations release findings pertaining to a particular tribe of Indians or civilizations of long ago. Recommendations for improving schools, homes, and other institutions in society are made by leading anthropologists in the United States.

Political science and current affairs instruction have much in common. The Security Council, General Assembly, and the Office of the Secretariat of the United Nations continually make news headlines in terms of decisions and recommendations made which affect various nations of the world. The United Nations, of course, is an attempt made at some kind of world government. It is rather common for listeners to news broadcasts on radio and television to hear of political leaders of different nations having left their positions for various reasons and a new government has stepped in. This presents opportunities for pupils to learn more about the forms of government of different nations of the world. When pupils study such units as "Living in Great Britain" or "Visiting Canada," They may be developing learnings in depth pertaining to Parliament, the Prime Minister, and other facets of government of these two countries. When listening to news broadcasts, one hears of decisions made by Parliament of either Great Britain or Canada. Thus, items pertaining to political science can well become an important part of the current affairs programme in the modern elementary school.

Using the Bulletin Board in Current Affairs

The social studies teacher needs to think of ways to stimulate pupil interest in current affairs instruction. To be sure, some pupils have little or no interest in this area. Thus, the teacher must provide interesting learning activities which will capture the interest of pupils. One way to do this would be to develop a bulletin board display pertaining to pictures of current happenings. An appealing caption should be a part of the display. The caption orientates the reader to the contents on the bulletin board. As an example, pictures pertaining to the following happenings can be neatly placed on the bulletin board:

1. conflict in the Middle East;
2. the President of the United States presenting the state of the union message;
3. the Security Council in session at the United Nations headquarters in New York;
4. the energy crisis.

Pupils with teacher guidance may ask the following questions pertaining to these pictures:

1. What will eventually happen in the Middle East between competing and opposing sides?
2. What recommendations did the President make in his annual state of the union message?
3. How are decisions made in the Security Council?
4. How can the energy crisis be solved?

Answers to the above problems should be discussed in an informal atmosphere. Respect for the thinking of others is of utmost importance. All pupils should participate in the discussion if possible. Pupils who dominate the discussion or participate excessively should be guided in sensing the importance of all pupils participating in the ongoing learning activity. The self-concept of each pupil is very important. Each pupil should be praised even if there is a very, very slight degree of improvement in performance. This helps pupils in developing self-confidence and in wishing to participate in current affairs programmes. By getting pupils interested in the ongoing current affairs programme in the elementary school, learners will transfer these learnings to situations involving listening to news broadcasts on radio and television in the home.

In Summary

Teachers, principals, and supervisors must study the following in working toward a modern social studies curriculum:

1. objectives in the social studies;
2. trends in teaching social studies;
3. scope and sequence;

4. materials used in teaching;
5. readiness for learning;
6. number of units taught in a year;
7. emphasis to be placed on the structure of knowledge;
8. balance in unit titles;
9. the use of specific objectives;
10. thorough evaluation of pupil achievement;
11. democratic living in the classroom;
12. the use of maps and globes in social studies units;
13. current affairs in social studies units;
14. developing pupil interest in current affairs.

REFERENCES

Ediger, Marlow and Digumarti Bhaskara Rao. *Teaching Social Studies Successfully*. New Delhi, India: Discovery Publishing House, 2003.

Ediger, Marlow and Digumarti Bhaskara Rao. *Elementary Curriculum*. New Delhi: Discovery Publishing House, 2003.

Issues in the Social Studies Curriculum

There are numerous issues in the social studies curriculum which educators should consider and attempt to resolve. Each issue must be understood in terms of its strengths and weaknesses. Thus, teachers, principals, and supervisors may be able to eliminate or modify identified weaknesses within an issue. Objectives, learning experiences, and evaluation procedures utilized in teaching-learning situations should be grounded in recommended principles of learning and teaching as well as in a consistent, sound philosophy of education.

Use of Social Studies Textbooks

Elementary school social studies textbooks have, in selected situations, been greatly misused in classroom settings. Thus, for example, in a class of thirty pupils, all students have been studying and reading content from the same page at the same time. This violates providing for individual differences among learners in a class who differ much from each other in capacity, achievement, interest, motivation, and socio-economic levels.

Elementary school social studies textbooks may be misused if the following methods of teaching are followed:

1. The content of the text is followed in sequence as written by the author with all learners being on the same page at the same time.
2. The teacher does not provide adequate readiness experiences for pupils prior to reading content.

3. A lack of creativity is in evidence in teaching when the teacher utilizing teaching suggestions contained in the teacher's manual section only, related to the elementary social studies textbook used by learners.
4. Pupils not reading up to the level of achievement demanded by the series of social studies textbooks being utilized hinder optimal achievement on the part of these learners.
5. Proficient readers reading well above the expectations of the content contained in the social studies texts may become bored and create discipline problems due to a lack of challenge in reading content.

Elementary school social studies textbooks may be wisely used if the following teaching procedures are utilized:

1. Prior to reading content from a social studies text, the pupil should have ample opportunities to gain related background information. The ideas will sound more familiar to pupils when reading content if needed background information has been developed.
2. While background information is being developed through viewing related pictures, filmstrips, and films, along with other needed learning activities, pupils should see new words in print which they will meet later on in reading a given selection. Through the use of audio-visual aids, pupils may attach meaning to these terms.
3. Ultimately, pupils should have some questions in mind whereby they would read selection from the social studies text to get related information.
4. Following the reading of a given selection in the elementary social studies textbook, pupils may reveal understandings in satisfying ways such as the following:
   (a) discussing the contents using higher levels of thinking;
   (b) developing an illustration, frieze, or diorama pertaining to content read;
   (c) dramatizing selected parts of content comprehended;
   (d) making models and objects related to information obtained from the social studies textbook;

(e) reading related library books and presenting content to other learners within a committee;

(f) developing a mural within a committee setting;

(g) writing a summary or outline over content read;

(h) reporting to the class selected relevant main ideas gained from the reading activity;

(i) developing a 'movie set' and putting in related content covering what had been read;

(j) letting pupils determine how they wish to reveal what has been gained in terms of content from the ongoing reading activity.

Inductive Versus Deductive Learning

Social studies educators have rather recently stressed the importance of pupils achieving learnings inductively. Thus, in inductive learning, the role of the teacher consists of:

1. guiding pupil achievement rather than serving as a lecturer or explainer of content;
2. stimulating pupils in identifying problems and working toward desired solutions;
3. being a good asker of questions rather than a dispenser of information. Questions need to be asked in proper sequence;
4. helping pupils realize desired generalizations and main ideas as a result of interacting with a variety of learning experiences;
5. developing positive attitudes within learners in wanting to discover facts, concepts, conclusions, and methods of working;
6. helping pupils obtain needed materials and aids necessary in inductive learning.

Disadvantages given for inductive learning include the following:

1. It may take much time in helping pupils achieve learnings inductively as compared to deductively.
2. It may not be necessary for pupils to discover content which has been discovered and recorded by others.
3. Deductive learnings may be presented to pupils in a purposeful and interesting manner.

4. A skillful and responsible teacher can teach well using either the inductive or deductive approach.

Group Work Versus Individual Efforts

There are plans in education whereby pupils could learn on an individual basis only. This would be true of the following plans in teaching-learning situations:

1. *Individualized reading*. Here pupils individually select and read a library book of their own choosing related to a social studies unit. Following the reading of the library book, the teacher may have a conference with the pupil to assess comprehension.
2. *Individualized spelling*. Pupils individually with teacher guidance identify a set of spelling words to master. The set of words could come from an ongoing unit of study in the social studies. Thus, in a unit on the Middle Ages, a specific learner may study the correct spelling of words such as manor, serf, nobleman, castle, knight, chivalry, crusaders, moat, drawbridge, and tournament.
3. *Writing activities*. At a writing centre, a pupil would select a picture of his or her own choosing to write about. Thus, if pupils are studying a unit of "Visiting a Farm," a learner may select from among the following a related picture to write about: tractors with air-conditioned cabs and power steering; dairy cows in a barn and a pipeline milker; sileage being augured down from a silo to a herd of hungry beef cattle; and laying hens in cages receiving mash using automated procedures.

There are many other good learning activities which may be mentioned pertaining to pupils learning on an individual basis only. However, there are selected questions which need to be asked concerning learning experiences whereby pupils develop learnings on an individual basis as compared to pupils working in committees or large group instruction.

1. How can balance in the curriculum be developed and maintained which emphasizes individual as well as committee work by learners?
2. How much emphasis should be placed upon pupils developing well individually as well as socially?

3. Which criteria should the teacher follow in teaching-learning situations pertaining to having pupils develop well individually as well as socially?

General Versus Specific Objectives

How specific should educational objectives be stated in the social studies? Advantages given for specific objectives in teaching-learning situations include the following:

1. Clearly stated objectives are necessary for good teaching to occur. Vague objectives, according to some educators, indicate a lack of clarity as to what will be taught.
2. With clearly stated objectives, it can be measured if pupils have or have not achieved the desired ends.
3. Quality learning experiences can be selected only if the objectives are clearly stated. Thus, learning experiences must relate directly to the chosen ends.
4. Measurable objectives and related learning experiences make it possible to determine the degree to which pupils are making progress.

Disadvantages given for utilizing behaviourally stated objectives are the following:

1. Relevant behaviours that pupils are to achieve cannot be stated precisely such as pupils developing an adequate self-concept or developing feeling of respect toward others.
2. Trivia may be taught if measurable objectives alone are used in teaching-learning situations.
3. Major emphasis should be placed upon selecting learning experiences rather than objectives for pupils to achieve.

When focusing upon learning experiences as compared to educational objectives in teaching-learning situations, the following kinds of learning activities would be better to emphasize:

1. those which require critical thinking, creative thinking, and problem solving;
2. those which develop feelings of appreciation and respect toward others;
3. those which aid pupils in developing a healthy self concept.

The Structure of Knowledge

Various educators in elementary school social studies have emphasized that pupils should achieve key structural ideas as identified by social scientists. These social scientists from colleges and universities include historians, geographers, political scientists, anthropologists, sociologists, and economists. The methods that each of these social scientists utilizes should also be used by elementary school children, according to select social studies educators. Advantages given for using this approach in teaching elementary school social studies would be the following:

1. Pupils would be achieving relevant social studies concepts and generalizations.
2. Learners need to use appropriate methods of gathering data, such as using primary sources of information as historians do or using and making maps and globes to gather and summarize data as geographers do.
3. Teachers have more security in teaching of selected vocabulary terms, main ideas, generalizations, and structural ideas pertaining to each social science disciplines. Thus, statements of structural ideas as gathered by social scientists would be available to public school teachers to implement in teaching-learning situations.

Disadvantages inherent in using the structure of knowledge concept in teaching the social studies would be the following:

1. Pupils may not be interested nor perceive purpose in gaining structural ideas.
2. Methods that social scientists use in gathering information may not harmonize with the needs and abilities of elementary school pupils.
3. Within each social science discipline, social scientists may not be able to agree upon relevant structural ideas.
4. An adult-centred social studies curriculum may be in evidence if pupils are to achieve structural ideas as identified by social scientists in their area of speciality.

New Disciplines in the Social Studies

Older disciplines making up the elementary school social studies curriculum include history, geography, and political science.

Newer disciplines more recently incorporated into the social studies programme include economics, anthropology, and sociology. Psychology and philosophy may also be included as newer disciplines. Reasons given for expanding the scope of the social studies curriculum include the following:

1. It was not adequate to study human beings from the point of view of history, geography, and political science only. Human beings should also be studied from the social science, disciplines of economics, anthropology, and sociology, as well as psychology and philosophy.
2. Pupils should learn and utilize the methods of gathering information that social scientists utilize who specialize in the different social science disciplines mentioned in number one.
3. The social studies would become more relevant in the lives of pupils if additional social science areas were added to the social studies curriculum, namely, economics, anthropology and sociology.

There are selected questions which may be asked pertaining to the different social science disciplines which provide content in the social studies.

1. How can balance be maintained among history, geography, political science, anthropology, sociology, and economics in the social studies curriculum?
2. How can the different social science disciplines become a part of an integrated social studies curriculum?
3. Which of these disciplines, if any, should become the basis for unit planning?
4. Can the classroom teacher have knowledge of diverse methods that social scientists in their area of speciality use?
5. Do public schools have aids and materials for pupils to utilize in working and inquiring as social scientists do?
6. Can the scope of elementary social studies become too broad when additional social science disciplines aid in providing content in the social studies?

The Child and the Teacher in Determining the Curriculum

An important issue in elementary school social studies that needs resolving pertains to who should select educational objectives, learning experiences, and evaluation procedures. There are selected questions which need appropriate responses.

1. Who chiefly should determine what pupils are to learn? The teacher? The child? The teacher and the child? Should other individuals be involved in deciding what pupils are to learn such as principals, supervisors, parents, members of boards of education, and diverse organisation within the community?
2. Who should select learning activities to achieve these desired objectives or ends?
3. Who should sequence learning experiences for pupils? Should the teacher or the child, or both, be involved in determining sequence in learnings for pupils? What role should the programmer have in sequencing learnings for pupils?
4. Who should be involved in assessing pupil achievement? What role should standardized achievement tests play in evaluating pupil achievement? Should pupil achievement be assessed in terms of specific or behaviourally stated objectives? To what degree should the learner and / or the teacher be involved in determining the achievement of pupils?

Programmed Learning and the Social Studies

Programmed learning using microcomputers or textbooks has contributed much toward thinking in education.

1. Pupils progress in very small steps, generally insuring learner success in each step of learning.
2. Pupils basically know immediately if they are right or wrong in terms of responses given in programmed learning.
3. Learners individually may work at their own optimal achievement in programmed learning.
4. Programmers develop their materials so that pupils feel rewarded by being successful at each step of learning.
5. Pupils can become independent learners when pursuing sequential steps in programmed materials.

There are selected differences in programmed materials that are sold on the market. However, there are also may basic agreements in philosophy as to what should comprise content in programmed learning. For example, a programmed book or booklet may follow these criteria:

1. Pupils look at a small picture or pictures.
2. Content is read by learners below these pictures.
3. Pupils then respond to a completion item.
4. Learners check their own response.
5. If a pupil is right, he is rewarded. If he is wrong in his response, he now knows the correct answer.
6. He then looks at the next picture, reads the related content, responds to an item, and then checks his own response.
7. Again, if he is right, he is rewarded. If the response given by the learner is incorrect, he now knows the correct answer.
8. The same steps may be followed over and over again when programmed materials are utilized in the class setting.

Programmed learning has been criticized by selected educators. Reasons given for the criticism are the following:

1. Programmed materials may become monotonous for pupils in ongoing learning activities.
2. Selected learners can advance at a more rapid rate in learning as compared to the small steps arranged sequentially by the programmer.
3. Relevant content may not have been selected by the programmer in writing programmed materials.
4. The child individually is a better determiner of sequential learning as compared to the programmer.
5. Achieving content in small steps may not meet the learning styles of selected learners.
6. Learning experiences need to be varied in the class setting.

Competition Versus Cooperation in the Class Setting

A very important issue that needs resolving in the elementary curriculum pertains to competitive versus cooperative efforts on the part of pupils in on-going learning activities. Reasons given for pupils engaging in competitive experiences include the following:

1. Life in society demands that individuals excel in performance.
2. Achievements in the United States have come about due to rugged individualism in society.
3. Competition between and among learners brings out the best within individuals.
4. Individuals take pride only in personal achievement and not group or committee work.
5. It is normal for individual to be competitive.
6. Not all individuals can get to the 'top' in achievement; thus survival of the fittest is important in school and society.

Disadvantages given for competition as a means of motivating learners in achieving well include the following:

1. Human beings in groups can do a better job of solving problems as compared to the efforts of individuals.
2. Progress in society has come about due to cooperative efforts of inventors, scientists, other professionals, and non-professionals.
3. Human beings must be educated to take pride in group efforts since this is more effective in scope as compared to the attempts of an individual in improving happenings in society.
4. Much merit can be placed on the statement "in union there is strength." Thus, achievement in society comes about due to united efforts of individuals determined to improve society.

It does seem necessary to emphasize balance between the concepts of competition and cooperation in the social studies curriculum. Individual efforts in positive achievement need to be rewarded in teaching-learning situations. Human beings need to find fulfillment in accomplishments on an individual basis. They, however, also must feel successful in group endeavours. Needed changes in society can come about through individual as well as group efforts. In the study of history, individuals and groups of individuals helped to change society from what it was to what exists presently. The following criteria are given to resolve controversies pertaining to individual and group efforts in achievement:

1. All individuals should feel successful in learning.
2. Individual achievement should definitely not be at the expense of others.
3. Respect for others is an important objective in the school curriculum.
4. Individuals working in committees and groups should feel rewarded in their efforts.
5. Good human relations should exist in group endeavours.

Pupil Involvement in the Community

Selected social studies educators have recommended that pupils' experience in the school setting should involve participating in community activities. Thus pupils' social studies experiences could involve the following pertaining to working in the community:

1. cleaning up the school and nearby environment when studying units on pollution;
2. making recommendations to the mayor or city manager and council on ways to avoid pollution in a city area;
3. participating in a mayor-council meeting by making specific recommendations.

There are selected issues involved in having pupils become directly involved in community participation:

1. To what degree should pupils become involved in community affairs?
2. How much of the school day should be given in having pupils participate in community activities?
3. How relevant can these learnings be made for pupils?

There are advantages in having pupils participate in community affairs.

1. Learnings can be highly realistic for pupils.
2. Pupils become actively involved in learning.
3. School and society become integrated entities.
4. Learners have opportunities to practice good citizenship.

Disadvantages which may be listed for pupils becoming actively involved in community work include the following:

1. Mundane tasks may be performed by pupils.
2. The lay public may question the values involved in having pupils participate in community work.

3. There is a question, of course, pertaining to priorities in the public school curriculum.
4. The cost may be high in terms of money when having pupils participate in community affairs, such as transportation costs.

Camping Experience and the Social Studies

There are selected elementary schools which provide camping experience for pupils away from the school setting. Boy scouts, girls scouts, and 4-H Club organisations have provided camping experiences for young people over the years. Thus, camping experiences for pupils may have the following opportunities to offer in relationship in the public school curriculum:

1. Pupils have opportunities to learn from a completely different environment as compared to the school setting.
2. Learning activities provided for pupils can be more varied as compared to those provided in the school setting only.
3. More facets of everybody living can be stressed in camping experiences as compared to what is experienced during a regular school day.
4. Teachers may get to know pupils in an informal environment and under different conditions.

Disadvantages which may be listed in having pupils participate in camping experiences involve the following:

1. There are adequate opportunities for pupils to participate in camping experiences through organisations such as boy scouts and girls scouts.
2. The cost of providing camping experiences for pupils may be excessively high.
3. It is not necessary for pupils to attend a campsite area to have worthwhile educational experiences.
4. Excursions can be taken to the community to aid pupils in experiencing reality.
5. There are other ways of having pupils experience reality such as having resource personnel come to the class setting. Teachers and pupils may bring objects and models to the class setting; thus, reality in degrees is brought into the classroom.

Performance Contracting

A few years ago performance contracting was given considerable limelight. Performance contracting emphasized the following:

1. The company doing the contracting guaranteed a given school a certain level of gain in pupil achievement within a specified time.
2. Terms of the agreement were stated in a contract.
3. The company was to receive no payment for those learners who did not achieve according to specified results in the contract.
4. Teachers were trained to use methods and procedures of teaching as emphasized by the company engaged in performance contracting.

Disadvantages given for performance contracting included:

1. No one in advance can predict needed pupil gains in a given school year.
2. It is difficult to determine which tests should be utilized to measure pupil achievement in a pretest-postest situation.
3. No test can measure all relevant achievement that pupils need to make.
4. Methods and materials used in teaching as recommended by companies may stress lower level cognitive learnings.
5. Pupils' needs may not be met in the school setting.

Advantages which may be listed for selected schools participating in performance contracting are the following:

1. The methods and materials utilized in teaching may provide for individual differences among selected learners with unique learning styles.

2. Attempts are made in pinpointing pupil gains in a given school year.

3. Parents may be more satisfied with the school setting if learner achievement can be verified.
4. Payment to schools for pupils' achievement is made only if predetermined levels of achievement have been acquired.

5. Teacher skills may be updated with appropriated recommended methodology and materials if the company engaged in performance contracting emphasized inservice education of teachers.

Criterion Referenced Supervision

With the use of specific behaviourally stated objectives, selected educators have recommended criterion-referenced approaches in supervision of instruction. Criterion-referenced supervision recommends utilizing the following criteria:

1. The supervisor assessing the quality of objectives with the teacher prior to observing teaching-learning situations.
2. Alternative objectives may be emphasized by the supervisor if the latter perceives this to be necessary.
3. The quality of teaching is evaluated in terms of how well pupils have achieved the desired objectives.
4. Harmful side effects on the part of pupils in teaching-learning situations are also evaluated by the criterion-referenced supervisor.
5. If pupils have not achieved stated objectives, the criterion-referenced supervisor may suggest alternative learning experiences.

Advantages given for using the criterion-referenced approach to supervising instruction include the following:

1. It can be an objective way of supervising instruction since teacher success is evaluated in terms of pupils achieving agreed upon objectives.
2. Stated objectives written by the teacher are further assessed by the supervisor in attempts at having pupils achieve the best objectives possible.
3. The success of learning activities is evaluated only in terms of pupils achieving desired objectives.
4. Pupil achievement can be assessed in terms of having achieved stated specific objectives.

Disadvantages which may be given in question form in relation to using criterion-referenced supervision include the following:

1. How far in advance do supervisors need to study teachers' selection of objectives before the observational visit is made?

2. Is the achieving of specific objectives by pupils the only reasonable criteria to emphasize when evaluating teacher performance?
3. Are supervisors adequately knowledgeable to recommend alternative objectives in a limited amount of time other than those stated in writing by teachers?
4. Are teachers and supervisors in the best position to specifically determine objectives that pupils are to achieve? Should pupils be involved in determining educational objectives which they are to achieve?
5. When observing teachers teach, can supervisors immediately notice harmful side effects on the part of learners in teaching-learning situations? (Detrimental learnings for pupils may be revealed more so over a longer period of time.)
6. Can all worthwhile objectives such as critical thinking, creative thinking, and problem solving be stated behaviourally?

In Summary

There are selected issues which teachers and supervisors should study, analyze, and appraise. Ultimately, a synthesis should be developed to implement a quality curriculum for each student.

These issues include:

1. how basal textbooks should be utilized;
2. the degree that inquiry methods of teaching should be emphasized;
3. committee as compared in individual tasks for pupils;
4. broad versus precise objectives in the curriculum;
5. structural ideas in the social studies;
6. emphasis upon anthropology, sociology, and economics in ongoing lessons and units;
7. teacher-pupil planning;
8. programmed learning in the curriculum;
9. competition versus cooperation in student endeavours;
10. student involvement in the community;
11. camping experiences for students sponsored by the school;

12. performance contracting;
13. the utilization of criterion referenced supervision to improve the social studies.

REFERENCE

Ediger, Marlow and Digumarti Bhaskara Rao. *Teaching Social Studies Successfully*. New Delhi, India: Discovery Publishing House, 2001.

20

Discipline in the School

Not much is written about the problem of discipline in the elementary school. One reason for this, perhaps, deals with the fact that children differ from each other in many ways and approaches to discipling one child may, of course, not work with another child. Another reason may be that the word 'discipline' has a negative connotation. Also teachers perceive things differently when identifying a child as being a discipline problem. Thus, teachers disagree with each other as to which child or children are discipline problems.

Approaches of the Past Used in Disciplining Learners

In colonial America, Puritans in New England felt that pupils were born in sin. Since Adam in the Garden of Eden had eaten fruit from the forbidden tree, Puritans thought that each human being was thus born in sin. The thinking then was that evilness or sin was inherited since each person was born in sin. It was of utmost importance to Puritans that teachers had correct beliefs pertaining to the Bible and the Puritan religion. Thus teachers would know what was correct for children to believe. Many teachers generally could then drive the evilness or sin out of pupils through the use of physical punishment, according to beliefs of the Puritans. Not all teachers in colonial days, of course, believed in using physical punishment in disciplining children.

Puritans, as a whole, generally did not believe in play as being a worthy goal for children. Thus, children being born in sin needed to be corrected and learn that which adults felt was important to learn. Materials used in teaching did not emphasize that which was in harmony with pupils' interests. For example, in learning to read, the pupil would first memorize the individual letters of the alphabet. Certainly, this activity generally did not get the interests of pupils. The memorization method of learning as emphasized here stressed the importance of pupils learning that which is abstract to begin with. The horn book which was first used to teach pupils in colonial New England had one page of content consisting of the upper and lower case letters of the alphabet plus the benediction and the Lord's Prayer. These were abstract learnings then that pupils developed through the methods of rote learning and memorization. Rote learning and memorization of content as a method of teaching, of course, generally does not capture the interests of pupils. Educators have long advocated that pupils begin with the simple and move to the more difficult gradually. Or, pupils should begin with the real or concrete and move to the semi-concrete and then to the abstract as their present achievement level will permit in developing meaningful learnings. It is small wonder that Puritan teachers used physical punishment in disciplining children if the following beliefs were adhered to:

1. Individuals were born in sin due to original sin committed by Adam in the Garden of Eden.
2. Sin had to be driven out of children.
3. Teachers could be obtained who had correct beliefs pertaining to the Bible and Puritan doctrine.
4. Individuals were predestined to be saved.

As individuals from diverse faiths entered colonial America, religious and educational thinking was revised. The harsh treatment given by Puritans of their own children and of others who did not adhere to their doctrine would soon aid in minimizing the importance of their thinking.

After the American Revolutionary War, the thinking of Americans turned gradually away from a heavy emphasis upon religion to more secular thought in the curriculum. With more diversity in religious faiths, modification of thinking was bound to occur. People would hear of the religious thinking of others and gradually change their own thinking. The Revolutionary War emphasized that the here and now was important in winning the war with Great Britain. Increased trade within and outside the original thirteen states of the United States stressed the importance of secular facets of living such as the study of arithmetic. Records, for example, needed to be kept of goods and services bought and sold as the United States in the beginning of its history increased its efforts in trade and commerce.

With the introduction of the Lancastrian Monitorial System of Instruction from England to the United States, new approaches to teaching were emphasized. In the area of discipline, emphasis was placed upon the use of more humane approaches other than the use of physical punishment. Thus, pupils were encouraged to behave 'properly' through the use of embarrassment. A child who did not behave as the monitor or master teacher wished him to behave could be paraded around the room so other pupils would clearly notice the offender. The offender then in the future would, no doubt, vow to never do the same thing again which caused this embarrassment. Children could also be punished in groups using the methods of embarrassment. They would then be seen by all other pupils in the room who could vividly observe the wrongdoers.

There are teachers today who still implement the outdated approaches of using physical punishment and/or embarrassment in disciplining pupils. In most cases, these approaches would not be used as rigidly today as compared to the days of colonial America or the Lancastrian Monitorial System. The following reasons would be given for not using these approaches in the 1980's:

1. Pupils are not helped in emotional development since positive attitudes cannot be developed when pupils are negatively affected by physical punishment or embarrassment in classroom teaching.
2. Learners cannot develop well socially if individual pupils are isolated from other children when negative approaches to disciplining are being used. Thus pupils may not respect those who are being punished in a negative way. Good teaching would help learners to be accepted by others.
3. It is very difficult for pupils to develop adequate self concepts when being threatened by physical punishment or embarrassment.
4. Positive efforts of pupils should be rewarded; learners then will want to get rewards, such as praise, and thus

put forth more effort in exhibiting positive behaviour in order to get needed recognition.

5. Some pupils may get needed recognition through negative ways of disciplining unwanted behaviour in the class. These pupils may not get recognition in any other way. Thus, the teacher is actually encouraging negative behaviour on the part of selected individuals.
6. Minimizing human beings is not in harmony with basic ideas relating to democracy as a way of life. Democratic living stresses the importance of human beings respecting each other.
7. If pupils are to become contributing members in a democratic society, they must develop positive attitudes towards others, the school, and society.
8. The teacher serves as a model to pupils in the area of democratic living. Pupils in the elementary school are always learning from their environment. The classroom teacher is a very important person in this environment.
9. Pupils should have a voice in determining standards of conduct for learners to follow. There should be frequent evaluation of pupil achievement in terms of these guidelines. Self-evaluation by pupils would be important in the evaluation process. The teacher should also continuously evaluate pupil achievement in developing self-discipline.
10. The teacher should evaluate his own teaching to determine if discipline problems arise because of faulty objectives, learning activities, or evaluation techniques.
11. Certainly, better approaches can be found to discipline pupils other than physical punishment or embarrassment.
12. The different curriculum areas of the elementary school should definitely not provide content to use when disciplining pupils.

Stimulus-Response Psychology and Discipline

Each school of thought pertaining to how pupils learn has some basic principles to suggest in disciplining pupils. The stimulus-response school of thought would emphasize reinforcement as a very important concept. A child who behaves well should be praised for his efforts in disciplining himself. Thus, the learner will do his best to exhibit proper behaviour since he generally will want recognition or reward. Most people desire praise for work well done and the child is no exception. Too frequently, teachers have hesitated in giving pupils recognition for good behaviour. The stimulus-response school of thought pertaining to how pupils learn emphasizes that undesirable behaviour will have a tendency to lose its power if the teacher and pupils do not pay attention to it. In some cases, this is very difficult to do. If the child continues to disrupt the class, certainly the teacher needs to approach this problem from the point of view that other children cannot realize their highest achievement in situations such as these.

Reinforcement of positive behaviour of learners has long been recognized as an important way of dealing with behavioural problems in school. The law of recency would also be important here in that all things being equal, the more recent reinforcement has been used in praising positive behaviour, the more effective this approach will be. This would also mean that continuous reinforcement of desired behaviour from pupils would have positive results. The law of effect would pertain to the more favourable the child responds to what is being learned, the sooner the learning will be achieved. This would be true if all other factors or variables could be kept constant. Thus, rewarding good behaviour should have positive effects upon pupils.

The gestalt school of thought in terms of how pupils learn emphasizes the total child in a given situation. The child who is scolded in front of the class for a misdeed generally will not feel positive over the incident. Continuous experiences such as these would make for poor emotional development. The child then will not like school as well as he should. The feelings a child has toward school will affect the total child. These feelings, positive or negative, will have their influence in how well a child achieves intellectually. If a child has a negative attitude toward school and himself, he will not do well in realizing understanding objectives. He will also lack in achievement in the area of skills development. If a child is reprimanded in front of others for misbehaviour, he may not be able to make the friends he would desire to make. His friends may minimize or desert him. Or, he may join others who feel rejected and left out of the mainstream of affairs. Thus, social development is being hindered in situation such as these. If learners feel negatively toward themselves and others, together with underachievement intellectually, the chances are the learner also will not develop as well physically as he should. Thus, gestaltists emphasize the total development of pupils. Negative approaches to disciplining a child then would have its effect upon the total development of pupils.

It is quite obvious that both the stimulus-response and gestalt schools of thought have important implications for disciplining pupils in the elementary school.

Don'ts in Disciplining Pupils

Practitioners in the field of education many times ask the question pertaining to how then should pupils be disciplined who disrupt others in the class. There is definitely no easy answer to this question. What works with one child may not work with another child with positive approaches that are utilized. Negative approaches, of course, have harmful effects upon pupils in terms of personality development. Reputable teachers, principals, supervisors, as well as writers in the field of education emphasize the following 'don'ts' pertaining to disciplining children:

1. Do not use subject-matter to punish children. For example, do not have a child work page 57 in his mathematics textbook for a misdeed. He may associate punishment with mathematics if this is done. Thus, he generally will learn to dislike mathematics in situations such as these.
2. Don't scold pupils for their shortcomings in front of other children. If this is done, the child being reprimanded has a tendency to be isolated from friends and peers. Children should rather be helped in the making of friends.
3. Don't have children stay in during play period for misbehaving. Pupils need variety in learning activities, and play makes for a definite change in daily routine. Learners need ample opportunities to engage in physical exercise in addition to those learning activities which require little or no physical movement.
4. Don't use physical punishment since this is not humane and better approaches are available to change pupil behaviour.
5. Don't use approaches in disciplining pupils which tend to minimize children. Each child needs to develop an adequate self concept so he can achieve to his optimum in school work as well as in society.

In the previous discussion, many references have been made as to what not to do in attempting to change negative behaviour of pupils. There are many things the teacher can try in attempting to improve pupil behaviour in the school setting. Among these ways would be the following:

1. Learn as much as possible about the home of the child. If parents do not get along or if there is illness in the home, this will definitely affect a child's behaviour. Abnormal disagreements and rivalry among children in a home will also affect a given child's behaviour in school. A neglected or an unwanted child in a home situation can definitely not exhibit the best kind of behaviour in school. Thus, teachers need to learn much about the home situation and try to understand the child from his very own point of view.
2. The teacher should evaluate his own teaching. A textbook centered approach to teaching does not provide for enough children. For some learners, the textbook is too difficult to learn from. For others, it is too easy. In other cases, the textbook is not the most interesting material to use in teaching. All pupils crave variety when it comes to materials and methods in teaching. Discipline problems can arise when approaches to teaching children need to be modified or changed completely.
3. A few teachers expect pupils to be passive individuals. Their thinking is that children need to sit very quietly at their desks in order for learning to take place. Learning then is equated with pupils being quiet and passive. Somehow, these teachers have not kept up with recent trends in teaching. They do not recognize that pupils should be actively involved in ongoing learning activities. When pupils in committees engage in conducting and discussing science experiments, there will be some noise in the class; however, learning in a positive direction may be taking place. Certainly, noise for the sake of having noise is a negative approach to teaching. Busy learners, however, will be making some noise. Learners in a committee sharing ideas obtained from using a variety of reference sources cannot do this in a quiet classroom environment where one could hear a pin fall to the floor.

4. The teacher should definitely not confuse creativity and misbehaviour of pupils. Some teachers have scolded pupils who ask many questions and do not like prescribed ways of doing things. These learners may also have been scolded for not giving exact answers to questions in words that the teacher wants to response to be in. Perhaps, the teacher has only asked questions where one word or several words are needed as answers. These are pat answers to questions. Creative children like questions where diversity of ideas can be discussed. Thus, unique answers to problems can be discussed. This gives opportunities for creative children to be playful with ideas. Teachers need to study characteristics of creative children and provide for these learners in the elementary school.
5. The teacher should use praise freely for those who are meeting proper standards of behaviour pertaining to a good learning environment. There are teachers who are afraid to praise positive behaviour. Perhaps, they feel that pupils will then misbehave as a result of having received praise. Other teachers have never engaged in the practice of rewarding learners for good behaviour. Teachers need practice in giving praise to pupils for better behaviour. They can tape-record their own teaching and notice if adequate rewards are given. In the analysis of the tape-recording, the teacher can notice if the verbal reward is varied or if it is the same. It gets rather monotonous for pupils unless there is variation not only of learning activities, but also of verbal rewards. The teacher can use the words "that's good!" to praise learners. Other varied expressions should also be used such as the following 'excellent!' 'Tremendous!' 'very good!' that's dandy!'

Nonverbal communication can also be used effectively in praising pupils for improved behaviour. The following, among others, can be used to reward pupils using nonverbal communication:

(a) a smile by the teacher;

(b) a positive nod of the head by the teacher.

6. Reasonable criteria or standards of conduct should be developed cooperatively between the teacher or teachers

and learners. Pupils entering a new class for the first time, in many cases, do not know what is expected of them in terms of standards of conduct. There are first grade teachers, for example, who have a permissive learning environment. They permit pupils to talk freely with each other during the school day pertaining to different learning activities. Learners here can get materials from different places in the classroom whenever the need arises. Also, pupils can move sequentially from one centre of learning in the class to another centre of their own choosing. The teacher serves as a consultant or helper to pupils but not as a lecturer or an explainer of knowledge. He is a friendly, secure person in dealing informally with pupils. Pupils leaving this class setting and moving to a second grade room for the next school year could experience the following as the year progresses:

- *(a)* Pupils sit in straight rows.
- *(b)* No one can get up from their desks without permission from the teacher.
- *(c)* There is no committee work.
- *(d)* Pupils are learning largely from the use of textbooks, workbooks, and duplicated materials.
- *(e)* The teacher does much lecturing and explaining.
- *(f)* There is basically no noise in the room.
- *(g)* A rigid time schedule is followed in teaching pupils.
- *(h)* Pupils line up to come into the room and to leave the classroom.
- *(i)* Exact one, two, or three word answers are given to questions asked them by the teacher.
- *(j)* The teacher is very formal in teaching much subject-matter to pupils.
- *(k)* Children basically are not praised for improved efforts and work.
- *(l)* The teacher is a very rigid individual expecting learners to complete all textbooks, workbooks, and duplicated materials in the allotted time he feels is just for the class as a whole.

It is no wonder that pupils having been in the previously described first grade room and now being members of this second grade class find it difficult to determine as to what makes for good behaviour. It certainly is necessary that all educators keep up-to-date pertaining to modern trends in the teaching of elementary school children. It is also necessary to discuss with pupils standards of conduct that will permit a good learning environment. Democratic living emphasizes that pupils be actively involved in developing theses standards with teacher guidance. Pupils need to know what criteria to follow in terms of standards of conduct in the class setting. The teacher, as well as pupils, need to evaluate these criteria frequently to determine if they stand in the way of each child realizing his optimum achievement. Quality standards of conduct in the class and in the general school environment should help each child achieve to his highest potential. The teacher should guide learners frequently to assess their behaviour in terms of these standards.

7. A common cause of misbehaviour in the class occurs when the teacher uses too much lecture. It is easy for pupils to refrain from listening in situations such as these. During the time the lecturer is in operation, it is difficult for the teacher to actually know if learners are comprehending. The child may even look at the teacher making it appear as if he is listening when this is not actually the case. Carefully selected questions should be used in teaching to determine pupils' present level of achievement as well as comprehension. The teacher must observe pupil behaviour carefully when teaching. If pupils appear to be bored or if they have turned off, the teacher can then change the kind of learning activity that is now being provided to something different thus avoiding many behavioural problems. The teacher must approach each pupil in terms of getting him involved on his present achievement level so that no time basically is available for misbehaviour.
8. The teacher can definitely not afford to have pupils lose interest in learning. If pupils are not interested in what is being taught, behavioural problems have a tendency to develop. The kinds of learning activities that generated

interest in learning a generation ago are no longer suitable for today's pupils in the elementary school. Too many teachers complain about pupils not wanting to learn when actually the teacher is not carefully selecting learning activities in terms of learner interest. These teachers, no doubt, may actually feel that pupils should be interested in learning no matter what is being taught. This is impossible! A few teachers actually feel that by piling work on pupils (way beyond what his capabilities permit), a challenge exists for completing the work. These teachers then may feel that this is a good way of challenging pupils. There are selected learning activities which are more interesting to pupils as compared to others. Among these would be the following on the appropriate achievement levels of pupils: using films, filmstrips, slides, excursions, pictures, discussions, resource personnel, tapes, replicas, and models. Thus it should encourage the teacher to assess prior to teaching, during teaching, and after teaching as to which learning activities capture pupil interest. Too many teachers are not willing to engage in self-evaluation and ask if their own teaching is at fault when discipline problems arise. Learners definitely will engage in more misbehaviour if they are not interested as compared to being interested in an ongoing learning activity. The teacher could involve pupils in evaluating learning activities which have a tendency to interest pupils as compared to those which do not capture pupil interest.

9. Pupils will also tend to exhibit problems in behaviour if they do not understand what is being taught. Thus, there is more time available for disrupting others since the learnings presented do not make sense. The teacher must assess learner achievement to determine where they are presently in achievement. The activities must then be provided in good sequence from the child's point of view. If this were done, discipline problems in the class could be cut down considerably. It, of course, will not eliminate all discipline problems, but it will tend to cut down on many of these problems.

10. Teachers perceive their roles incorrectly. The task of the teacher is to teach all children. Too frequently, teachers

have thought of their responsibilities consisting of sorting learners in terms of those who should be successful as compared to those who are to be failures in life. These teachers may even verbalize that everything possible is being done to provide for individual differences in the class setting. They may use slogans like "making learnings interesting, meaningful, purposeful, and meeting the needs of learners." However, careful observation of these same classes may reveal that all pupils are at the same place at the same time with reading materials being utilized predominately. Those pupils that do not meet the arbitrary standards of the teacher are called down in front of other children and scolded in a rude manner in class. What is actually done in teaching pupils is much different from the verbal statements that are made. There are numerous causes for this situation:

(a) Teachers may actually not know what it means to provide for individual children in a class.

(b) They may be biased toward pupils who are below average in capacity or who underachieve in different curriculum areas of the elementary school.

(c) Selected teachers do not like pupils who come from disadvantaged homes. These pupils may not dress neatly and may not have good clothes in terms of teacher expectations.

(d) There are teachers who, unfortunately, are biased toward pupils who come from minority groups. They may even feel these pupils should be flunked rather than taught. There certainly is a big difference in attitudes between teachers who are positive and feel that all children should be taught to realize their highest potential versus teachers who are negative and have the concept of failing pupils in their minds continuously.

(e) A few teachers having taught in a specific district for some time have felt that a child cannot do well in school because one or both of the parents were failures in the different curriculum areas of the elementary school. Sometimes, the feeling exists on

the part of these teachers that the father and/or mother of a pupil never "amounted to much," so how can the offspring be any different.

(f) The mental health of selected teachers certainly is not what it should be. The teacher may have a personal need to dominate children. It would be excellent if there were a test which could very accurately measure the mental health of teachers in relationship to liking all pupils and wanting to help learners realize their optimum achievement.

(g) Too many teachers after having received a baccalaureate degree in teaching do not keep up with modern trends in teaching the different curriculum areas of the elementary school. They lack information pertaining to the psychology of teaching and learning. If the teacher has this information, it may not be utilized in the teaching-learning situations. Thus teachers need to study recent trends in elementary education. The school must have a professional library for teachers to use. Good teaching must be identified and rewarded, thus spurring other teachers on in improving their own skills. Workshops should be conducted to improve the curriculum. Improving the curriculum deals with a good learning environment for pupils where all can realize their potential!

In Summary

Outdated approach in disciplining elementary school pupils would pertain to the use of physical punishment and embarrassment of pupils. The approaches are still used by some teachers in public schools of the United States. There are many reasons which can be given for not using negative techniques in dealing with discipline problems in the public schools. Among these would be the following: (a) emotional and social development are not developed to their optimum; (b) it is difficult to develop feelings of adequacy; (c) it may actually give pupils needed recognition; (d) democratic living is then not in evidence; (e) teachers do not present good examples for learners to follow; (f) the teacher may be at fault for discipline problems existing in the class setting; and (g) pupils can learn to dislike the school and what it stands for.

Teachers, principals, and supervisors need to study positive methods in disciplining pupils. These approaches include assertive disciplines, behaviour modification, logical consequences, positive peer culture, reality therapy, social literacy training, teacher effectiveness training (TET), and transactional analysis (TA).

With the utilization of quality procedures in the area of discipline each student needs to be assisted to achieve optimally.

REFERENCES

Ediger, Marlow and Digumarti Bhaskara Rao, *Relevancy in Elementary Curriculum*. New Delhi, India: Discovery Publishing House, 2004.

Ediger, Marlow and Digumarti Bhaskara Rao, *Elementary Curriculum*. New Delhi: Discovery Publishing House, 2003.

21

Reporting Pupil Progress to Parents

Most parents are highly interested in the achievement of their offspring. They want to know how well their children are doing in school. Parents also want to know what they can do to help their offspring achieve to the best degree possible. Thus, faculty members of an elementary school must find the best ways to communicate pupil achievement to parents. This presents a difficult problem.

The curriculum of an elementary school should continuously be evaluated and modified if evidence warrants the making of changes. One way to improve the curriculum is to study, evaluate, and change the approaches used to report pupil achievement to parents. Certainly, the methods used to report pupil progress to parents does affect learner achievement. In some cases, parents have used information obtained from conferences with teachers as a club against their children. The club is used as a lever to get pupils to work 'harder' and achieve at a higher level. Perhaps, parents misinterpreted statements made in the evaluation of their child's progress. If a teacher says that child is not working up to potential, the parent may pressure the child to 'work up to capacity.' It is difficult to determine which pupils are or are not working up to their highest potential. First of all, it is difficult to assess what the capacity of individual pupils are. Intelligence tests are not perfect determinants of the capacity of any child. Even if one could evaluate the capacity of a child with no flaws involved, a further problem would be to evaluate if a child is working toward his revealed intelligence level. Achievement tests which are standardized have their weaknesses thus making the problem complex indeed in determining if a child is working up to capacity. Teacher observation, of course, also has its many weaknesses in determining if a child is working to capacity.

If parents are pressuring a child to work 'up to capacity', the pupil presently could really be trying to do his best work. Thus, parental pressures upon the child could have negative consequences. There are a number of reasons why a pupil is not doing better than it appears his mental maturity would permit:

1. The child faces personal problems which reflect upon his being able to benefit more from ongoing learning activities. He worries much about these problems and thus loses out on valuable learnings that could be achieved.
2. Parents are not as accepting of a particular child as compared to other children in the family. Perhaps, the child's total personality development is not what the parents appreciate as compared to other children in the family.
3. Perhaps, poverty or low income is a problem in the home. A child then does not receive the benefits from living an enjoyable life due to inadequate income in the home.
4. Illness, death, divorce, and separation of parents can take its toll of a child being able to benefit from the curricular offerings of an elementary school.
5. Cruel and/or unusual punishment given by one or both of the guardians can do much to hinder pupils from achieving to their highest potential. A guardian using abusive language, hitting pupils physically, screaming at the child, and sending a child to his room frequently as punishment can only assist the child in disliking the home, and what it stands for.
6. Teachers using outdated methods of teaching and emphasizing the irrelevant and unimportant can definitely keep pupils from doing well in an elementary school.
7. Instructors who are in poor mental or physical health which is not conducive in helping learners to achieve can definitely take its toll in learner performance in the school setting.

8. Administrators emphasizing 'quiet classrooms as being good learning environments' can influence the classroom teacher into thinking that continually clamping down on children is the major objective to be achieved in teaching. Pupils then can become passive learners who lack interest, curiosity, purpose, and zest for learning.
9. The child may lack friends. An elementary school is a social institution. There are many human beings in the school setting. Thus, it is important that learners enjoy being together with each other. The teacher must assist learners in developing good human relationships. Teachers should enjoy children and have a desire to help all learners achieve to their optimum. A prejudiced, biased, emotionally unstable classroom teacher has no business in the classroom attempting to teach children!

An approach must be developed whereby pupil achievement and progress can be reported in an objective way. The method used should help pupils to achieve at their own highest unique rate possible. It should emphasize the total growth of the child which includes the following facets—intellectual, social, emotional, and physical. If parents use information properly of reported learner achievement, the child should develop positive attitudes toward himself and others. Reporting to parents of learner achievement should assist pupils to achieve to their maximum development intellectually. Punishment given by parents to offspring based on information obtained from report cards, for example, will not help pupils to develop positive attitudes toward self and others. It will not help pupils, generally, in achieving at a higher level intellectually. Instead the pupil may learn to dislike the different curriculum areas of the elementary school as well as teachers and the entire school setting. Thus, different methods of reporting pupil progress to parents should not defeat its own purpose. The purpose should be to keep parents informed of their child's achievement in terms of each individual learner. The home and the school should work together in which a curriculum will be developed to fit the needs, interests, and abilities of each individual child. In a democracy, the individual is of utmost importance. Democratic living stresses the importance of all human beings being respected by others. It emphasizes the importance of the uniqueness of each human being.

Using Report Cards to Report Pupil Achievement

Many elementary schools use report cards in reporting pupil progress to parents. Educators have long questioned the values of reporting learner progress in this way. Many disadvantages can be given for reporting pupil progress with the use of report cards.

1. It is difficult to do a thorough job of reporting pupil progress covering all facets of development.
2. Parents, in many cases, perceive the marks given in the report card differently from the way they are perceived by the teacher.
3. If a child is given an 'A' grade in reading, it is difficult to determine what this means. For example, this could mean that the child is one of the best readers in the class. It could also mean that the child reads poorly, but he is improving over previous efforts. It could also mean that the child is achieving to his optimum efforts. The best reader in a class could get grades below an 'A' if he is goofing off or is lacking in effort.
4. A single grade given in a curriculum area is not sufficient to determine how well a child is doing. For example, if a child gets an 'A' grade in social studies, what does this mean? Is he doing better in social development or working in committees? Or, is he achieving at an optimum rate in using reference materials? There are many more questions that could be raised as to what the one letter grade would mean in elementary school social studies as well as the other curriculum areas in the elementary school.
5. Negative attitudes have been developed by the pupil when he or she perceives marks received as unfair.
6. Parents have used the results of the report card as a lever to pressure pupils to higher levels of achievement.
7. Parents have become dissatisfied with teachers and the school as a result of having observed the report card of their child.
8. It is difficult and arbitrary to determine the marks or grades that a particular child should receive.
9. Sometimes there are too many categories for a teacher to evaluate pupil achievement in. For example, reading could

be divided into many categories in which pupils could be assessed such as using context clues, configuration clues, phonetic analysis, syllabication, and picture clues. The teacher could check how well the learner is doing in each of these areas. Further divisions, other than using word recognition techniques, could be made of the curriculum area of reading. These could include different purposes in reading such as being able to read for facts, main ideas, generalizations, a sequence of ideas or events, directions, and being able to skim content. The reader will readily notice that there are too many areas for teachers to evaluate pupil achievement in reading when reporting many categories of information to parents. Other curriculum areas of the elementary school would add to the number of categories. Parents, no doubt, would not understand the meaning of all these different categories.

10. Many complaints reach the school due to marks or grades that have been given on report cards. The time spent in handling grievances had report cards not been issued could have been given to improving the total elementary school curriculum.
11. It is a oneway street of communication.

Report cards have existed for a long time in American educational history to report pupil achievement to parents. The philosophy back of using the report card has changed over the years as have the different categories or areas that students are assessed in. Thus, reports cards also have their many advantages:

1. This is one way that the school can communicate pupil achievement to all parents.
2. Report cards can be used with other approaches in reporting pupil progress to parents. This then has a tendency to minimize some weakness that report cards have.
3. If report cards convey information incorrectly as perceived by parents and guardians, the faculty of an elementary school should invite reactions to categories that learners have been evaluated in.
4. No approach in reporting pupil achievement to parents is perfect. Thus, report cards also have their strengths and weaknesses.

5. Parents should feel free to come to school and inquire about their child's achievement if the marks or grades received were perceived to be low.
6. Faculties of elementary schools should continuously revise the report cards used in order that weaknesses can be eliminated or minimized. Important facets of a pupil's achievement and development should appear on the report card.

No doubt, report cards will be with us for some time to come in reporting pupil achievement to parents. Thus, it behooves faculty members of an elementary school or several elementary schools to provide the best and most important information about each child's progress on the report card. The following questions are important to answer when revicing or modifying the report card as it is presently being utilized in a public school system:

1. Does the report card reflect up-to-date thinking in terms of what facets of each child's achievement is being reported to parents?
2. Are the contents of the report card too difficult for parents to interpret?
3. Could the report card be filled out by teachers in a reasonable amount of time?
4. Could the report card convey misinformation to parents?
5. Are the categories for pupils to be evaluated are free from duplication?
6. Is the philosophy of the school clear pertaining to basic ideas in back of the issuing of grade cards?
7. Have parents been informed as to the meaning of each of the categories pupils are being evaluated in on the report card?
8. Is the terminology used in the report card clear, concise, and free from ambiguous statements?
9. Is space available on the report card for parents to respond to marks or grades given to pupils?
10. Does the report card invite parents to come to school to confer with the teacher and principal about their child's progress?

11. Could teachers justify the grades or marks given to pupils which appear on the grade card?
12. Is there adequate justification in terms of how frequently pupil achievement should be reported to parents when using report cards?
13. Should other approaches be used simultaneously with the grade card when reporting pupil progress? Should parent-teacher conferences occur at the same time report cards are issued?
14. Do the contents of the report card clearly convey to parents needed information about each child's progress?
15. Has the faculty of an elementary school studied and evaluated an adequate number of report cards from various school systems to determine what a good report card should contain?

Improving the quality of report cards can be one approach, among others, in which an elementary school can improve the curriculum.

Having Parent-Teacher Conferences to Report Pupil Progress

Many elementary schools conduct parent-teacher conferences at least once a year. This gives parents opportunities to ask questions of the teacher in a face-to-face situation. Problems and questions can be identified by parents as well as the teacher. It is not a one-way street of communication. Both the parent or parents as well as the teacher can be actively involved in the parent-teacher conference. There are certain standards that the teacher should follow in conducting parent-teacher conferences.

1. The ideas of parents must be respected since good communication comes about in an atmosphere of positive consideration for the thinking of others.
2. The teacher should be well prepared prior to conducting each parent-teacher conference. Otherwise, parent-teacher conferences can be a waste of time. The teacher should have important knowledge about the child's general capacity and achievement, home background information, and general emotional and physical health.
3. It is good to show parents work samples of their child's achievement. Thus parents can get some data about the

achievement of their children. Teachers and parents must understand that all materials used in teaching pupils should be on the instructional level of the child. Objectives must be reasonable so that they can be achieved by pupils. Thus learning activities need to be on the instructional level of pupils and not the frustrational level.

4. After report cards, if used, have been issued for the first time in a given school year, results can be discussed with parents in a parent-teacher conference.
5. Agreed upon criteria should be established with teacher-parent cooperation in a conference to help in improving the curriculum for each child.
6. If a second parent-teacher conference is held somewhat toward the end of a given school year, these criteria could be referred to in the conference when making comparisons from the first to the second conference.
7. The teacher must use terminology which parents understand. Technical vocabulary used only by educators has no place in a parent-teacher conference. If these terms are used, they should be explained to parents. Parents must sense that meaningful communication is taking place in a parent-teacher conference.
8. The teacher should jot down some major generalizations and conclusions from the conference. The summaries can be placed in a folder for each child. It is important that the date appear on the papers which are filed for each child in a folder.
9. Information obtained from a conference should be kept strictly confidential. The purpose of the conference is to guide learner achievement to the optimum.
10. All conferences should have a positive emphasis to provide for a free flow of ideas.

Parent-teacher conferences have many advantages over the report card as a means of reporting pupil progress:

1. The plan is good psychologically in that a one-to-one relationship exists between parent or parents and the teacher.
2. If the atmosphere provides for freedom of expression, many misunderstandings could be minimized due to being able

to clarify ideas between parents and the teacher in a face-to-face situation.

3. Numerous opportunities exist for the identification and solution of problems pertaining to each child's achievement.
4. Parent-teacher conferences can be held whenever it is feasible and appropriate. There is no limitation on the number of conferences that can be held in a given school year. The school should invite parents to discuss their child's achievement with the teacher whenever it is desirable.

Using the Telephone in Reporting Pupil Progress

The telephone can be used effectively in reporting pupil progress to parents. Too often, the negative is reported to parents about their child's achievement. Thus, parents and the child may come to feel that the school has nothing positive to report on learner progress. The telephone can be used quickly to compliment a given child on his performance on a particular lesson or test. It can also be used to compliment a selected child's attitude toward others in a specific situation. Thus, the telephone can be used to communicate ideas rapidly and effectively.

The giver of information on the telephone cannot see the receiver of the message. This, of course, is a disadvantage in using the telephone. However, there is a one-to-one relationship between the sender and the receiver of the message. The following standards are important in conducting a parent-teacher conference using the telephone:

1. Politeness is important in conducting the conference.
2. The teacher, principal, or supervisor should listen carefully to the thinking of others.
3. A pleasant tone of voice should be used.
4. Ideas that are communicated should be to the point.
5. Words and sentences used should be on the understanding level of parents.

It is important that more elementary school teachers use the telephone to communicate ideas quickly in a parent-teacher conference. Parents, of course, do not need to come to school in order to use this approach to communicate ideas. Thus, much time is saved in the scheduling and conducting of conferences of this kind.

Writing Letters to Report Pupil Achievement

Some schools have adopted the practice of writing letters to parents in order to report pupil achievement. Guidelines to follow in writing letters to report pupil progress could be the following:

1. Ideas must be communicated accurately when putting statements in writing.
2. The mechanics of writing are important, such as spelling, handwriting or neat typing, punctuation, and capitalization.
3. Statements must be written which are meaningful to the reader.
4. Respect for the parent and child must be an inherent part of ideas to be communicated.
5. Due care must be taken to refrain from putting in content which can be misinterpreted.
6. Ideas in the letter should pinpoint learner achievement being reported to parents.

There are numerous advantages of written statements pertaining to pupil achievement which is reported to parents.

1. Content can be written down just the way it is desired before mailing the letter to parents. In speaking to parents, ideas are expressed and cannot be changed unless verbal clarification occurs.
2. Letters can be written to parents at any point during a given school year.
3. Any facet of pupil achievement can be put in the letter, not just the categories as they appear in a report card.

Disadvartages of writing letters pertaining to reporting pupil progress to parents are quite in evidence.

1. Once content has been sent out, it cannot be revised by the sender.
2. Misinterpretation of content in the letter is definitely a possibility.

3. It is difficult for many to put ideas in written form which communicate ideas clearly to readers.
4. Seeing content in written form leaves much room for a variety of interpretation pertaining to words, phrases, and sentences. Ample time must be taken to evaluate what has been written at the time the information is sent.

In Summary

There are numerous ways to report pupil achievement to parents. The grade card or report card is, perhaps, the most common approach used. There are advantages and disadvantages in using this method of reporting pupil progress to parents. It is difficult to convey accurately to parents what grades mean on a report card. Teachers differ much in their thinking pertaining to how pupils should be evaluated. In other words, should the top achievers in a class get A's, the next best achievers receive B grades, and so on? Or, should learners be evaluated in terms of effort? This would mean that pupils doing poor quality work could get A grades if they are trying to do the best work possible in terms of their capacity and past achievement. A major problem in using report cards to report pupil achievement related directly to the number of categories in each curriculum area that teachers would assess pupil progress in.

Parent-teacher conferences can be an excellent means of reporting pupil progress depending upon the quality of interactions between and among those involved. Respect for human beings is important in these conferences. The teacher must be a good listener to understand the concerns, goals, and aspirations that parents have for their children. Parents should be involved in solving problems pertaining to their child's achievement. The home and the school be brought together in cooperative planning so that the best curriculum can be developed for each child.

The telephone can be a good means to inform parents about learner progress. This approach can be used at different intervals when necessary and desirable. It is an inexpensive approach to use which takes a minimum amount of time. Parents then do not need to take time in making arrangements to come to school. Neither do teachers need to arrange a time schedule as to when parents should come to school for conferences. Parents should be informed about their child's achievement at numerous intervals.

Letters can be written to inform parents of their child's achievement. Numerous problems exist here. A major problem is that it is difficult to write ideas clearly. Secondly, words, phrases, and sentences leave considerable room in many cases, for a variety of interpretations. Thirdly, once content has been written down and mailed, it cannot be revised.

Additional Reading

Bhaskara Rao, Digumarti (1994). *Scientific Aptitude*, New Delhi: Ashish Publishing House. pp. 100. ISBN 81-7024-658-X.

Bhaskara Rao, Digumarti (1995). *Animal Kingdom*. New Delhi: Discovery Publishing House. pp. 135. ISBN 81-7141-274-2.

Bhaskara Rao, Digumarti (1995). *Batracology*. New Delhi: Discovery Publishing House. pp. 174. ISBN 81-7141-279-3.

Bhaskara Rao, Digumarti (1996). *Scientific Attitude vis-à-vis Scientific Aptitude*. New Delhi: Discovery Publishing House. pp. 143. ISBN 81-7141-308-0.

Bhaskara Rao, Digumarti, Editor (1996). *Encyclopaedia of Education for All*, 5 volumes. New Delhi: APH Publishing Corporation. pp. 1460. ISBN 81-7024-759-4 (set).

Vol. I *Education for All: The World Conference*. pp. 440. ISBN 81-7024-760-8.

Vol. II *Education for All: The EPA-9 Summit*. pp. 340. ISBN 81-7024-761-6.

Vol. III *Education for All: Quality Education for All*. pp. 250. ISBN 81-7024-762-6.

Vol. IV *Education for All: Planning and Monitoring*. pp. 170. ISBN 81-7024-763-4.

Vol. V *Education for All: The Indian Scenario*. pp. 260. ISBN 81-7024-764-0.

Bhaskara Rao, Digumarti, Editor (1996). *Global Perceptions on Peace Education*, 3 volumes. New Delhi: Discovery Publishing House. pp. 980. ISBN 81-7141-319-6.

Bhaskara Rao, Digumarti, Editor (1996). *National Policy on Education*, 2 volumes. New Delhi: Anmol Publications Pvt. Ltd. pp. 710. ISBN 81-7488-323-1.

Bhaskara Rao, Digumarti, Editor (1997). *Care the Child*, 2 volumes. New Delhi: Discovery Publishing House. pp. 616. ISBN 81-7141-394-3.

Bhaskara Rao, Digumarti, Editor (1997). *Education for the 21st Century*. New Delhi: Discovery Publishing House. pp. 288. ISBN 81-7141-389-7.

Bhaskara Rao, Digumarti, Editor (1997). *Reflections on Scientific Attitude*. New Delhi: Discovery Publishing House. pp. 980. ISBN 81-7141-319-6.

Bhaskara Rao, Digumarti (1997). *Scientific Attitude*. New Delhi: Discovery Publishing House. pp. 120. ISBN 81-7141-381-1.

Bhaskara Rao, Digumarti, Editor (1997). *Success Story of a Primary Education Project*. New Delhi: APH Publishing Corporation. pp. 260. ISBN 81-7024-850-7.

Bhaskara Rao, Digumarti, Editor (1997). *World Food Summit*. New Delhi: Discovery Publishing House. pp. 153. ISBN 81-7141-386-2.

Bhaskara Rao, Digumarti, Editor (1998). *Adolescence Education*. New Delhi: Discovery Publishing House. pp. 238. ISBN 81-7141-432-X.

Bhaskara Rao, Digumarti, Editor (1998). *Community and School Nutrition Education*. New Delhi: Discovery Publishing House. pp. 425. ISBN 81-7141-435-4.

Bhaskara Rao, Digumarti, Editor (1998). *District Primary Education Programme*. New Delhi: Discovery Publishing House. pp. 506. ISBN 81-7141-396-X.

Bhaskara Rao, Digumarti, Editor (1998). *Earth Summit*, 2 volumes. New Delhi: Discovery Publishing House. pp. 930. ISBN 81-7141-435-4.

Bhaskara Rao, Digumarti, Editor (1998). *National Policy on Education: Towards an Enlightened and Humane Society*, New Delhi: Discovery Publishing House. pp. 542. ISBN 81-7141-426-5.

Bhaskara Rao, Digumarti, Editor (1998). *Reforming School Education*. New Delhi: Discovery Publishing House. pp. 575. ISBN 81-7141-403-6.

Bhaskara Rao, Digumarti, Editor (1998). *Teacher Education in India*. New Delhi: Discovery Publishing House. pp. 424. ISBN 81-7141-406-0.

Bhaskara Rao, Digumarti, Editor (1998). *World Summit for Social Development*. New Delhi: Discovery Publishing House. pp. 278. ISBN 81-7141-420-6.

Bhaskara Rao, Digumarti, Editor (2000). *Education for All: Achieving the Goal*, 3 volumes. New Delhi: APH Publishing Corporation. pp. 830. ISBN 81-7648-152-1.

Vol. I *The Global Consensus*. pp. 285. ISBN 81-7648-155-6.

Vol. II *Mid-Decade Review Reports of Regional Seminars*. pp. 198. ISBN 81-7648-154-8.

Vol. III *Issues and Trends*. pp. 346. ISBN 81-7648-155-6.

Bhaskara Rao, Digumarti, Editor (2000), *International Encyclopaedia of AIDS*, 11 volumes in 13 parts. New Delhi: Discovery Publishing House. pp. 676. ISBN 81-7141-6 (set).

Vol. 1 *Introduction to HIV/AIDS*. pp. 246. ISBN 81-7141-523-7.

Vol. 2 *HIV/AIDS—Issues and Challenges*, 2 parts. pp. 805. ISBN 81-7141-524-5.

Vol. 3 *HIV/AIDS—Socio Economic Realities*. pp. 436. ISBN 81-7141-524-3.

Vol. 4 *HIV/AIDS—Law Ethics and Human Rights*, 2 parts. pp. 589. ISBN 81-7141-526-1.

Vol. 5 *AIDS and NGOs*. pp. 215. ISBN 81-7141-527-X.

Vol. 6 *AIDS and Home Care*. pp. 183. ISBN 81-7141-528-8.

Vol. 7 *STD Case Management*. pp. 223. ISBN 81-7141-529-6.

Vol. 8 *HIV/AIDS Prevention and Care—Teaching Modules for Nurses and Midwives*. pp. 183. ISBN 81-7141-530-X.

Vol. 9 *HIV Prevention Education for Education for Educational Institutions*. pp. 75. ISBN 81-7141-531-8.

Vol. 10 *Instructional Modules for AIDS Education*. pp. 111. ISBN 81-7141-532-6.

Vol. 11 *School Health Education to Prevent AIDS and STD—A Package for Curriculum Planners*. pp. 298. ISBN 81-7141-5338-4.

Bhaskara Rao, Digumarti, Editor (2000). *International Encyclopaedia of Science and Technology Education*, 11 volumes, New Delhi: Discovery Publishing House. pp. 4892. ISBN 81-7141-548-2 (set).

Vol. 1 *Science and Technology Education*. pp. 557. ISBN 81-7141-568-7.

Vol. 2 *Science Education in Developing Countries*. pp. 334. ISBN 81-7141-570-9.

Vol. 3 *Organisational Structure of Science*. pp. 334. ISBN 81-7141-570-9.

Vol. 4 *Science Education in Asia and the Pacific*. pp. 249. ISBN 81-7141-571-7.

Vol. 5 *Science and Technology Education for All*. pp. 464. ISBN 81-7141-572-5.

Vol. 6 *Values, Ethics, Talent and Girls in Science and Technology Education*. pp. 463. ISBN 81-7141-573-3.

Vol. 7 *Popularization of Science and Technology Education*. pp. 334. ISBN 81-7141-574-1.

Vol. 8 *Science, Power and Society*. pp. 357. ISBN 81-7141-575-X.

Vol. 9 *Information Technology*. pp. 442. Rs. 775. ISBN 81-7141-576-8.

Vol. 10 *Teacher Training in Science and Technology Education*. pp. 536. ISBN 81-7141-577-6.

Vol. 11 *Teacher Training in Science and Technology: A Curriculum Framework*. pp. 642. ISBN 81-7141-578-4.

Bhaskara Rao, Digumarti, Editor (2001). *Distance Education in Different Countries*. New Delhi: APH Publishing Corporation. pp. 574. ISBN 81-7648-229-3.

Bhaskara Rao, Digumarti, Editor (2001). *Decentralised Management of Education (Management of Education in Panchayati Raj and Municipal Bodies)*. New Delhi: Discovery Publishing House. pp. 116. ISBN 81-7141-617-9.

Bhaskara Rao, Digumarti, Editor (2001). *Electrochemistry for Environmental Protection*. New Delhi: Discovery Publishing House. pp. 208. ISBN 81-7141-619-5.

Bhaskara Rao, Digumarti, Editor (2001). *Global Educational Studies*. New Delhi: Discovery Publishing House. pp. 145. ISBN 81-7141-616-0.

Bhaskara Rao, Digumarti, Editor (2001). *Global Synthesis of Educational Assessment*. New Delhi: Discovery Publishing House. pp. 152. ISBN 81-7141-613-6.

Bhaskara Rao, Digumarti, Editor (2000). *International Encyclopaedia of Human Rights*. 7 volumes in 13 parts. New Delhi: Discovery Publishing House. pp. 6500 (Royal size). ISBN 81-7141-567-9 (set).

Vol. 1 *International Instruments of Human Rights*, 2 parts. ISBN 81-7141-595-4.

Vol. 2 *Regional Instruments of Human Rights*. ISBN 81-7141-604-7.

Vol. 3 *Human Rights and the United Nations*, 2 parts. ISBN 81-7141-605-5.

Vol. 4 *Fact Files of Human Rights*, 3 parts. ISBN 81-7141-605-3.

Vol. 5 *Study Stories of Human Rights*, 3 parts. ISBN 81-7141-607-3.

Vol. 6 *International Meetings on Human Rights*, 2 parts. ISBN 81-7141-608-X.

Vol. 7 *Professional Training in Human Rights*. ISBN 81-7141-609-8.

Bhaskara Rao, Digumarti, Editor (2001). *Jomtein Decade of Education*. New Delhi: Discovery Publishing House. pp. 106. ISBN 81-7141-618-7.

Bhaskara Rao, Digumarti, Editor (2001). *Nuclear Materials: Issues and Concerns*, 2 volumes. New Delhi: Discovery Publishing House. pp. 1100. ISBN 81-7141-611-X.

Bhaskara Rao, Digumarti, Editor (2001). *World Conference on Education for All*. New Delhi. APH Publishing Corporation. pp. 380. ISBN 81-7141-274-9.

Bhaskara Rao, Digumarti, Editor (2001). *World Conference on Higher Education*. New Delhi: Discovery Publishing House. pp. 306. ISBN 81-7141-610-1.

Bhaskara Rao, Digumarti, Editor (2001). *World Conference on Science*. New Delhi: Discovery Publishing House. pp. 85. ISBN 81-7141-612-8.

Bhaskara Rao, Digumarti, Editor (2004). *Chernobyl: Never Again*. New Delhi: Discovery Publishing House.

Bhaskara Rao, Digumarti, Editor (2004). Habitat Agenda. New Delhi: Discovery Publishing House.

Bhaskara Rao, Digumarti, Editor (2003). *Inspiring Experiences in Teacher Education*, New Delhi: Discovery Publishing House. pp. 256. ISBN 81-7141-656-X.

Bhaskara Rao, Digumarti, Editor (2003). *International Studies in Education*, 3 volumes. New Delhi: Discovery Publishing House. pp. 912. ISBN 81-7141-647-0. (set).

Bhaskara Rao, Digumarti, Editor (2003). *Military Conversion: Impact on Science and Technology*. New Delhi: Discovery Publishing House. pp. 200. ISBN 81-7141-578-4.

Bhaskara Rao, Digumarti, Editor (2004). *Virology and Immunology*. New Delhi: Discovery Publishing House.

Bhaskara Rao, Digumarti, Editor (2003). *United Nations Millennium Summit*. New Delhi: Discovery Publishing House. pp. 112. ISBN 81-7141-632-2.

Bhaskara Rao, Digumarti, Editor (2003). *World Assembly on Aging*. New Delhi: Discovery Publishing House. pp. 88. ISBN 81-7141-637-3.

Bhaskara Rao, Digumarti, Editor (2004). *World Conference on Human Rights*. New Delhi: Discovery Publishing House.

Bhaskara Rao, Digumarti, Editor (2003). *World Education Forum*. New Delhi: Discovery Publishing House. pp. 336. ISBN 81-7141-639-X.

Bhaskara Rao, Digumarti, Editor (2004). *Education Employment and Human Resource Development*. New Delhi: Discovery Publishing House.

Bhaskara Rao, Digumarti, Editor (2004). *Learning to Live Together*, 3 volumes. New Delhi: Discovery Publishing House.

Bhaskara Rao, Digumarti, Editor (2004). *Successful Schooling*. New Delhi: Discovery Publishing House.

Bhaskara Rao, Digumarti, Editor (2004). *European Education and Teachers*. New Delhi: Discovery Publishing House.

Bhaskara Rao, Digumarti, Editor (2004). *Teachers in a Changing World*. New Delhi: Discovery Publishing House.

Bhaskara Rao, Digumarti, Editor (2003). *All For Education: Sharing Strategies and Experiences in Education*. New Delhi: APH Publishing Corporation.

Bhaskara Rao, Digumarti, C.A.P. Swamy and B.S.V. Dutt (1997). *Self-Evaluation in Student Teaching*. New Delhi: Discovery Publishing House. pp. 762. ISBN 81-7141-374-9.

Bhaskara Rao, Digumarti and Digumarti Pushpa Latha (1994). *Achievement in Biology*. New Delhi: Discovery Publishing House. pp. 102. ISBN 81-7141-264-5.

Bhaskara Rao, Digumarti, C. Sridevi and K. Vijaya (1995). *Achievement in Social Studies*. New Delhi: Discovery Publishing House. pp. 102. ISBN 81-7141-281-5.

Bhaskara Rao Digumarti, and Digumarti Pushpa Latha (1995). *Achievement in English*. New Delhi: Discovery Publishing House. pp. 214. ISBN 81-7141-283-1.

Bhaskara Rao, Digumarti and Digumarti Pushpa Latha (1994). *Achievement in Science*. New Delhi: Discovery Publishing House. pp. 159. ISBN 81-7141-280-70.

Bhaskara Rao, Digumarti and Digumarti Pushpa Latha (1995). *Achievement in Mathematics*. New Delhi: Discovery Publishing House. pp. 125. ISBN 81-7141-278-5.

Bhaskara Rao, Digumarti and Digumarti Pushpa Latha, Editors (1998). *International Encyclopaedia of Women*. 5 volumes. New Delhi: Discovery Publishing House. pp. 2172. ISBN 81-7141-410-9.

Vol. 1 *Status of World's Women*. pp. 427. ISBN 81-7141-494-X.

Vol. 2 *Women, Education and Empowerment*. pp. 467. ISBN 81-7141-498-1.

Vol. 3 *Women Challenges in Advancement*. pp. 354. ISBN 81-7141-497-4.

Vol. 4 *Women and Family Health*. pp. 470. ISBN 81-7141-497-4.

Vol. 5 *Women and International Action*. pp. 453. ISBN 81-7141-498-2.

Bhaskara Rao, Digumarti, Digumarti Pushpa Latha and Digumarti Harshitha, Editors (2001). *Biological Warfare*. New Delhi: Discovery Publishing House. pp. 422. ISBN 81-7141-597-0.

Bhaskara Rao, Digumarti, Digumarti Pushpa Latha and Digumarti Harshitha, Editors (2001). *Women as Educators*. New Delhi: Discovery Publishing House. pp. 112. ISBN 81-7141-602-0.

Bhaskara Rao, Digumarti, Digumarti Pushpa Latha and Digumarti Harshitha, Editors (2001). *Education in India*. New Delhi: APH Publishing Corporation. pp. 280. ISBN 81-7648-207-2.

Bhaskara Rao, Digumarti, Digumarti Pushpa Latha and Digumarti Harshitha, Editors (2001). *Assessing Learning Achievement*. New Delhi: Discovery Publishing House. pp. 128. ISBN 81-7141-601-2.

Bhaskara Rao, Digumarti, Digumarti Pushpa Latha and Digumarti Harshitha, Editors (2001). *Energy Security*. New Delhi: Discovery Publishing House. pp. 564. ISBN 81-7141-598-9.

Bhaskara Rao, Digumarti, Digumarti Harshitha and K.R.S.S. Rao, Editors (1999). *Advanced Biotechnology*. New Delhi: Discovery Publishing House. pp. 335. ISBN 81-7141-516-4.

Bhaskara Rao, Digumarti and D. Sridhar (2002). *Job Satisfaction of School Teachers*. New Delhi: Discovery Publishing House. pp. 104. ISBN 81-7141-652-7.

Bhaskara Rao, Digumarti and K.R.S. Sambasiva Rao, Editors (1996). *Current Trends in Indian Education*. New Delhi: Discovery Publishing House. pp. 234. ISBN 81-7141-311-0.

Bhaskara Rao, Digumarti and K. Vijaya (1995). *A Text Book Evaluation*. Ambala Cantt: The Associated Publishers. pp. 100.

Bhaskara Rao, Digumarti and N.V.M. Mohana Rao (2002). *Problems of Mentally Handicapped Children*, New Delhi: Discovery Publishing House. pp. 96. ISBN 81-7141-645-4.

Bhaskara Rao, Digumarti and S. Chandra Mohan (2002). *Student Participation in Sports and Games*. New Delhi: APH Publishing Corporation.

Bhaskara Rao, Digumarti, V.V. Rao, V.V. Lakshmi and V.V. Krishna, Editors (1999). *Status and Advancement of Women*. New Delhi: APH Publishing Corporation. pp. 570. ISBN 81-7648-169-6.

Babu, P.C., Author and Digumarti Bhaskara Rao, Editor (2004). *Flowers of Wisdom*. New Delhi: Discovery Publishing House.

Bhagya Lakshmi, Lingineni, Author and Digumarti Bhaskara Rao, Editor (2000). *Reading and Comprehension*. New Delhi: Discovery Publishing House. pp. 108. ISBN 81-7141-543-1

Bhuvaneswara Lakshmi, Gadde, Author and Digumarti Bhaskara Rao, Editor (2002). *Attitude towards Science*. New Delhi: Discovery Publishing House. pp. 128. ISBN 81-7141-541-6.

Devraj, T.A.S., Author and Digumarti Bhaskara Rao, Editor (1997). *Trace Analysis of Uranium and Thorium*: Discovery Publishing House. pp. 195. ISBN 81-7141-375-7.

Durga Rani, K., Author and Digumarti Bhaskara Rao, Editor (2000). *Educational Aspirations and Scientific Attitudes*. New Delhi: Discovery Publishing House. pp. 130. ISBN 81-7141-555-55.

Dutt, B.S.V. and Digumarti Bhaskara Rao (2001). *Empowering Primary Teachers*. New Delhi: Discovery Publishing House. pp. 283. ISBN 81-7141-615-2.

Ediger, Marlow and Digumarti Bhaskara Rao (1996). *Science Curriculum*. New Delhi: Discovery Publishing House. pp. 309. ISBN 81-7141-321-8.

Ediger, Marlow and Digumarti Bhaskara Rao (2000). *Teaching Mathematics Successfully*. New Delhi: Discovery Publishing House. pp. 279. ISBN 81-7141-552-0.

Ediger, Marlow and Digumarti Bhaskara Rao (2001). *Teaching Science Successfully*. New Delhi: Discovery Publishing House. pp. 320. ISBN 81-7141-600-4.

Ediger, Marlow and Digumarti Bhaskara Rao (2001). *Teaching Social Studies Successfully*. New Delhi: Discovery Publishing House. pp. 296. ISBN 81-7141-596-2.

Ediger, Marlow and Digumarti Bhaskara Rao (2002). *Philosophy and Curriculum*. New Delhi: Discovery Publishing House. pp. 224. ISBN 81-7141-631-4.

Ediger, Marlow and Digumarti Bhaskara Rao (2002). *Improving School Administration*. New Delhi: Discovery Publishing House. pp. 240. ISBN 81-7141-633-0.

Ediger, Marlow and Digumarti Bhaskara Rao (2002). *Elementary Curriculum*. New Delhi: Discovery Publishing House. pp. 490. ISBN 81-7141-658-6.

Ediger, Marlow and Digumarti Bhaskara Rao (2003). *Language Arts Curriculum*. New Delhi: Discovery Publishing House. pp. 348. ISBN 81-7141-657-8.

Ediger, Marlow and Digumarti Bhaskara Rao (2003). *The Holy Land*. New Delhi: Discovery Publishing House.

Ediger, Marlow and Digumarti Bhaskara Rao (2004). *Psychology and Curriculum*. New Delhi: Discovery Publishing House.

Ediger, Marlow and Digumarti Bhaskara Rao (2004). *Teaching Language Arts Successfully*. New Delhi: Discovery Publishing House.

Ediger, Marlow and Digumarti Bhaskara Rao (2004). *Psychology and Curriculum*. New Delhi: Discovery Publishing House.

Ediger, Marlow and Digumarti Bhaskara Rao (2004). *Teaching Mathematics in Elementary Schools*. New Delhi: Discovery Publishing House.

Ediger, Marlow and Digumarti Bhaskara Rao (2004). *Teaching Science in Elementary Schools*. New Delhi: Discovery Publishing House.

Ediger, Marlow and Digumarti Bhaskara Rao (2004). *Teaching Social Studies in Elementary Schools*. New Delhi: Discovery Publishing House.

Ediger, Marlow and Digumarti Bhaskara Rao (2004). *School Curriculum and Administration*. New Delhi: Discovery Publishing House.

Ediger, Marlow and Digumarti Bhaskara Rao (2004). *Relevancy in Elementary Curriculum*. New Delhi: Discovery Publishing House.

Ediger, Marlow, B.S.V. Dutt and Digumarti Bhaskara Rao (2004). *Teaching English Successfully*. New Delhi: Discovery Publishing House.

Jayasree, Kandi, author and Digumarti Bhaskara Rao, Editor (1999). *Correlates of Socialiation*. New Delhi: Discovery Publishing House. pp. 160. ISBN 81-7141-517-2.

John Babu, Chikati, Author and T.J.R, Prasad, G.M. Madhukar and Digumarti Bhaskara Rao, Editors (1996). *Problem Solving in Mathematics*. New Delhi: APH Publishing Corporation. pp. 125. ISBN 81-7648-273-0.

Jyothi, Nirmala M., Author and Digumarti Bhaskara Rao, Editor (2003). *Non-detention System in School Education*. New Delhi: Discovery Publishing House. pp. 400. ISBN 81-7141-654-3.

Marja, Talvi and Digumarti Bhaskara Rao, Editors (1996). *Educational Leadership and Social Changes*. New Delhi: Discovery Publishing House. pp. 236. ISBN 81-7141-320-X.

Prabhakaram, K.S., Author and Digumarti Bhaskara Rao, Editors (1998). *Concept Attainment Model in Mathematics Teaching*. New Delhi: Discovery Publishing House. pp. 122. ISBN 81-7141-424-9.

Prasanth Kumar, J., Author and Digumarti Bhaskara Rao, Editors (1998). *Effectiveness of Distance Education System*. New Delhi: Discovery Publishing House. pp. 152. ISBN 81-7141-437-0.

Prasanth Kumar, J., Author and G. Sundara Rao and Digumarti Bhaskara Rao, Editors (2000). *Open University Student Support Services*. New Delhi: Discovery Publishing House. pp. 100. ISBN 81-7141-550-4.

Ramatulasamma, K., Author and Digumarti Bhaskara Rao, Editor (2002). *Job Satisfaction of Teacher Educators*. New Delhi: Discovery Publishing House. pp. 160. ISBN 81-7141-655-1.

Rama Krishnaiah, D., Author and Digumarti Bhaskara Rao, Editor (1998). *Job Satisfaction of College Teachers*, New Delhi: Discovery Publishing House. pp. 251. ISBN 81-7141-438-9.

Rathaiah, Lavu and Digumarti Bhaskara Rao, Editors (1996), *International Innovations in Education*. New Delhi: Discovery Publishing House. pp. 513. ISBN 81-7141-359-5.

Ramesh, Ganta and Digumarti Bhaskara Rao, Editors (1998). *Environmental Education: Problems and Prospects*. New Delhi: Discovery Publishing House. pp. 324. ISBN 81-7141-423-0.

Rathaiah, Lavu and Digumarti Bhaskara Rao (1997). *Achievement Correlates*. New Delhi: Discovery Publishing House. pp. 116. ISBN 81-7141-385-4.

Reddy, Sudhakar Y., Author and Digumarti Bhaskara Rao, Editor (2003). *Creativity in Adolescents*. New Delhi: Discovery Publishing House, pp. 430. ISBN 81-7141-659-4.

Reddy, M.S., Author and Digumarti Bhaskara Rao, Editor (2004). *Creativity in College Students*. New Delhi: Discovery Publishing House.

Rudramamba, B., Author and Digumarti Bhaskara Rao, Editor (2003). *Problems of Teaching*. New Delhi: APH Publishing Corporation. pp. 203. ISBN 81-7648-462-8.

Sanjeeva Rao, P.C., Author and Digumarti Bhaskara Rao, Editor (1996). *A Text Book of Geology*. New Delhi: Discovery Publishing House. pp. 320. ISBN 81-7141-313-7.

Satya Narayana, V., Author and Digumarti Bhaskara Rao, Editor (2001). *Physical Education, Social Attitudes and Leadership Qualities*. New Delhi: Discovery Publishing House. pp. 296. ISBN 81-7141-593-8.

Srinivasulu Reddy, M. and K.R.S. Sambasiva Rao, Authors and Digumarti Bhaskara Rao, Editor (1999). *A Text Book of Aquaculture*. New Delhi: Discovery Publishing House. pp. 296. ISBN 81-7141-482-6.

Srinivasa Rao, Mandalapu, Author and Digumarti Bhaskara Rao, Editor (2004). *Achievement Motivation and Achievement in Mathematics*. New Delhi: Discovery Publishing House.

Vanaja, M., Author and Digumarti Bhaskara Rao, Editor (1999). *Inquiry Training Model*. New Delhi: Discovery Publishing House. pp. 189. ISBN 81-7141-515-6.

Valeri V. Koustiouk, Author and Digumarti Bhaskara Rao, Editor (2002). *A Text Book of Cryogenics*. New Delhi: Discovery Publishing House. pp. 288. ISBN 81-7141-642-X.

Valeri V. Koustiouk, Author and Digumarti Bhaskara Rao, Editor (2004). *Refrigeration and Environment*. New Delhi: Discovery Publishing House.

Veena Kumari, Balusu and Digumarti Bhaskara Rao (1996). *Operation Black Board*. New Delhi: Discovery Publishing House. pp. 140. ISBN 81-7141-711-X.

Veena Kumari, Balusu, Author and Digumarti Bhaskara Rao, Editor (2000). *Psycho-Social Correlates of Achievement*. New Delhi: Discovery Publishing House. pp. 36. ISBN 81-7141-547-4.

Venkata Rao, P. and Digumarti Bhaskara Rao (1989). *A Text Book of Zoology—Junior Intermediate*. Guntur: Vignan Publishers. pp. 370.

Venkata Rao, P. and Digumarti Bhaskara Rao (1989). *A Text Book of Zoology—Senior Intermediate*. Guntur: Vignan Publishers. pp. 480.

Venugopala Rao, K., author and Digumarti Bhaskara Rao, Editor (2000). *Teacher Morale in Secondary Schools*. New Delhi: Discovery Publishing House. pp. 300. ISBN 81-7141-551-2.

Vidya, C., Author and Digumarti Bhaskara Rao, Editor (1996). *A Text Book of Nutrition*. New Delhi: Discovery Publishing House. pp. 438. ISBN 81-7141-309-9.

Vidya Bharathi, D., Author and Digumarti Bhaskara Rao, Editor (2000). *Educational Philosophies of Swami Vivekananda and John Dewey*. New Delhi: APH Publishing Corporation. pp. 200. ISBN 81-7648-309-9.

Books in Telugu Language

Bhaskara Rao, Digumarti (1986). *Dhrushya Sravana Bodhanopakaranalu* (Audio Visual Teaching Aids). Guntur: Nagarjuna Publishers.

Bhaskara Rao, Digumarti (1993). *Jeevasashtra Bodhana* (Teaching of Biology). Guntur: Nagarjuna Publishers.

Bhaskara Rao, Digumarti (1995). *Vignanasasthra Bodhana* (Teaching of Science) Guntur: Nagarjuna Publishers.

Bhaskara Rao, Digumarti (1997). *Vidya Manovignana Seshtram* (Educational Psychology). Guntur: Creative Press. pp. 434. Rs. 79.

Bhaskara Rao, Digumarti (1998). *DSC Study Material*. Guntur: Nagarjuna Publishers.

Bhaskara Rao, Digumarti (1998). *Upadhyayudu Vidya*. (Teacher and Education) Guntur: Nagarjuna Publishers.

Bhaskara Rao, Digumarti (1998). *Vidya Drukpadalu* (Perspectives of Education). Guntur: Nagarjuna Publishers.

Bhaskara Rao, Digumarti (1999). *EdCET Teaching Aptitude*. Guntur: Nagarjuna Publishers.

Bhaskara Rao, Digumarti (2001). *Bharata Samajamulo Upadyayudu Vidya* (Teacher and Education in Emerging Indian Society). Guntur: Nagarjuna Publishers.

Bhaskara Rao, Digumarti (2001). *Bhoutika Sastra Bodhana Paddathulu* (Methods of Teaching Physical Science). Guntur: Nagarjuna Publishers pp. 324.

Bhaskara Rao, Digumarti (2001). *Jeeva Sastra Bodhana Padhathulu* (Methods of Teaching Biology). Guntur: Nagarjuna Publishers. pp. 344.

Bhaskara Rao, Digumarti (2001. *Vidya Manovignana Sastram* (Educational Psychology). Guntur: Nagarjuna Publishers. pp. 344.

Bhaskara Rao, Digumarti (2003). *Patasala Yajamanyam/Paripalana* (School Management and Administration). Guntur: Nagarjuna Publishers.

Bhaskra Rao, Digumarti (2004). *Vidya Sanketika Sastram Mariyu Computer Vidya* (Educational Technology and Computer Education). Guntur: Nagarjuna Publishers.